16-96 BK Bud Jan 96

NORTH CAROLINA
STATE BOARD OF COMMUNITY
LIBRARIES
SOUTHEASTERN COMMUNITY COLLEGE

P9-CND-823

BACKWOODS
ETHICS

SOUTHEASTERN COMMUNITY
COLLEGE LIBRARY
WHITEVILLE, NC 28472

NORTH CAROLINA
STATE BOARD OF COMMUNITY COLLEGES

GV
199.4
.W38
1993

Second Edition, Revised

BACKWOODS ETHICS

Environmental Issues for
Hikers and Campers

SOUTHEASTERN COMMUNITY
COLLEGE LIBRARY
WHITEVILLE, NC 28472

Foreword by Bill McKibben

Laura and Guy Waterman

THE COUNTRYMAN PRESS
Woodstock, Vermont

Backwoods Ethics
Copyright © 1979, the Stone Wall Press; © 1993 Laura and Guy Waterman
Foreword © 1993 Bill McKibben

All rights reserved. No part of this book may be reproduced in any form or by any electronic
or mechanical means including information storage and retrieval systems without permission
in writing from the publisher, except by a reviewer who may quote brief passages.

The first edition of *Backwoods Ethics* was originally published in 1979 by
the Stone Wall Press, Inc. (ISBN 0-913276-28-6)

Published by The Countryman Press, Inc.
P.O. Box 175
Woodstock, Vermont 05091

Cover and text design by Karen Savary
Cover art and interior art by Beth Krommes
Printed in the United States of America by Gilliland Printing
Printed on Recycled Paper

10 9 8 7 6 5 4 3 2

Library of Congress Cataloging-in-Publication Data
Waterman, Laura.
Backwoods ethics: environmental issues for hikers and campers/Laura and Guy Waterman;
foreword by Bill McKibben. —2nd ed. rev.
p. cm.
Includes index.
ISBN 0-88150-257-X
1. Hiking—Environmental aspects—United States—Case studies.
2. Backpacking—Environmental aspects—United States—Case studies.
3. Camping—Environmental aspects—United States—Case studies.
4. Nature conservation—United States. I. Waterman, Guy.
II. Title
GV199.4.W38 1993
333.78'0973—dc20 93-18435 CIP

Extracts from the following sources have been reprinted with kind permission: Leigh
Marlow, letter–to–the–editor, *Appalachia Bulletin*, May 1991; Raymond H. Fadner,
letter–to–the–editor, *Appalachian Trailway News*, May–June 1986; Dan Orlinski,
letter–to–the–editor, *Appalchian Trailway News*, March–April 1987; William Harlow,
"Stop Walking Away the Wilderness," *Backpacker*, August 1977; letter from Emily
Benson to the authors; "Uncle Sam Raises His Eyebrows," (Editorial) *Climbing*,
April–May 1991; Martin Hackworth, "Perspectives: One of Fifty Classic Landfills in
North America," *Climbing*, October 1988; Ron Amick, letter–to–the–editor, *Climbing*, April–May 1991; Mark Robinson, "Rude Boys," *Climbing*, August–September
1990; Alison Osius, "The Steel Magnolia," *Climbing*, February–March 1991; Stuart
Pregnall, "Access," *Climbing*, August–September 1990; paper by Eugene Daniell III,
"Routes to New England's Hundred Highest Peaks"; Laury Marshall, "Barbless Hooks:
Conscience or Cops?" *The Izaak Walton League of America Outdoor Ethics Newsletter*,
Spring 1991; letter from Fred Kacprzynski to Lee Tibbert; paper by Edwin H.
Ketchledge, "The Crisis in Summit Stewardship"; letter from Allen Koop to the
authors; paper on Vermont's ranger–naturalist program by Rick Paradis; letter from
Nancy Rent to the authors.

For Chuck
. . . and, of course, for Ralph
two of the best companions in the mountains

Contents

Foreword

AT THE TAIL END of a long day's hike, you reach a wilderness lake and start looking for a campsite. There is the easy and obvious way to do it—find the spot with the best view, chop out some saplings that are in the way, build a nice big blaze in a circle of rocks. And then there is the low-impact way, which the Watermans were among the first to describe in the original edition of their *Backwoods Ethics*.

The reason this choice matters, I think, is not because of the people who will come next and have to live with your scars. The reason it matters—and the reason all the other choices, about boots and tent colors and latrines and so forth, matter—is because, for a moment, you are placed in the role of an early settler of a wild land. Will you make your decisions based on your convenience and comfort, thinking only about the next 10 hours? If so, you will reenact the patterns of your ancestors who settled this continent, and the result will be the same—far more devastation than necessary, the slow impoverishment of the place.

On the other hand, if you will put yourself out a little bit you will not only "preserve the environment," an abstract and negative proposition, but you will also find yourself reaping great immediate benefits. You will find yourself *fitting in*. There are backpackers who have never really seen the long slow arc from blue sky to a little less blue, to definitely darker, to there's a planet, to black, because they've built a good blaze as soon as they've made camp.

The difficult task for modern Americans is not to show we can impose our wills on the natural world—we've long since proved we can do that. The difficult task is blending in, and here the Watermans provide great insight throughout their fine book. Take it to heart and not only will you leave the woods in better shape, you will leave the woods with better memories.

Bill McKibben

Acknowledgments

FOR GETTING US started on the original columns for *New England Outdoors*, which ultimately grew into this book, we are greatly indebted to Mike Pogodzinski, Mike Ricciuto, Jim Barry, and especially Lyle Richardson. This colorful quartet urged us to write what we thought, and then they published what we wrote.

For conceiving the idea of and then skillfully producing the original edition of *Backwoods Ethics*, we shall be eternally grateful to Henry Wheelwright of Stone Wall Press—also for his generosity in allowing us to proceed with this revised edition with another publisher.

For the vision of this new edition as part of a companion set, along with *Wilderness Ethics: Preserving the Spirit of Wildness*, we are very thankful equally for the imaginative ideas and for the professional competence and practical good sense of the wonderful people at The Countryman Press, especially Carl Taylor and Robin Dutcher-Bayer.

For factual information we are indebted especially to Ned Therrien of the White Mountain National Forest and to many staff people in the chief hiking and conservation organizations of our region, the Green Mountain Club, Adirondack Mountain Club, Adirondack Forty-Sixers, and the Appalachian Mountain Club.

For kind permission to adapt materials originally appearing elsewhere we thank Bill Kemsley of *Backpacker* and Fran Belcher of the *Mount Washington Observatory News Bulletin.*

For the birth and growth of our ideas about the backwoods, we are conscious of a deep debt to many influences. Going way back are early family mentors, most of all Alan Waterman. Over the years many, many people have taught us, exchanged ideas, challenged theories, illuminated possibilities, explained the errors of our ways, and otherwise ignited and fanned our perceptions of the outdoor world. We think especially of those gentle teachers and constant friends, the Smileys—Ruth and Keith and, years ago, Dan and Virginia. Of the legion of others over the years, some who stand out in our memory and in our special gratitude are Louis Cornell, Dan Allen, Ed Ketchledge, Jeanie Cooley, and Nat Scrimshaw, and most of all the friend who has for 25 years discussed and debated back and forth practically every idea (and some of the grammar) in this book, Brad Snyder.

Our sources of facts and ideas are many, but the final responsibility for how they all come out, with whatever errors or misconceptions may have crept in, is exclusively that of the authors.

Introduction

The Preservation of Wildness

IN APRIL 1976 we began contributing a monthly column on camping and hiking to *New England Outdoors* magazine. Into those columns flowed all manner of anecdotes, observations, reflections, cries of outrage, melancholy mutterings, confused chuckles, and woebegone warnings that occurred to us during the next three years. In 1979 Henry Wheelwright of Stone Wall Press suggested that we impose some semblance of order on the accumulating chaos of those columns, so as to produce the first edition of this book, under the title *Backwoods Ethics: Environmental Concerns for Hikers and Campers* (Stone Wall Press, 1979).

Now, 14 years later, the editors of The Countryman Press, neighbors of ours in Vermont, have suggested that many of the issues that we discussed in 1979 merit rethinking and restatement. (We suppress the suspicion that they just wanted to give us a chance to see if we could get things right this time around.) Also, new issues have arisen. As we thought about Countryman's suggestion, we decided that there was much, much more to say, as well as some things now better discarded.

Therefore, this revised edition of *Backwoods Ethics* is considerably altered and amended, addressing the issues of the 1990s and looking ahead to those of a new century.

A major change in the organization of this book results from a growing conviction that there are two separate but equal concepts that urgently need the attention of all backcountry recreationists and managers alike. One is protection of the physical environment of the mountains and backcountry in general; the other is preserving the spirit of wildness out there.

This is a distinction that we recognized in the first edition. The problems and urgent requirements for action have grown in both areas, however. So now we have written two books, one addressed to each of these concerns. Each is too important to be relegated to second place in any one book.

The present volume addresses primarily the needs of the physical environment—protecting the plants, soils, waters, wildlife, and the total interconnected ecology of the mountains and forest and desert and arctic world. If you are interested in the spiritual side of the backcountry, and we very much hope that you are, you may want to have a look at the companion volume, *Wilderness Ethics: Preserving the Spirit of Wildness.* But please do not overlook or bypass the first important step, the sine qua non of wildness, preserving the physical environment.

Our hiking experience is largely regional, but the problems that confront the backwoods of New England have come to the Smokies and the Everglades, the Badlands and the Rockies, the deserts and the High Sierra, and even the arctic vastness of Alaska. The issues that stir the consciences of hikers and campers are found nationwide, indeed worldwide.

This book expresses strong views sometimes, and many may question or disagree. That's fine. While we may sometimes sound cocksure or arrogant, we are fundamentally perplexed and humbled by the difficulty of some of the questions confronting backwoods hikers and those who have the complex and thankless responsibility of managing the wildlands of this country. The aim of this book is not to provide answers so much as to provoke questions in the minds of all those who are concerned about the future of the backcountry environment.

A few words on terminology: As if backcountry issues weren't complex enough in substance, they are vastly compounded by semantic confusion.

To begin with, we say "New England" when we often mean the northeastern corner of the United States, including New York State's Adirondacks, Catskills, and Shawangunks, and the Hudson Highlands.

We use "backwoods" and "backcountry" almost interchangeably, since most of our region's backcountry is wooded. Elsewhere, great expanses of above-treeline or desert zones would make "backcountry" the preferred general term.

Like a lot of others, we overwork the word "ethics." Often our agenda for backwoods ethics is really more a catalog of backwoods etiquette, or manners, actions we should all take or refrain from. Strictly speaking, ethics concern the underlying set of values, the code of moral beliefs about the natural world and our relationship to it, from which our actions should proceed.

Readers will note we refer much more to wildness than to wilderness. The words "wild," "wildness," and "wilderness" have created more confusion than clarity over the past three decades. The term "wilderness" has a specific legal meaning in the Wilderness Act of 1964; therefore it seems helpful to limit use of that term most of the time to legally defined wilderness areas. On the other hand, when referring to wildlands in general, regardless of legal status, we prefer the terms "wildness" and "wild" because to us they conjure up the spirit that is a fundamental appeal of backcountry: the sense of being away from civilization's softening influences, of being in predominately natural surroundings (woods, mountains, waters), and of relying on one's own resources in a natural world where our human powers and accomplishments seem puny in comparison with nature's.

The word "stewardship" expresses to us an obligation that we would like to see recognized by all outdoor recreationists. This term rubs some concerned ecologists the wrong way: to them it implies an arrogance on the part of humanity, an attitude of dominion over the natural world, rather than acceptance of a limited role within the world of nature. We honor that viewpoint, and agree that humanity is within, not above, nature. But as we view the effects of human civilization on the world of nature—the wholesale destruction of forests, pollution of oceans, paving of hundreds of square miles of metropolises, and the imposition of human presence on every corner of the globe and every species of flora and fauna therein—we have to conclude that the impact of our presence imposes on us an obligation that indeed sets us apart from other species. Some argue that we have already blundered our way into destroying any independent integrity in the natural world. We are not quite that pessimistic. But we are certain that if something in the world of nature is to be preserved, it must be by our accepting the role of stewards. This need not, must not, be undertaken in a spirit of arrogance, but on the contrary in one of humility and recognition that we often do not really know what we should do. But we must try to learn, and to act responsibly.

If you seek a more in-depth discussion of this issue, you are probably looking in the wrong book. Profound philosophers we are not. We are simply two people who spend as much time as we can manage in the backcountry and who have been fortunate enough to arrange our lives so we can manage to spend a lot more time out there than most people. And we recognize that our good luck carries with it a heavy responsibility.

But safeguarding this heritage of wild country is a responsibility for everyone. If we want our children's children to have the same opportunities to enjoy the backwoods, we have to do the right things. In a broader perspective, if we want the natural world of the 21st century to retain the fine qualities and delicate balance that it has always known, we have to act responsibly—as hikers and climbers, as backpackers and campers, as voters and concerned citizens.

The question of how to exercise this stewardship may lead to disagreements as well. For example, we have heard it said that one prime weapon in defending the backwoods is a loud voice with which to accost anyone you meet who violates the new backwoods ethics (or etiquette)—for instance, anyone who discards a piece of litter, sets up a tent on a fragile stream bank, walks off-trail on alpine vegetation, and so forth. Well, maybe a stern word spoken to other hikers now and then may be appropriate and timely, but we have to confess that as a general procedure it just isn't our style.

We wonder whether the good word is always accepted when presented in such a package. If we find someone about to tent right on a delicate stream bank or cut a bough bed, we try to fall into a friendly conversation first and gently work it around to a question about the offending practice. Once we found a couple just finishing setting up their tent right on a trail where it was illegal to do so, as the last light was fading and a violent thunderstorm was obviously about to break. We did not tell them they had to move. Some people may be able to come on with the more direct approach and still make it palatable. We know a ranger for a private landowning agency who can tell anybody to do or not do anything and still come out on friendly terms—a rare quality (especially among park rangers). But unless you have that golden touch, you have to weigh, as we do, zeal for land stewardship with good manners. You could harm the good cause by creating a backlash reaction; more-over, the backwoods is not, in our opinion, a good place for arguments and unpleasantness, but a place for serenity and goodwill.

Nevertheless, we remain fundamentally committed to the concept of stewardship, and we earnestly hope that the messages of this book will help preserve wildlands and the wild spirit that goes with them—and that an adequate level of tact has been maintained in presenting these messages, even when our strong feelings may have made us a bit enthusiastic in preaching the good gospel and smiting the heathen.

Thoreau's oft-quoted injunction—"In wildness is the preservation of the world"—is apt enough. If it remains as true today as when Thoreau wrote it, the question that this generation must concern itself with is *the preservation of wildness*. The spirit of wildness can be threatened from many sources—"development" speculators, unrestrained economic exploitation, tourist mania, overuse by thoughtless hikers, needless restrictions by wilderness managers, and others. Recreation itself can be just another form of exploitation, or it can be undertaken in a spirit of stewardship of the land. The choice is ours.

Laura and Guy Waterman
East Corinth, Vermont

I

HIKERS: WHO ARE WE?

A fine kind of madness...
WARREN G. HARDING

A fine and pleasant misery...
PATRICK F. McMANUS

HIKERS AND BACKPACKERS are a breed apart. What they do provides ample reason to question their good sense, if not their sanity.

Many sensible Americans spend their weekends in rational, socially responsible pursuits like pushing (or riding) a lawn mower in concentric circles, staring at football on television, or getting plastered at neighborhood cocktail parties. Not so the hiker/backpacker of the neighborhood, whose weekend is divided roughly into four parts:

1. Grunting and puffing uphill carrying a load on the back that can only be good news to the nation's back doctors
2. Plunging jerkily downhill, drumming up trade for the nation's knee doctors
3. Sitting on damp logs, slapping mosquitoes, eating (if not digesting) partially cooked dehydrated or freeze-dried inedibles, before sleeping on an uneven surface of roots and stones, only to arise at an ungodly hour when his rational neighbor remains fast asleep, secure in the knowledge that the first pro game won't start till noon

4. Sitting behind a steering wheel, careening through Friday
   and Sunday night darkness, to get to and back from what
   our Puritan ancestors sagely called "that dismal wilderness"

Who is this backpacker? Studies tell us that he or she is apt to
be from the upper end of the income scale (but *not* the top end), to
live in an urban setting during the week, and to have a string of
diplomas that would make you think that somewhere along the
line this person might have learned enough to stay in out of the
rain, but didn't. Very often he or she is of college age, though many
backpackers are considerably older. This much is statistically
ascertainable.

But *who* is this backpacker? What kind of person would self-
inflict this strange weekend-and-vacation life of hardship and
deliberate avoidance of the amenities with which Thomas Edison,
Alexander Bell, and Sir Thomas Crapper went to so much thought
and trouble to provide us all? Who is it that would give up technological blessings like televised football and premixed martinis for a
life of blisters, downpours, and gorp?

Is the average backpacker an aspiring mountaineer? Do
backpackers dream about feats they know they'll never pull off, of
conquering Himalayan heights? Are they latter-day Thoreaus,
seeking to contemplate the richness of the natural world? Or are
they more related to their ancestral outdoor cousins, the hunters
and fishermen, but have merely discarded rod and gun in the
interests of doing more walking? Tenzing Norgay, who climbed
Mount Everest with Sir Edmund Hillary and spent a lifetime
observing the passing parade of expeditionary mountaineers in the
Himalayas, described them all as "odd people, idealists, eccentrics,
men with curious obsessions." Does this description fit the American hiker and backpacker?

We raise these questions not because we can fully answer them,
but because groping toward answers is essential if we are to come to
grips with some of the issues we discuss in this book: the new backwoods ethics of concern for the environment, the kind of backwoods
environment we want to preserve, the values that ought to shape
management policies in the woods and hills where hikers go.

We need to know who the backpacker is, what motivates him and her, if we are to preserve the right values in the backcountry.

One thing seems clear: The backwoods trampers we're talking about are not seeking physical comfort. They are deliberately leaving the easy life to go where they'll get rained on, eaten by bugs, and exhausted by the physical effort of getting themselves and their backpacks there and back. Whatever the specifics of their motives, they're obviously seekers of challenge and difficulty. If they weren't they'd stay in the cities or suburbs. With the British explorer Sir Francis Younghusband, who walked across the deserts and ranges of Central Asia, the weekend backpacker takes joy in "the pride in his prowess that is such a satisfaction to his soul."

Those who would construct backcountry facilities with all the comforts of home are missing the essence of the experience that true outdoorspeople seek. If we wanted hot water and brightly lit weatherproof interiors, sumptuous meals, and sociable crowds, we'd stay at home or go to road-accessed resorts. The backcountry is a world apart, and one distinguishing characteristic is that it is *not* a world of indolent ease.

It's not just sitting on a remote summit that matters. It's how hard it was to get there. It's getting there on your own power, testing your knowledge and experience of the woods trails, your judgment, your physical condition, and most of all your drive and desire to overcome the difficulties. "The summit's in the climb," writes the mountain poet M. W. Borghoff.

Not that every weekend hiker is out there to set speed records or attain summits at all costs. Quite the contrary. Most of today's outdoorspeople seem deliberately contemptuous of the minority who push themselves hard in the backcountry. Peakbagging is definitely out of style these days. The backwoods majority set themselves modest trip goals and try to enjoy the scenery along the way. They try to be reasonably comfortable in their outdoors homes.

Nevertheless, they wouldn't be there at all if comfort and ease were their goals. Whatever the grade of their hair shirt, they're still out there to enjoy being tough.

Another quality that seems common to all this breed is a "sense of place." If exercise were the sole goal, they could walk around the block all weekend long—or even mow their lawns with old hand mowers. If suffering were the sole goal, the Marquis de Sade devised a number of tools and techniques that would suffice to hold attention. But our backpacker seeks exercise and hardship in a particular setting: a world of natural surroundings.

The deserts of Arizona, the mountain ridges of the Sierra, the wetlands of the Everglades, the trodden paths of the Catskills, the vast forests below the Brooks Range are greatly different worlds—but in underlying spirit they are similar.

The backpacker seeks wildness. He or she wants to look at mountains, streams, deep woods, jagged rock formations. He or she has visions of the caribou that once roamed the spectral barrens of Katahdin's high tableland, and still migrate in untold numbers across the vast Alaskan tundra. He or she wants to feel the thin, cold air, to hear the pure whistle of the white-throated sparrow, to see the delicate lacework of green moss on a boulder, to sense the solitude of remote places.

Whether he or she seeks real solitude is a question that's more difficult to answer. Backlands managers assume that he does, and the Wilderness Act proclaims that goal. Yet the tendency of so many to head for so few choice wilderness meccas, to hike the same trails, climb the same summits, sleep in the same campgrounds, makes one wonder how much solitude they really want. A rough life in a natural setting, yes. Solitude? Doubtful.

...which is fortunate. If backpackers are seeking true solitude in the backwoods today, they are not generally finding it. The woods are overrun with solitude seekers. But that's getting ahead of our story.

In this first section we present a few thoughts that have occurred to us over years of watching that curious breed, the hikers and backpackers of this country, and their principal preoccupation. The breed may be viewed as fundamentally mad and their pastime as an absurd form of self-imposed misery—but their affliction is, as Warren Harding said of that other ridiculous avocation, rock climbing, "a fine kind of madness," and in the words of the hunting-and-fishing humorist Patrick F. McManus, "a fine and pleasant misery."

1

That Pack on the Back: Mae West vs. Twiggy

And seeing the snail, which everywhere doth roam
Carrying his own house still, still is at home,
Follow (for he is easy pac'd) this snail,
Be thine own palace, or the world's thy jail.

JOHN DONNE

WE MEET TWO distinct types of hikers in the woods: the kitchen sink and the hair shirt. Maybe you know them too. Maybe you're one or the other. Some people carry more than you can possibly use on a two- or three-day weekend; others less than you need to enjoy a reasonably good time.

The kitchen sink believes in carrying it all, everything to make himself comfortable in the woods, along with every precaution against a wide range of possible emergencies, from hypothermia to hangnail. With his pack bulging and stuff sacks strapped on top or hanging below, he grunts along, sweat pouring from his overworked body. Maybe you can't take it with you, but this fellow will obviously try.

The hair shirt subscribes to the go-light school, toothpick-and-a-match, survive on as little as possible. He drills holes in the handle of his toothbrush and bivouacs in a rain poncho.

These two traditions have deep roots. It's Atlas versus Mercury. He who bears the weight of the world on his shoulders versus he of the winged foot. It's Paul Bunyan versus John Muir. Goliath versus David. Connie versus Big Stoop (remember, you "Terry and the Pirates" fans?). Late Gothic versus Rococo. Mae West versus Twiggy. (As we said, some people carry more than you can possibly use on a two- or three-day weekend; others less than you need to enjoy a reasonably good time.) The difference is more than a matter of pack weight; it's a contrast in approach to the outdoors, a divergence of personal style, almost a split in philosophy.

On his pioneering explorations of Yosemite Valley and the Sierra Nevada, John Muir carried incredibly little—sometimes just a couple of blankets and a food box small enough to strap to his belt, containing only grain meal, sugar, and tea. Muir is not only one of America's greatest champions of conservation, he is also the patron saint of the go-light school.

Muir's modern-day successor as lord of the Sierra backcountry was Norman Clyde, who spent 40 years exploring hidden valleys and making solo first ascents of difficult routes almost right up to his death at age 87, in 1972. But Clyde was the opposite of Muir as a backpacker. His typical 100-pound pack might include elaborate fishing gear, two pistols, camera equipment, extra pairs of boots and clothes, several large kettles, a wide assortment of dishes, bowls, and cups, canned food, and perhaps a few chunks of firewood if he were going above timberline; plus the famous Clyde library of books. "The pack that walked like a man," he was called. Surely Clyde was the patron saint of the kitchen sink breed.

The New England inheritors of the Clyde legacy have traditionally been the hut men of the Appalachian Mountain Club's chain of huts in the White Mountains. These college-age lads used to stock all the food and equipment for huts that were as far as six miles from the road over mountain trails, with as much as 3,600 feet of elevation to be gained. Their packs of well over 100 pounds humbled many a tired vacationer whom they steamed past on the trail. Back in the 1950s, the hut boys at the 4,900-foot Madison Springs Hut began packing all the parts of a Model T up to that remote and rocky windswept col, intending to assemble it among the boulders. Sober authorities intervened, and a helicopter flew out the parts as part of a cleanup campaign in the 1960s. These days the AMC is deemphasizing the load-carrying legend of hut life; modern hut men are hired more for their hospitality or their ability to interpret the ecology around the hut, and there are now female "hut persons." Loads are still respectable, but packs over 100 pounds are frowned upon. An era has passed.

The modern backpacking ideal is to cut weight ruthlessly. The western outdoors painter Roy Kerswill says he gets along fine for five days on a 16½-pound pack, including camera, sketch pad, and brushes. He carries no cooking gear because he eats cold food only, and has worked it out so that he survives comfortably on a half pound of food per day.

Many years ago a New Englander of outsized legends, a fiery eccentric by the name of Arthur Comey, boasted of multiday trips with his famous "Ten Pound pack." Incredibly, Comey's 10 pounds found room for many items we would scarcely consider necessary today—razor and shaving soap, washcloth, bathing trunks, moccasins, and axe, with sheath and whetstone.

Confessions of a Weight Lifter

Considering the obvious advantages of the go-light approach, we wish we could report that our normal packs are models of how to go superlight. Not so. Part of our problem is that we do a good deal of winter camping, when some heavy gear is unavoidable. Somehow we can't bring ourselves to part with it in summer.

For example, for years we were accustomed to a roomy, stormproof tent. It's very useful in winter, especially in exposed campsites or spots where you may have to sit out a storm for a full

day or more. Being accustomed to this luxury in winter, we went
on enjoying it year-round. We carried the Bauer Expedition model,
with the front *and* back vestibules, snow flaps (in July?), and a
weight of 12 pounds (grunt!).

It took the "new ethic" of clean camping to wean us away
from our beloved Bauer for summer camping. Now we swing along
the trail with somewhat lightened loads (and fewer backaches),
since we made the switch to hammocks. We'll tell you more about
that in chapter 10.

For winter camping, we've discovered the delicious advantage of
the sled over the backpack. As long as you aren't trying to climb too
steep a slope, it is much, much easier to drag your overnight gear on a
simple plastic sled. When you stop walking with a pack on, that 50
pounds is still on your back unless you struggle to set it down and heft
it back on again. With a sled, when you stop pulling, that 50 (or even
100) pounds sits there on the snow, not on your back.

Otherwise, we have learned the lessons of weight too slowly.
For many years we were hung up on a model of headlamp that gives
strong light while leaving both hands free; but it ran on four D
batteries, while the handy miniature flashlights run on two tiny
AA batteries. Today we're content with the little flashlights and a
jerry-built head rig for converting them to headlamps if we need to.

We were very reluctant to give up the marvelous Optimus
111B camping stove. We knew it was great for melting large
amounts of snow (again…in July?), but it was also virtually the
heaviest of the myriad models of backpacking stoves on the market. We'll have more to tell you about this in chapter 11.

Last fall we noticed that in an obscure corner of our pack
we'd been carrying—all summer—a file for sharpening crampons
on ice-climbing trips…

An anthropologist named Woody Allen claims that there are
tribes in Borneo that do not have a word for "no" in their language
and turn down requests by nodding and saying "I'll get back to
you." Well, our ability to reject articles from backpacking trips
sometimes seems about as effective. So, for years in went the extra
batteries, the extra sweater, the extra fuel.

What You *Don't* Need

If you want to avoid getting into this bind, we can suggest a number of things that we've seen in the backcountry that you don't need:

1. A folding foxhole shovel, an old Boy Scout favorite; it might have been great in World War I, but who needs the weight in today's backwoods?
2. A mallet for driving tent pegs; you'll need it to set up a circus tent, but not for the typical weekend camping setup.
3. A tool kit, including a wrench, needle-nose pliers, screw drivers (regular and Phillips), and scissors; we find that a four-ounce Swiss Army knife, plus a little parachute cord, will suffice for emergency repairs.
4. Various camp stools and folding chairs—even folding toilets, as if these matters can't be taken care of without specialized equipment.
5. Cosmetics for the ladies. One handbook for women in the woods advises that "using a deodorant daily in the backwoods is a must." And we've seen recommended equipment lists that include a nail file and clippers (again, these are handy on a Swiss Army knife).
6. Carbon monoxide detection kits. No kidding—one widely quoted authority on camping says that you should never use a portable cookstove inside a tent without a carbon monoxide detection kit. Who wants to lug a kit around when thoroughly ventilating your tent will solve the problem?

Ten Tiny Tips for Weight Carrying

If you eliminate all such non-necessities, but you still find that your pack outweighs a Notre Dame linebacker, we could suggest 10 tiny tips on how to coexist with the enemy. Alas, these ideas grow from long personal experience. If your pack is heavy:

1. Keep the weight high; load the heavier items near the top of your pack.
2. Keep it all close to your back; avoid bulky items strapped on the outside in such a way as to pull you over backward.
3. Get everything into or onto the pack; don't try to carry anything in your hands, unless you go in for a walking staff (or in winter, an ice ax or ski pole).
4. Use a waist strap to transfer most of the load from your shoulders to your hips: on most modern packs this is standard.
5. Once you put the pack on, plan to walk steadily for long periods and not to stop for "rests" very often; frequent rest stops, taking the pack off and wrestling it back on, will delay your progress interminably and use up more energy than the rests restore.
6. Adopt a slow, sustainable pace, with a steady rhythm of regular steps; if you can sort of roll your weight from one foot to the other you can get a momentum that eases the strain. A stop-and-go, herky-jerky motion continually makes the full presence of the pack felt.
7. In winter, try using a sled for most of the weight, although this approach may be appropriate for some itineraries and not others.
8. Winter or summer, plan itineraries that fan out from base camps, so that you aren't always carrying all the weight. Enjoy a light day pack for most of your upper-elevation walking, and camp low—which eases the impact on fragile alpine ecologies as well as on your back.
9. Cultivate strong young companions who like to show that they can carry enormous weights. Then, as you walk uphill, ask them short questions that require long answers, so they have to do the talking while you gasp for breath as unobtrusively as possible. ("I didn't quite follow the theory of relativity. Would you go through it again?")
10. If all else fails, and you must carry weight, grin as you bear it. Think positive; like so many activities that seem purely physical, packing a heavy load is 75 percent mental. If you can pick up a pack, you can walk all day with it—if your frame of mind is right.

We know a marvelous fellow, Win Thratchett, with whom we've been on several winter camping trips in the Adirondacks. Thratchett's the kitchen sink type, par excellence. He carries an enormous pack, but he's ready for anything. In fact, he's never so happy as when some unusual emergency requires some obscure item that only a pack of his size could possibly provide. When a trip goes smoothly, Thratchett's unhappy—all that extra weight for nothing.

On one trip a young friend broke a snowshoe and was be-moaning the inadequacy of his planned patch job, which made use of a stick, a strip of rawhide, and tape. Along came Thratchett and asked (somewhat eagerly, we thought) if he could help. Our young friend allowed as how what he really needed was a pair of wood screws just the right size.

Thratchett looked delighted. "What size?" he asked as he swung off his enormous pack and started into it.

The other man felt this was just too much and remarked somewhat acidly: "Five-eighths inch, and only flat heads will do."

Thratchett looked momentarily nonplussed, but buried deeper into the dark recesses of the pack. When he came up, triumphantly clutching his tool kit, you could sense his satisfaction as he said:

"Brass or steel?"

2

Backpackers' Favorite Lies

*They that are serious in ridiculous matters will be
ridiculous in serious affairs.*

PLUTARCH

"THERE WE WERE! Hadn't seen a sign of other people for six days.
The temperature that morning was 20 below and the wind was gusting
to 90 miles per hour, but we shouldered our 80-pound packs and…"

If anyone tried to feed you that story, you'd wisely be suspicious of half of what he said. Yet he'd be only slightly overplaying a
game that most of us backwoods hikers play.

We're normally an honest enough crowd. You meet few
outright car thieves or embezzling accountants in the backcountry,
and we don't recall that backpacking was listed as the hobby of any
of the Watergate or Iran-Contra conspirators. Still, there are
certain subjects that a hiker simply can't discuss without Twainsian
exaggeration at the least. If fishermen are more renowned for their
estimates of the one that got away, it's only because we backpackers have not articulated our own stories adequately yet. But, God
knows, some of us try.

For your guidance (and protection) we identify half a dozen favorite subjects for loquacious backpackers' tall-tale telling.

Pack Weight

This ploy has two versions. The first version consists of grossly overestimating your pack's weight and thereby gaining points for superior strength and stamina. The figures usually given for this purpose range, for men, from 70 to 90 pounds; for women, 60 to 80 is the preferred range. Over 100 strains credibility and you lose points.

In the second version, instead of implying strength, you gain points by demonstrating your resourcefulness and toughness in surviving on practically nothing—which you indicate by underestimating your pack's weight. For instance, you went out for six days in the wilds and the pack weighed under 20 pounds.

We've seen many a relatively inexperienced backpacker come to ruin by playing the first version of this game in a crowd that turned out to have the experience and shrewdness to pull the second on him unexpectedly. Just when the poor duffer thinks his hearers are impressed with his tales of 80-pound packs lugged over Continental Divides, someone in the group remarks coolly that he used to carry weights like that but now he's got it down so that he can go five days on 13.5 pounds and have food left over. Others in the group then start in on how they cut handles off toothbrushes and remove the cardboard from inside the toilet paper, and pretty soon the air is dripping with scorn for the utter oafishness of anyone who'd carry 80 pounds even were he headed for Outer Mongolia from Singapore.

The old-time hard men still can't resist the lure of the 90-pound pack. Once when we were in the Carter Range of New Hampshire's White Mountains, one of the hut boys of the Appalachian Mountain Club had just packed 135 pounds up to Carter Notch Hut. That figure was authentic: they had scales right there. An hour or so later, he started down the trail to return to AMC's base camp at Pinkham Notch. Unbeknownst to him, one of us was sunning himself on top of a tall boulder next to the trail. As this young husky passed underneath alone, we heard him say quietly to himself: "How much did you take up to Carter today?" (Pause—then in casual tones:) "One hundred and thirty-five pounds." (Pause—then with hushed awe:) "Wow!" Evidently we were the unsuspected audience for a rehearsal of a conversation to which our young friend looked forward with all the relish of a true back-packer.

Distances Hiked

Here is another ploy that can cut both ways: You'll hear some braggarts tell you about covering 25 miles of rough mountain terrain with full packs. But the more sophisticated gamesmen have learned how to lay waste the opposition by describing what a formidable bushwhacking trip they struggled through: "All day we fought through dense growth, with only the compass to guide us, and in 10 hours of monumental effort we'd covered less than two miles." The latter's listeners are cowed by the implication that only superhuman strength and resolution could keep a person going through such incredibly tangled jungle.

Days away from People

Most of us hikers yearn for the wilderness to be wilder than it really is in this day and age. Part of the true pleasure of hiking is the illusion of getting into a country where few people are or, better yet, ever have been. We speak wistfully of "mountain solitude."

Perhaps this is why some backpackers go in for the fantasy that "we didn't see a sign of other people for six days." It's still possible to go places where you can really escape all evidence of humans, present or past. But few really get there. More likely you're bound to hear a plane overhead at some point, find a worn track that isn't just deer or moose, or, worst of all, kick up a Vienna sausage can on the edge of a clearing that you thought was your aboriginal discovery.

Stand on a remote New England mountaintop and look out over miles of rugged, heavily forested ridges, and you can be tempted to speculate that much of it is country where no one has

ever been. As you sit staring at those ridges, you slowly realize that
many of them show faintly discernible patterns of horizontal lines.
These are the tracings of old lumber roads switchbacking up the
ridges from the days when loggers crisscrossed the entire area.
Instead of your dream that no humans have ever set foot on those
ridges comes the realization that 100 years ago they were crawling
with logging teams.

So when someone tells you that they were out in country
where no one had ever been before, control your envy. The nine-
teenth-century loggers, as well as hunters and trappers, combed
over this grand country from east to west pretty thoroughly, and
your pioneer friend was probably stalking the ghosts of several
generations of outdoorsmen who never heard of Kelty packs or
Mountain House freeze-dried food.

Wind Speed

If you've ever been above the treeline when the wind was
really hitting 60 miles per hour, you turn a benevolently skeptical
ear to the tales of crossing rugged terrain with heavy packs in 90-
mph winds. We don't know very many people who carry an
anemometer with them. Those that do develop a conservatism in
estimating wind speed that seems to elude the rest of us.

Once five of us were climbing on Maine's Katahdin in winter.
It was one of those wild days above treeline. When we climbed out
of our snow gully onto that remarkably flat tableland plateau of
Katahdin's upper elevations, we were engulfed in clouds. Visibility
was reduced to 50 feet at best, and there was no place to hide from
the wind or cold. Before starting out on a compass course, we
huddled together for a bit of lunch, numbed by the cold and
buffeted by the wind, which seemed stronger than most of the party
had experienced before. At this point one of our group produced an
anemometer from his pack and invited our guesses on the wind
speed. The other four of us guessed speeds ranging from 30 to 50
mph; no doubt, had there been no instrument around, the Monday
morning office stories would have definitely fixed the speed at least
at 50. (Usually speed increases in memory from the already exag-

gerated estimates of the actual moment.) Then our iconoclastic
friend gave us his reading: 18 mph.

Once, when we were coming down from New Hampshire's
Presidential Range, we met another party at the trailhead, who asked
how it was above treeline. "Windy!" we said. "How fast?" they asked.
Clearly we were being invited to spout a figure, but out of what whole
cloth are such figures supposed to be concocted? We didn't know, and
we suspect that few people have any real ability to judge wind speed.
Our refusal to give a dramatic figure, though, seemed to disappoint the
other hikers: we weren't playing the true backpackers' game.

Temperature

You might think that Doc Fahrenheit's handy invention
might keep us all honest when reporting the temperature extremes
in which we've camped or hiked. But the resourceful tale teller has
carefully sanded down the sharp edges of his memory so that he can
leap gracefully from hard observed reading to speculations about
what it "probably" was—and thus come up with some astonishing
tales of extreme cold or heat.

We've been winter camping in northern New England for
three decades, yet we've seen the thermometer actually reach -20°F
on nights that we've been camped out on only three or four
occasions. Still, we've regularly heard novices who took up winter
camping for a year or two during that period regale their friends
with what it's like to camp at –20°F above treeline. Well, *maybe*
they saw the red line sink to –20°F—but we're skeptical.

We've been told by our western friends that desert hikers
become just as imaginative in exaggerating the high temperatures
they've walked through. ("We had to walk 15 miles carrying 80-
pound packs in 120-degree heat with no water.")

Bird Species

This is a highly specialized branch of the art. The very fact
that backpackers who know anything about birds are as rare as
Kirtland's warbl—oops, sorry, we mean they're very rare—gives lots
of leeway to those who have little more than a nodding acquain-
tance with a Peterson Field Guide.

If you hear some far-off chirp, you'll rarely be caught off base if you say, "Hey, did you hear that? Black-throated green warbler." If your companions ask you to point it out, the bird can generally be stuck with the blame for not repeating the call, if it ever issued it in the first place. Of course, you risk having some unsuspecting amateur Audubon turn up among your companions and challenge your identifications. If you've just confidently snapped "yellow-throated vireo" as a winged creature flitted momentarily in and out of view among some hemlocks, you may be aghast to have someone in the group venture an apparently better-informed view that it was in fact a robin. (Sometimes you can get out of this predicament by smilingly observing that the female immatures are not always readily distinguished.)

Variants of the bird species ploy may be explored in such areas as tree identification, ferns, rock types, and especially alpine flowers.

These are just a few of many areas in which the joys of the hiker's memory may transcend the confines of mere experience. Hiking speed, angle of slope climbed, and wild food foraged are some other possibilities.

We do not offer these suggestions in any critical sense, nor as definitive. Backpackers are still developing the state of the art, and we have much to learn from our fishing and hunting cousins. You might want to work up your own subjects and refine your own tips for successful playing of the game. After all, this activity will provide interesting employment for your mind while you're ticking off the miles on those 50-mile day hikes...

3

Peakbagging

He's got 'em on the list—he's got 'em on the list, and they'll
none of 'em be missed—they'll none of 'em be missed.
W. S. GILBERT

PEAKBAGGING IS A CROSS between outdoor recreation, competitive athletics, and religion. Originally, climbing mountains was primarily a recreational experience, and for many people it still is. Its overtones of aesthetic appeal and communion with nature make a formal listing of peaks "bagged" seem harshly inappropriate. However, when a mountain range has, let us say, 46 summits over a given height—and for some reason it seemed for a while as if a disconcerting number of the world's ranges did have precisely 46 such peaks—it is only human nature to want to climb them all. Thus is born the sport—eventually the religion—of peakbagging.

Northeastern Peakbagging

The first known peakbagger in our northeastern mountains was a man by the name of Alden Partridge. Founder of the military school at Norwich (now moved to Northfield), Vermont, Partridge climbed peaks all over New England during the first quarter of the nineteenth century. That was when there were virtually no trails, and certainly no superhighways to whisk you to the trailheads for your peak. Partridge would walk from his home in Norwich to Crawford Notch in the White Mountains, 76 miles, in one day. On the next day he'd bushwhack up Mount Washington and back to his inn. On the third day he'd walk 76 miles home. In rainy spells he'd get soaked thrashing through the thickets, but persist for days on end anyway. He was a most remarkable peakbagger, and fit forefather for the rest of the madcap breed.

Two of the most attractive personalities that ever walked a wooded mountain ridge are associated with the formal codification of peakbagging in the Adirondacks.

Herb Clark was one of scores of Adirondack canoeing, fishing, and hunting guides, and probably never would have found a distinctive niche in outdoor recreation history had he not one day been given an unusual assignment. His client, the great civil liberties New York lawyer Louis Marshall, wanted someone to entertain his two overly energetic teenage sons, Robert and George, by taking them on mountain climbs during vacations in the Adirondacks. So Herb Clark began to climb various peaks with the boys. Then they got the fatal idea: why not climb all of the peaks over 4,000 feet in elevation? They studied the maps and picked out 46 such eminences.

Thus began the first systematic bag-'em-all peakbagging extravaganza. Between 1918 and 1925 Clark and the Marshall brothers climbed those 46 mountains. It was a magical adventure.

George Marshall was probably a great fellow, but his older brother, Bob, had to have been one of the sweetest, most exuberant, unmistakable cutups that ever walked this earth. And how he walked this earth! A cragged six-footer crackling with "great gusto and infectious enthusiasms," he not only pioneered on the Adirondack "46," but went on to explore Alaskan wilderness, repeatedly (over 50 times, by actual count) logging 40 wilderness miles per day in the most uncompromising terrain. He threw himself into wilderness preservation with the same relentless but good-humored zeal, as cofounder of the Wilderness Society and a key Interior Department official during critical decision-making times for wilderness all over the country. There's one story, during that original Adirondack peakbagging spree, when Herb Clark kidded him about carrying a huge log for firewood from a ridge far removed from their campsite; undaunted, Bob shouldered the log and made Clark and his brother eat their words as they watched him wrestle that huge log over mountaintops for hours and finally into camp for the evening's fire.

As for Clark, he was an original too. When they were walking a lone dusty road toward the base of one of their Adirondack peaks, he solemnly assured the brothers that this road was the original site of the battle between the *Monitor* and the *Merrimac*, pointing out holes where shells had landed as proof. Bob Marshall, himself one of the funniest men of the mountains, called Clark "the happy possessor of the keenest sense of humor I have known."

With this joy-lit trio began the zany pursuit of the Adirondack 46. According to the official records, eight years passed before the feat was repeated by a fourth person. In the eight years after that, however, 21 more stalwart Adirondack trampers had reached all 46 summits. In the next eight years, there were 43 more successful peakbaggers, and the race was on. Today the number is over 2,000, and they have their own club, the Adirondack Forty-Sixers, complete with officers, dues, and an official magazine.

By coincidence, the White Mountains over in New Hampshire, when first counted, also turned out to have 46 peaks over 4,000 feet in height. By the 1930s ardent lovers of the Whites were keeping their list of peaks climbed too. Ultimately a group within the Appalachian Mountain Club organized the "Four Thousand Footer Committee" and began handing out scrolls and patches and decals for those who had been to the tops of the New Hampshire "46."

Peakbaggers zealously pursuing membership in either the Adirondacks or White Mountains group climb mountains with a religious dedication like that of monks resolutely repeating their rounds of prayers or good works.

The Conflict of Science and Religion

Over the years the mapmakers of the US Geological Survey have not treated the sacred number 46 with proper veneration and respect. Relatively early in the game, the impious triangulations of the USGS uncovered the heretical revelation that the holy roll of 46 summits originally climbed by the Marshall brothers included four peaks whose elevations were several embarrassing feet short of 4,000. One (Couchsachraga) was only about 3,800 feet. Not only that, but another mountain, which the Church Fathers had completely overlooked (McNaughton), was in fact *over* 4,000 feet high.

Like all uninvited scientific discoveries, the impact of this revelation on the organizational hierarchy of the revealed religion—in this case, the peakbagging Forty-Sixers—was traumatic. Like many ecclesiastical orders before and since, the High Priests decided that the best way to deal with this new fact was to ignore it. To this day the anti-Darwinian Forty-Sixers gallantly carry on with the original tablet of 46 peaks handed down by the Marshalls.

Edward Gibbon, surveying his completed life's work, *The Decline and Fall of the Roman Empire*, is said to have summarized his 2,442-page effort with the words, "I have described the triumph of barbarism and religion." Those twin forces perhaps won the day in the Adirondacks. And so, with religious zeal and barbaric energy, aspiring Forty-Sixers must still climb those three 3,900-footers and little scrubby 3,800-foot Couchsachraga, while the offending McNaughton may be omitted.

For many years the rival High Priests over in New Hampshire smirked behind their vestments about this humiliating inaccuracy of the Adirondack "46." Then the anticlerical forces of the USGS slipped into the temple of the White Mountains and smashed another icon. The Four Thousand Footer Committee had overlooked, it seemed, a 4,000-foot eminence called Galehead. Sorry, reported the cynical scientists, you have 47, not 46.

Consternation and dissension struck the upper priesthood of the Four Thousand Footer Committee, to the undisguised amusement of the Adirondack Forty-Sixers' fathers. One might have thought the state of the *Manchester Union Leader* and "Live Free or Die" to be safe from the machinations of modern science. An editorial in the Appalachian Mountain Club's official publication called for leaving Galehead off the formal list, whatever the spurious findings of the surveyors. Dark suggestions were whispered about omitting the apostate mountain from the AMC maps. Meetings and correspondence flew back and forth. Finally the duly authorized Four Thousand Footer Committee met in close recess and secret conclave and, sending up the white smoke, announced that henceforth there were indeed 47, not 46, 4,000-foot summits that aspiring peakbaggers must climb.

Let a hog in your house and he'll walk on your table. The scientists, having won their point, had to rub it in by "finding" yet another 4,000-footer, the rugged and exciting Bondcliff, hitherto regarded as a mere subsidiary ridge on Mount Bond. So now we're up to 48 in New Hampshire. The cocky surveyors stalk the shadows just beyond the official list with rumors of still more to come. (That northwest peak of Hancock? Guyot? Others as yet unrevealed?)

Thus the two groups are now in somewhat the position of baseball's major leagues relative to the designated-hitter rule. One accepts the findings of science and requires initiates to climb the 48 (*sic*) measured 4,000-footers; the other clings to tradition and the memory of the Marshalls, and hews to its beloved 46 summits despite the cold water thrown by the surveyors.

Listing to Port and Starboard

Meanwhile, down in the Catskills, the devotions of peakbagging were slower in coming. There are only two 4,000-foot summits in the land of Rip Van Winkle, but the impulse to form a club overcame nature's oversight by dropping the cutoff point 500 feet. For the "Catskill 3500 Club" you must bag the 34 Catskill peaks over 3,500 feet in elevation...*and* climb four of them in winter. The Catskill group never has taken its orders quite as seriously as the more prestigious Adirondack and White Mountain faiths. "After all," wrote Catskill tramper Henry Young, "when you are grabbing peaks that are only 3,500 feet high, you have to have a sense of humor."

The mania for peakbagging in the Northeast has spread beyond the mystical limits of 46. Maine, it appears, has a dozen 4,000-footers. Vermont has five more. This gives the New Englander a total of 63 peaks to shoot for—whoops, make that 65— and many do, to become members of the Four Thousand Footer Club of New England.

Put these together with the Adirondacks' 46 and the Catskills' two, and you have (or had originally) the Northeast 111 (now 113).

About 10 years ago, not satisfied with reclimbing their 4,000-footers (like the Adirondacks' Jim Goodwin, who has climbed his 46 eighteen times each), a New England group drew up a list of the 100 highest in New England. There followed lists of 100 highest by state. Finally someone came up with the inevitable list of 3,000-footers; there are 445 of those in New England. Sure enough, a few folks have climbed them all.

We asked one of the 3,000-footer peakbaggers whether anyone was working on the list of 2,000-footers. His response was: "Do you think we're crazy?" We thought the answer to that question was clear a long time ago.

Vermont, with only five 4,000-foot mountains, has set up a somewhat different goal of its own. The Green Mountains' gentle contours are traversed north to south by the celebrated Long Trail stretching 265 miles from Massachusetts to the Canadian border. First cut all the way through in 1930, the Long Trail now has over 2,000 End-to-Enders.

The end-to-end mania is more widely associated with the world-famous Appalachian Trail. This 2,000-mile feat now has become so much of a status symbol that trail traffic presents serious erosion and overcrowding problems. About 700 miles of the AT run through New England, from its northern terminus at Maine's Katahdin, over such celebrated summits as Mount Washington and Mount Greylock, and crossing the Bear Mountain Bridge into New York on its way south toward Georgia. (More on this in the next chapter.)

There are other north-south supertrails in the West, such as the Pacific Crest Trail and the Continental Divide. These are both over 2,000 miles long. Some years back an aggressive walker named Eric Ryback pulled off the first grand slam by hiking the AT, the Pacific Crest, and the Continental Divide.

Back here in the Northeast, a further challenge has been discovered: climbing the "46" in winter. With heavy snow, formidable temperatures, and the wind that sweeps loftier summits, winter climbing is a considerably more challenging undertaking than summer trail walking. Miriam Underhill, considered by many to be America's greatest woman mountain climber, after a distinguished career in the Alps and other remote ranges, set herself the goal of doing all of New Hampshire's (then) 46 between December 21 and March 21. During the 1950s Miriam and her husband, Robert, a formidable climber himself during the 1920s, succeeded in pulling off this difficult achievement—the first two to do so. Their feat was made even more astonishing by the fact that the great lady was 62 years old and Robert over 70 when they finally stood atop 5,715-foot Jefferson, having done all 46 on snowshoes, crampons, or skis. Today there are more than 100 people who have achieved this remarkable goal. Some have even done all of them more than once, and one incurable has done them each from all four points of the compass in winter.

Naturally, when New Hampshire's 46 had been climbed in winter, some hardy snow lovers set their sights on the New England list, including the Maine and Vermont summits. Interestingly enough, one of the first four to achieve this tough objective was also a woman—Penny Markley, a Maine apple grower.

The Adirondacks' 46 have also been done in winter, and

those who have climbed in both ranges in winter rate the
Adirondacks as tougher. This is because many of the New York
peaks are without formally maintained trails and must be climbed
as genuine map-and-compass bushwhacks. In winter that can be
super rough. Nevertheless, almost as many have climbed this list as
that of New Hampshire.

Inevitably the toughest goals of all have attracted the aspira-
tions of the most confirmed of peakbaggers. On January 2, 1971,
Jim Collins, the second man to do the Adirondack 46 in winter,
reached the summit of remote North Brother in Maine, to become
the first conqueror of the Northeast 111 in winter. It is noteworthy
that, despite the boom in winter climbing, it was not until 1977
that a second man, Guy Huse, achieved this goal. During the 1980s
various indefatigables knocked off the various 100 highest lists in
winter, and in 1993 it appeared likely that the greatest peakbagger
of New England, a man with the unlikely name of Tom Sawyer,
would complete all 445 of New England's 3,000-footers in winter, a
truly remarkable odyssey.

There is no end to the imaginativeness of the dyed-in-the-
wool certified peakbagger.

Fred Hunt, an Adirondack hiker of prodigious ground-
covering talents, has climbed both New Hampshire and
Adirondack lists in winter—at night.

Ed Bean, the first hard man to climb the Adirondacks' 46 in
winter, then began going back with different parties of climbers,
surreptitiously hoping to become the first man to kiss a different
woman on the summit of each of the 46.

The resourceful and ingenious Bean also set himself a goal
that once proved very helpful to these writers. It seems that Ed
wanted to take a leak on the summit of each of the 46 in winter.
One blustery March day, the two of us were snowshoeing up
Santononi's windswept ridge, having heard that Ed had been there
the day before with another party. As we emerged on the summit
ridge itself, we were surrounded by dense clouds and terrific winds.
Visibility was reduced to a few feet. We groped our way along the
ridge, buffeted by those cyclonic gusts, trying to figure out how we

could be sure that we were on the true summit. Suddenly at our feet we saw—yellow snow! Old Ed Bean had left his trademark the day before. We knew we were on the summit.

Another incurable peakbagger, the Reverend Henry Folsom, set out to do all of the New Hampshire peaks in one continuous walk, rather than driving to different trail heads. The resulting 244-mile trek took him 19 days. He dubbed his feat "The Four Thousand Footer Directissima."

We heard of one young woman who was out to climb the New Hampshire 46—oops, 48—in bare feet. We don't know whether she made it.

Several dogs have done each of the two 46s. Our own dog, Ralph, had climbed all of the New Hampshire peaks at least three times (some much more often) before his death in 1976.

One of the great pranksters of the AMC's White Mountain hut system, the late Tony MacMillan, once organized what he called the Six Thousand Footer Club. Since there is only one true 6,000-foot mountain in the Northeast, Tony contented himself with locating three or four outcroppings of boulders somewhere near the top of Mount Washington. Devotees of high living as well as high mountains, Tony and his epicurean friends would gather annually to parade from bump to bump, fortified by champagne and lavish hors d'oeuvres at each "summit." The hilarious venture in peakbagging would climax when the celebrants tottered back to the summit buildings to collapse in merriment among the bewildered tourists—perhaps a suitably iconoclastic approach to the often overbearing posture of peakbaggers.

National and International Peakbagging

The mania for climbing many peaks in a short time or in unusual ways is not confined merely to New England's back hills.

Colorado has 54 mountains that are over 14,000 feet. Two hikers climbed these peaks in 21 days, which they figured made a cumulative climb of 147,000 vertical feet (an average of 7,000 feet per day) and a total of 300 miles. Their main purpose was not to speed-run the "Fourteeners" (the peaks *could* be done faster—although the hikers' time was very good), but to make an endurance test out of the stunt and document their medical histories. One of the climbers was a doctor.

Some hikers play the game of trying to reach the highest point in each of the 50 states. One can go from the lofty mountain bulwark of Mount McKinley in Alaska, at 20,320 feet, to a record low of 345 feet in Florida. This "peak" is not even a mountain, just the highest sand hill in a flat state. Colorado has the distinction of having the highest lowest latitude: 3,350. In other words, wherever you are in Colorado, you can't be lower than the summit of New Hampshire's Mount Monadnock.

One zany couple set out to walk the entire perimeter of the contiguous United States—roughly 19,000 miles! They started in July 1975 and finished in late 1978.

By an almost unbelievable coincidence, the Alps have 46 peaks that are over 4,000 meters. Except for the metric conversion, the good old White Mountains and Adirondacks have something in common with the snowy Alps of Europe, though not their glaciers and crevasses. As we all know, Mont Blanc is the highest at 15,771 feet. Many people have climbed all of these 4,000-meter peaks. The trick is to do them all in one season. We understand that Fritz Wiessner, a Vermonter born in Germany and one of this century's greatest climbers, did just that.

What happens if we move this game to the great mountains of Asia, the Himalayas? This is the home of Mount Everest, at 29,028 feet the highest point on the globe. Two mountaineers (as of 1992) have climbed all 13 of the 8,000-meter peaks. When mountains get this high—the lowest of the 13 is 26,287 feet—they get a lot harder to climb.

What if someone, stuck on the number 46, wanted to climb the 46 highest peaks in the Himalayas? That *would* be a feat. These would be, of course, the 46 highest in the world, and the elevation of the lowest would be a cloud-splitting 23,890 feet.

There is one more stunt for world record makers. That is

climbing to the highest point in each of the seven continents, including such stunning peaks as Everest, McKinley, Mont Blanc, Africa's Kilimanjaro, and Antarctica's Mount Vinson, at 16,860 feet. That last is not so terribly high for fellows who have already climbed Everest, but it is very hard to get to. The seven summits have been "done" by several globe-trotting peakbaggers.

Scotland has its own special game—or inanity. This mountainous country has 280 peaks over 3,000 feet, which the Scots call "Monros," after the man who first listed them. One climber of these was a dog, who not only chaperoned his master on the climbs but also ascended the 3,000-footers in England, Wales, and Ireland, a feat only about a dozen humans could claim at that time.

Critics of Peakbagging

In 1972 two strong hikers set out to see how fast they could hike all 46 Adirondack peaks. They were careening along at a pace that would have knocked them all off in five days, or more than nine 4,000-footers per day. An unkind fate intervened to pronounce a harsh judgment on their folly: crossing over the summit of Marcy in the teeth of a hurricane, one of the pair suffered a massive heart attack and died. Suddenly he went from young, strong, buoyant, ambitious, to…just plain dead.

When death struck this peakbagger the outcry against the mania for speed records was predictable. Nor was that the first such protest. Benton MacKaye, the man who is credited with having more to do with creating the Appalachian Trail than any other, years ago deplored those who tried to cover the 2,000-mile trail in the fewest number of days. "What I hope is that it won't turn into a racetrack," grieved MacKaye in *Backpacker* magazine. "I for one would give the prize to the person who took the longest time."

Conservationist Edward Abbey is another who has spoken out against speedy traverses of trails and peaks. "Stopwatch hiking," Abbey called it.

Even everyday hikers can sometimes take offense at trail

speedsters who pass them at a breakneck clip. One hiker was heard to remark to a group of trail runners: "Why do you people hate the woods so much?" He explained his question by acidly commenting that they seemed in such a hurry to get through the woods that they must not enjoy them very much.

Influential leaders of the Appalachian Mountain Club began calling for the abolition of the Four Thousand Footer Committee. (For example, see the article by Phil Levin in the AMC's journal, *Appalachia*, June 1973.) The critics charged that peakbagging clubs tended to lure people out onto remote summits that would otherwise remain less heavily trampled, causing trail erosion, damage to vegetation, and overcrowding problems. Critics also contended that peakbagging was a deplorable motive for going to the mountains.

Systematic peakbagging is "a numbers racket," according to one critic, and "seems sacrilegious" to another. The growth of peakbagging clubs introduces "an undesirable artificiality into the natural scenery of the mountains," according to the articulate Levin. The gist of this attack on peakbaggers is the charge that they rush breathlessly from one mountaintop to the next without enjoying the view or contemplating the details and mystery of the mountain environment. "I often wonder if they ever appreciate any of the beauty that surrounds them," sighs one observer.

We'd like to rise to the defense of the peakbagger. Unquestionably there are those who grind through their list of 46 peaks with little of the spirit of appreciation that most of us think the mountains deserve. But we would guess that they are the minority. The ranks of overt peakbaggers include many people whose deep and lasting love of and commitment to the mountain environment is beyond dispute. Let's cite some examples:

1. *Robert Marshall*—the man who started the whole game back in the 1920s with his brother and their guide-friend, Herbert Clark. Yes, Marshall was a peakbagger—he never would have denied it—but he also devoted his all-too-short life to conservation and wilderness preservation. He climbed mountains because he loved them.

2. *Dr. Orra Phelps*—a grand lady whose dedication to peakbagging was so strong that she was among the first to climb all the Adirondack 4,000-footers. That was way back in 1947. Then she went on and "bagged" them all again. Peakbagger, yes—but Dr. Phelps is also a botanist of exceptional knowledge and insight. She has probably led more people to share her appreciation of mountain flora than anybody in the Adirondacks through her talks, slide shows, writings, personally led walks, and work as a ranger-naturalist at the Adirondacks' Nature Museum and Nature Trail.

3. *Miriam Underhill*—an inveterate peakbagger, the first to do the New Hampshire 46 in winter, and early conqueror of all 111 four-thousand-foot peaks in the Northeast. Her abiding affection for the mountains she climbed stands out on every page of her autobiography, *Give Me the Hills*, and in her work as both an editor of and photographer for *Mountain Flowers of New England*.

4. Almost any of the great peakbaggers we know, whose love for the hills keeps taking them back to the high ridges to feel the thin, cold air and see the wild, uncompromising scenery and hear the clear call of the white-throated sparrow in a mist-clouded alpine landscape.

An odd psychology infects many people in the mountains when they see other hikers moving rapidly along a mountain trail. Some people resent the fast hiker with a depth of resentment that's difficult to understand. Most of these people are not so narrow-minded as to insist that everyone should enjoy the mountains in precisely the same way as they do; yet they seem to want to exclude the hiker who gets enjoyment from maintaining a fast pace on a rugged trail.

We plead for tolerance—and caution the critic not to jump to conclusions when he sees someone move past him rapidly on a ridge. It's been our experience that most of the fast hill-walkers we know are people who deeply appreciate the mountain environment. They may be going fast, but they're taking it all in.

Yet we've seen people become actually angry at the sight of a hiker moving fast. This "vague prejudice," as Mr. Levin calls it, even found its way into print in a Green Mountain Club brochure on "guidelines" for use of the Long Trail. One of its 15 instructions, along with such useful admonitions as carry out all trash and stay on the trail above treeline, is: "Take your time: The Long Trail is no place to break speed records."

We're sorry to see people with one approach to hiking try to impose their personal prejudices on people with another approach. The mountains are a place for people to enjoy themselves in their own way as long as that doesn't interfere with enjoyment by others or do damage to the mountain environment. The fast hiker isn't making noise, or littering, or doing anything else to interfere with anyone else's enjoyment. We wish his critics would get off his back.

We find that we go to the mountains for many different reasons. Sometimes we poke along slowly to look at the wildflowers or gaze on an exceptional view. Sometimes we travel with one or a few friends and enjoy leisurely companionship in the mountain setting. Often we're working on trail maintenance, devoting many hours to a fraction of a mile. Sometimes we push off-trail to explore valleys or ridges we've never been to before. Sometimes, however—not as often as when we were younger, alas—we like to push ourselves and take in a considerable amount of trail mileage and several summits in a single day. On some of our "biggest" days, when we've covered lots of miles and peaks, we've also treasured moments of spectacular scenery, or cloud effects, or unusual wildlife sightings, or hard-to-define moments of exaltation absorbing the majesty and mystery of the hills around us. Neither peakbagging nor fast hiking are inconsistent with complete appreciation of the mountain scene.

We are unreconstructed peakbaggers, no question. One of us is working on her seventh round of the New Hampshire 48; the other on his sixteenth. We've done them and the Adirondacks' 46 in winter too. Once we did all the New Hampshire peaks in a continuous two-week trip. This kind of thing may strike many people as silly. That's OK. But we see no reason to dispute the spirit in which we or anyone else may approach the hills—as long as nothing is done to downgrade the experience of others or of the mountain environment.

A more sophisticated argument against peakbagging relates to the existence of official "clubs" that pass out badges or scrolls to people who climb all 46 or whatever number. The charge is made that such clubs lure more people to the already overcrowded mountains or encourage "artificial use patterns" and spread a lot of traffic onto peaks and trails that otherwise might remain relatively pristine.

This is a respectable argument that deserves to be thought about. Four-thousand-footer clubs probably do bring more people to some of the lesser-known high peaks. This is a problem that ought to concern the clubs. It seems unlikely, though, that such clubs increase total traffic in the mountains significantly. People who hear about a club and start trying to "bag" peaks are probably people who already had taken up hiking seriously.

We do deplore groups that attract more crowds to the mountains, because we think that many ranges are already reeling from the effects of too many people. We also deplore large parties at any time, because of their impact, especially their psychological impact, on the experience of others and the spirit of quiet and solitude. We'll have more to say about these things later, a lot more. But we don't believe the peakbagging clubs attract people who wouldn't otherwise be there anyway. Others are guilty of that.

At any rate, whether or not clubs and their attendant publicity are valid, there seems to be no defensible argument against the pursuit of peaks as an individual's objective. It's all part of that "fine kind of madness."

4

The 2,000-Mile
Community-on-the-Move

'Tis a long road knows no turning.

SOPHOCLES

ONE FALL DAY on top of Maine's great mountain Katahdin, we saw
two young men stride the last few steps to the summit rock cairn,
exchange a warm handshake and then produce a bottle of champagne.

We knew right away what the occasion was: here were two
hikers just at the moment of completing a six-month 2,000-mile-
plus walk from Georgia to Maine—the Appalachian National
Scenic Trail.

The world's first long-distance footpath organized for purely
recreational pursuit, the Appalachian Trail, including its 700 miles
in New England, has become an immensely popular and prestigious
test piece.

This famous footpath from Maine to Georgia was the inspired
brainchild of one man: New Englander Benton MacKaye, who died
at the advanced age of 96 in 1975.

In 1921 MacKaye, who was a forester as well as a city planner by profession, conceived the idea of the Appalachian Trail and wrote an article about it for the *Journal of the American Institute of Architects*.

His idea caught fire, and the first work began at Bear Mountain Park in New York. MacKaye and those early trail-building pioneers tried to link up already-existing trail systems to form the continuous footpath. But of all the 14 states the trail runs through, only a few, mainly in New England, had such systems in place. From there on the trail-clearers were on their own, and work was not completed until 1937—15 years and more than 2,000 miles later.

Along the way, the trail acquired many friends, including the Appalachian Trail Conference, founded in 1925, which greatly boosted construction by dividing up sections and parceling them out to local hiking organizations.

The finished product is marvelously diverse, a walker's longitudinous paradise. For the length of the Eastern seaboard it traverses mountains, forests, valleys, small towns, remote wildernesses, stately tall hardwoods, dense scrubby coniferous thickets, southern "balds," subarctic tundra, mosquito-infested wetlands, and much more.

In New England the Appalachian Trail reveals the many faces of this region's backcountry. You experience at least four different outdoor worlds as the trail passes through five of the region's six states. (We'll give mileage in round numbers; with many minor trail relocations in process, precise figures keep changing.)

Maine: 280 miles. The north woods. Here you get as big a sense of endless forest as anywhere on the trail. There's more AT mileage in Maine than in any other state save Virginia. It's not all idyllic woods-walking, as much of it is boggy and wet, while Maine's insect army is bigger and meaner than any. But that's all part of the true north woods scene.

New Hampshire: 150 miles. Spectacular mountain scenery. The rugged, rocky ridges of the White Mountains afford views

without parallel. It's a tough, uncompromising granite world up
there.

Vermont: 135 miles. Deep green forest. This is the pure
hiker's (as distinct from the mountaineer's) ideal state. Lush green
vegetation enfolds the woodsy miles of Vermont, whose famed
Long Trail (Canada to Massachusetts) coincides with the AT most
of the way.

Massachusetts and Connecticut: 135 miles. Man-modified
landscape. Instead of "wilderness," the characteristic views in these
states are of alternating fields and woods, with many stone walls
and old cellar holes, along with entrancing views over small
villages.

In the course of this 700-mile odyssey, the trail passes over or
near most of New England's outstanding scenic wonders—Maine's
mighty Katahdin, the spiny ridge of the Bigelow Range, Mount
Washington (highest point in New England), the spectacular
Franconia Ridge, Vermont's celebrated ski meccas Pico and
Killington, Mount Greylock in Massachusetts, and the tristate
Taconic Range at the junction where Connecticut, Massachusetts,
and New York come together.

Besides these big and famous attractions, many quieter vales
and vistas become personal favorites of hikers who grow to know
them as old friends—places like Carter Notch, tucked away in one
of the White Mountain's more impressive cols between the Carter
and Wildcat ranges; Sage's Ravine, a deep quiet glade at the
Connecticut-Massachusetts border; Deer Leap, an overlook of
massive buttresses in Vermont.

Then there's "the most difficult mile"—a wild jumble of
boulders strewn through the gorge of Maine's Mahoosuc Notch.

The trail doesn't hit everything there is to see in New England—it misses Vermont's best peaks, Mansfield and Camel's
Hump, and it neglects New Hampshire's picture-book Chocorua
and ever-popular Monadnock, just to cite a few examples. But it
covers more than it misses.

For many years the outside world, and even many of the AT's
active supporters and maintainers in the Appalachian Trail Con-

ference, have viewed the great trail primarily in physical terms, as a silvan corridor of precious backcountry coursing the spine of this end of the continent. Its physical properties are of course vital, and they sorely need to be defended from encroachment, maintained from erosion, and appreciated for their natural beauty.

But along that quiet corridor has grown, over the past generation, something more than the physical world of nature. A human component has been grafted on. We refer to the community of people who walk the trail, most especially that singular colony who walk it in one long continuous walk, the so-called through-hikers.

Our dictionary defines "community" as "all the people living in a particular district, city, etc.," or "a group of people living together as a smaller special unit within a larger one, and having interests, work, etc. in common," or "(*ecology*) a group of animals and plant species living together and having close interactions, esp. through food relationships."

The community of AT through-hikers is not, of course, living in one stationary place like the communities we normally think of. They are a community in constant motion, never all in the same place at once, the individuals rarely spending more than one or two nights in the same spot. But they are emphatically "a group of people living together as a smaller special unit within a larger one, and having interests, work, etc. in common,"—as long as you allow that at any one moment no more than half a dozen members of this community are physically "together." They certainly have "close interactions, esp. through food relationships."

The month of April has a special significance for the AT through-hiker community. In fact, when you think of it, April is one of your more interesting months. April is income tax showdown, baseball's Opening Day, and T. S. Eliot's cruelest month. It's the birth month of Charlemagne (743) and Hitler (1889), the sinking of the Titanic (1912) and the time the boys fired on Fort Sumter (1861). On the brighter side it's also the birth month of Buddha (563 B.C.), Leonardo da Vinci (1452), Shakespeare (1564), and Duke Ellington (1899).

More to the point for our outdoor perspective, it's the month the world first saw John Audubon (1785), John Burroughs (1837), and John Muir (1838). It's the month Admiral Peary reached the North Pole (1909) and Mount Washington recorded the highest wind man has ever been pushed around by—231 mph (1934). It's also when Pocahontos married John Rolfe (1614).

But to get back to our subject, April is also Appalachian Trail month. This is the time when legions of walking enthusiasts set off from Springer Mountain in Georgia with the intention of hiking continuously for the next few months. Ahead of them lies a footpath that wends its way northward through the Southern Appalachians, the Great Smokies, the Shenandoah Ridge, the Alleghenies, the Kittatinny, the Berkshires, the Green Mountains, and the White Mountains, before finally reaching lonely and aloof Katahdin way up in the northeast corner of Maine's north woods, farther north than Montreal.

Time was when the AT was seldom attempted as a single long walk. Trail users were primarily there for a single day's outing, or maybe a long weekend or occasionally a two-week vacation devoted to walking some small and particularly scenic stretch of it. The AT saw only two or three "end-to-enders" for its first generation of existence.

Then came the outdoor back-to-nature, backpacking boom of the 1960s. By 1968 and 1969 ten people a year were "doing" the whole trail. That was only a beginning. No one really knows how many people walk the AT now, but the Appalachian Trail Conference documented the following numbers of known through-hikers, painting a vivid picture of that boom in outdoors walking:

1970 16
1971 46
1972 68
1973 166

After that incredible spurt between 1970 and 1973, the experts figure that long-distance hiking has settled down to something like 100 per year.

It is still true that the overwhelming majority of trail users are there for much shorter distances—day trips, overnights, or short vacations. The end-to-enders are a small minority. Furthermore, it should be pointed out that the foregoing figures include a great many AT enthusiasts who "do" the trail in little sections at a time over a period of years. Sometimes whole families will decide to devote their vacations regularly to hiking a different section every year. After 10 or 20 years they may fill in all the gaps. The unvarnished, one-shot, 2,000-miles-in-one-walk purists are still a minority within a minority.

But they sure are a fascinating breed. The formal statistics yield little generality about who these unique individuals are. They are both male and female: perhaps the most famous end-to-ender yet was a woman, Grandma Gatewood, the original little old lady in tennis shoes. Many of them are young, but a surprising number are middle-aged or even in retirement years, if you call that retiring. By occupation, you could say they're all the same: unemployed. At least for several months. But their career interests before and after their marathon jaunt show wide diversity.

Personality characteristics are probably equally inconsistent— but by definition they must all share a certain long-range vision, clinically known as nuttiness. They think in long cycles. And they are monstrously cruel to their pedal extremities.

Planning the Campaign

Planning for a continuous 2,000-mile walk is half the battle—well, at least for the mind if not the feet. No one is yet known to have lugged all his or her food for 2,000 miles, for example. That means careful planning for how to reprovision along the way.

Food logistics are handled in an ingenious variety of ways. Some of the early trail walkers carefully deposited caches of food, sealed in metal containers either buried in the ground or wired high in trees. Others cajoled bemused relatives into meeting them at specified points along the way. Those with a little more ready cash take advantage of the fact that the trail never goes too many miles without swinging fairly close to little towns where mom-and-pop stores may provide passable fare, though unfortunately much of the better grub is canned or frozen and thus not too helpful to those who carry it all on the back. The most common solution these days lies with the US Postal Service. Along the 2,000-mile route, accessible post offices have been identified where end-to-enders may mail their provisions marked "hold for arrival." The chosen postmasters are deluged every March and April with these care packages; they have taken on a stoic philosophy and extra storage space, knowing that at a certain point in the summer dirty and hairy figures, clad in indecent shorts, will tramp boots into their East Halffrog Post Office to pick up their provisions.

Besides food, the planning process involves a rigorous attention to weight and space saving. Compared with weekend or vacation backpackers, the end-to-ender quickly becomes the archetypal Spartan. While packing, the word "essential" undergoes repeated and relentless redefinition. Does toothbrushing really require toothpaste? Does a toothbrush really need a handle? Do teeth really need brushing? Does freeze-dried food really require teeth? So it goes. Weight is the dread enemy, space the golden commodity.

The Community Assembles

Planning and packing completed, now comes the cruelest month, and the hitherto-unrelated community assembles at Springer Mountain. Fewer than one hundred each year may not sound like many, but don't forget, that's the number that comes out the end of the tube in Maine. Several times that number start each year in Georgia, hopes raised high, spirits eager to adopt the nomad life, boots well oiled, feet unblistered, packs well filled, real-world responsibility banished.

Reality returns with the first southern rain. They call them the Great Smokies because the perpetual misty clouds that drift around look like smoke. Those are the good-weather days. But all that moisture means something. Before long come the all-day rains, then the all-week rains. That's when the dropout rate steps up.

End-to-enders say that if you can get through the first two weeks, your odds of doing the whole trail go way up. It's during those first two weeks that a number of things happen:

1. You find out just how wet you can get if you can't ever go indoors in bad weather.
2. You find out just what you smell like when you're wet that long.
3. Your pack still feels like an imposition.
4. Two thousand miles seems like a long way to walk.
5. You have to ask yourself whether there is really nothing more fruitful or enjoyable or at least more comfortable to be doing for the next few months; during the first all-day rain you find yourself asking that question all day long, and during the first all-week rain you think perhaps you've found the answer.

Many successful trail walkers come close to quitting in those first two weeks. Good judgment, fortunately, is overcome, and they continue. A much greater number do quit. "Dear Postmaster, East Halffrog: Can you return..."

"You'll Never Walk Alone"

Those that remain settle into a serenity about bad weather; they have to. The pack ceases to be a burden and feels like just part of the clothes you put on each morning. The rhythm of the daily walk actually becomes a satisfying pleasure, almost a need. The daily tasks absorb attention; starting each dinner becomes more important to the through-hiker than it does to any of the rest of us, not because he likes to eat but because it's something he must do to go on and there is something terribly and awesomely absorbing about things in life that absolutely must be done, a feeling that many city dwellers never get to feel.

The chances of staying with it seem greatest for those who walk alone. Those who have watched the first 200 miles of the AT in the spring—remember, 200 miles gets you only 10 percent of the way to Maine—say that the groups tend to fall apart and quit. A few pairs, usually mixed, stay with it, but most are by themselves.

On one level, they stay by themselves too, spiritually, even though inevitably they may travel together for many miles, and rest at the same trailside shelters for many nights in a row. One end-to-ender told us how he and six others walked together for two weeks, but each night seven different stoves came out of seven different packs, and seven different individual dinners were cooked. Never did anyone suggest combining a meal or saving stove fuel. All instinctively guarded their independence and shunned attaching themselves to anyone else, for fear of the practical or emotional problems that would inevitably arise.

Yet, each traveling jealously alone, they do develop a sense of community. The experience, all 2,000-plus miles of it, is too powerful and unique not to be shared. Each summer, a social unit is formed of those walking the trail. Though most travel separately, they read each other's names every night in trail registers, hear reports from hikers catching up or overtaken or traveling the reverse direction. They pass along news of a washed-out bridge, or a troublesome dog at a certain farmhouse that must be passed, or a cheap pizza place 0.3 miles off the trail where it crosses Route 16. They gossip about the others on the trail. They feel differently toward one another versus all other hikers or humans, just as any townsperson feels a unique bond with others from his hometown.

Each year's crop of through-hikers has indeed become a community, not of place but of experience. This community has many of the same problems faced by other communities, like East Halffrog or Boston—traffic, housing, water supply, sewage disposal, and interpersonal relations—albeit in a different form.

The through-hiker community has actually taken a modest step toward formalizing its sense of cohesion. An organization known as the Appalachian Long Distance Hikers Association has been formed. Each year ALDHA holds a "gathering," with a program of speakers, panel discussions, social events, and a chance for past through-hikers to congregate and exchange stories, reminiscences, and ideas about the problems and prospects of the great trail. ALDHA has also provided a chance for through-hikers to "give something back" by working on trail maintenance teams. Because the Appalachian Trail Conference has always seemed just a bit formal and high level, maybe sometimes a little too stuffy for the scruffy set of through-hikers, ALDHA provides an alternative organizational home. It's important, but not vital: the sense of community must be earned, not in meeting rooms, but by being one with the moving flow of hikers along the woods and ridges of the AT itself.

One of the interesting images of the annual April AT opening is the scramble for post position that takes place at the start. With everyone starting at the first good spring weather, the shelters in Georgia, Tennessee, and North Carolina become crowded every night. Many have taken to starting in March, still wintry at upper elevations, but now that means a crowd too. Each year the stronger hikers put on a push to get ahead of the pack. Very often these are likely to be strong prospects to finish. Their confidence and camaraderie are strengthened as they move ahead of the others together. That's not to say that speed is directly related to likelihood of sticking it out—far from it. Many of the best AT walkers are not in any hurry.

One pleasant eccentricity of the AT through-hiker community is their passion for "trail names." In the shelter registers, which form such a vital link of communication between them, they sign in with messages of varying length, regularly employing a specially selected nickname or alias or, as they call it, their trail name. Some of these are colorful indeed: Kaptain Wilderness, the Boston Strollers, Rambling Rat, Redbeard and the Gypsy, the Trail Tots, the Hobbit, the Cheshire Cat, the Irish Wonder, the Hog, A Pilgrim in Progress, Minnesota Two-Sticks, the Connecticut Connection, Rockhopper, Droopalong, Flatfoot, Bumbles, and the Bag Lady.

A very low proportion of the AT hikers start from the north end. Several excellent reasons argue for the preponderance of south-to-north migration.

1. In typical winters (forget some recent ones), the snow depth in New England's mountains makes much of the trail very hard to walk until May.
2. It's still cold, if not actually winter, until well into April.
3. It's hard to get permission even to enter Baxter Park, where Katahdin is located, at that time of year; much less of a problem in the autumn.
4. If you started from Maine in April, you'd be in New Hampshire and Vermont in May and June for the height of the black fly season; 'nuff said?
5. Anyway, who eats dessert at the beginning of the meal? Save the best for last, right?

Thus it is that most of the survivors of April's mad scene in the south stroll separately or in little groups into New England in the last of summer or early fall. Here they find magnificence. After high summer's heat and all the dull, sweaty stretches of Virginia and those awful rocky stretches in Pennsylvania, the AT hiker comes to the East's crown jewels: the lovely low ridge of the Taconics, with its classic pastoral views; outspreading Greylock, with its high spruce forest just south of Massachusetts's highest eminence; the southern half of Vermont's venerable Long Trail, with its long-established tread (the LT preceded the AT by almost 20 years); the incomparable Franconia Ridge, if you've the luck to hit it on a clear blue day or the sensitivity to appreciate its wildness on a windracked, cloud-tossed howler; lordly Mount Adams, number two in height but so much grander than the building-and-crowd-dominated Mount Washington; the long wilderness experience of Maine's north woods, culminating in the rugged scramble up the steep slopes to Katahdin's moonscape tableland, then that last gentle rise to the true summit, there to look down the dizzying precipice to gemlike Chimney Pond 2,000 feet below, the endless vistas of Maine's lakes and forests stretching out to Canada and the Arctic itself. Journey's end...well, journey's end for most. During the early 1980s Stephen ("Yo-Yo") Nuckolls walked from Georgia to Maine, touched the cairn on Katahdin and turned around to walk back, turned around again at Georgia and returned to

Katahdin, surely one of the first uninterrupted walks of more than 6,000 miles and a remarkable demonstration of the magnetic power of this way of life.

But All Is Not Splendor

Only an ostrich would paint a picture of the AT as all idyll and romance, and ostriches are notoriously clumsy painters, especially in April. The Appalachian Trail faces some muddy problems these days that dim its splendor in the eyes of many hikers. Among these are:

- Overcrowding. Just too many people. It's sometimes hard to find solitude on the AT, and many wilderness-loving hikers prefer to get off onto the less-frequented byways.
- Regulations. In part resulting from the aforementioned overcrowding, Maine's Baxter State Park is the worst offender when it comes to telling the hiker what he or she can and cannot do. They insist on knowing where everyone is in the park at all times, "close" the mountain when weather is dubious (incredible!), and otherwise play Big Brother to one and all.
- Expense. One recent booklet composed by a through-hiker for the benefit of the rest of that community is entitled: "How to Get through the White Mountains without Losing Your Socks." Use of the backcountry facilities in the Whites now carries a charge, and the fee seems steep to through-hikers who have camped for free almost all the way for the preceding 1,600 miles. AMC's huts, at more than $50 per night, are simply out of the question for down-at-the-heels through-hikers, but even the shelters and tent platforms in the Whites have inflated to what seem like outrageous levels.
- Physical damage to the trail. This is a direct result of the crowds of hikers. The alpine zones above treeline are the most fragile, as are the beautiful but delicate high-level bogs that can be found at intervals among the high ridges that the trail traverses. But there is scarcely a mile of the AT that doesn't show some damage from overuse.

- Overengineering. In an effort to protect the environment, trail tenders have been forced to "harden" the tread with log bridges through the bogs, rock steps on steeper slopes, and other devices. A lot of this work is necessary, and much of it is thoughtfully and subtly done, but some of it is overengineered, tending to impair the sense of wildness that hikers go to the mountains to find.
- Uniformity. In recent years the federal government has stepped into the act and come up with guidelines for trail management. One of the charms of the AT has been the diversity of its character along the way. The Feds have now decreed, for example, that the trail should always be off-road. So gone are some of those charming strolls along country lanes and by people's backyards. Some of the through-hikers lament this change. Comments one: "The diversity of the trail is one of its special charms....Keep a few road walks." Another: "Why is it a sin for a hiker to see a house?" Another: "Why are we working so hard to make the trail as monotonous as possible?"

Still They Come

Despite all these problems, the through-hikers still come. The spring still sees them converge on Springer Mountain, the fall sees them straggling upward toward Katahdin. The mountains still gleam before them, the forests are as green as even, the brooks still sparkle cold, the chickadees still flit sociably among the spruces, the white-throated sparrow yet raises his soulful sound high in the alpine mists. The Appalachian Trail is ever there. And so is the community that represents perhaps this country's greatest collectivity of pure walkers.

5

Winter Camping Idyll

If you're comfortable on a northeast winter hike, you'll survive—yes, even flourish—just about anywhere in the world.
HARRY ROBERTS, *MOVIN' ON*

GOING BACKPACKING IN February? Sleeping out at –20°F?
Covering 10 miles over snow five feet deep?

Most New England hikers know better. They hang up their
lug-soled boots in November and leave them alone till April.

But then there are fishermen who like all-day downpours,
skiers who deliberately pick those suicidal downhill runs, baseball
players who enjoy batting against Nolan Ryan, book lovers who
choose to read *Paradise Lost*, gourmets who like to add more hot
peppers to Indian dishes...and hikers who enjoy winter camping
and climbing. Count us among this fraternity of nuts.

Most of our friends, when we mention plans for winter
outings, look as dismayed as Mrs. Daniel must have looked when
her husband announced that he was going into the den for a while
before dinner. (Before whose dinner?)

Unquestionably there is a strain of masochism in the winter
backpacker. Unless you can decide that you like to be cold and to

have a devil of a time trying to make one mile per hour if snow conditions are good, unless you want a challenge just to carry on life's normal operations of walking, cooking, sleeping, tying a shoelace, unzipping a fly, looking at your watch—all of which take excruciatingly longer on the third day out below zero—then you won't really enjoy the northeastern backcountry in February. In that case, take up chess, or yoga, or *Paradise Lost*.

"Many human beings say that they enjoy the winter, but what they really enjoy is feeling proof against it," wrote Richard Adams in *Watership Down*. That's a perceptive observation for a rabbit.

The early Icelandic saga writers conceived of hell as a place of intense cold and ice. They were right. Even the orthodox Christian view of hell in the aforementioned *Paradise Lost* had room in it for a corner where

> Beyond this flood a frozen continent
> Lies dark and wild, beat with perpetual storms
> Of whirlwind and dire hail, which on firm land
> Thaws not, but gathers heap, and ruin seems
> Of ancient pile; all else deep snow and ice.

—which may prove that John Milton's been on Mount Washington on a typical February day.

Trying to explain the attractions of winter camping and climbing is about as unprofitable as trying to raise money for a memorial to Joe Stalin in Moscow in the 1990s.

Just walking along the trail isn't the simple pleasure it was in summer. Now in our mountains it's covered with three or four feet of snow, five or six feet or more as you get up in elevation. This means the first problem is that your booted feet alone would flounder hopelessly.

So you wear cross-country skis or snowshoes. The former are becoming popular and chic, and an expert skier can travel smoothly over rough country. On a moderate downgrade, a glide on skis is 10 times as fast as a waddle on snowshoes.

Still, for climbing the steeper trails or bushwhacking, as we like to do, skis can't make it. It's unbelievable what you can get up, through, and over with snowshoes. Not the long Alaskan models, built for covering flat or rolling open country, but the short flat bear paws or modified beaver tails that you can work with in steep, broken terrain and through dense trees and shrubs.

But now you begin to learn some of the "attractions" of winter travel.

In the first place, that trail was cut in summer, blazes marked about four feet off the ground, and branches clipped to a height of maybe seven feet. You do the arithmetic with, say, five feet of snow: few blazes are visible, and a loose weave of snow-laden branches obscures the trail at many points. Furthermore, the snow has covered all the thick undergrowth that told you where the trail *wasn't* in summer. So now all ways look equally open—or tangled.

In short, staying on trail is in itself a major challenge. We think you can tell an experienced winter traveler more by his or her ability to stay on an unbroken trail, somehow sensing the right way, than by almost any other indicator of winter experience.

To add to your troubles, your pack, which is bulging with winter-required gear, much heavier than your normal summer load, is now there in the branches getting tangled and shaking snow down your neck.

Next discover the pleasures of the spruce trap. This invention of an ill-humored Norse frost god on a morning when his wife had burned the toast is based on the principle that falling snow doesn't pack in nearly as tightly around the branches of a small evergreen as it does elsewhere. Once a small tree is covered with loosely consolidated snow, the unwary snowshoer won't see it as he tromps along an otherwise fairly well consolidated surface. One enthusiastically slammed snowshoe in the vicinity of those covered branches and the whole fragile structure of unconsolidated snow gives way in a whoosh.

Oh, the fiendish fate of a spruce trap victim! At upper elevations where snow is really deep, we've seen an entire adult with full pack disappear below the surrounding surface into a spruce trap. (At that elevation the true villain is likely to be a fir, not a spruce, but who wants to hear botanical niceties when you're floundering with a 50-pound pack five feet below where you'd like to place your foot next?)

Once you've plummeted down inside a spruce trap, malicious little snow elves go to work far down there somewhere, weaving the tree's lowest branches around your snowshoes in lacework of intricate complexity that defies your most vigorous efforts to extract your feet, to the accompaniment of language you never knew you had in you. Then there's always the inconsiderate soul who wants to document your absurd contortionist acrobatics on film. "Great," the would-be cinematographic artist cries. "Can you hold that position a second?" Curses!

Get out from down in there, dust off the snow, stop whimpering, and carry on till the grade steepens. You've strapped minicrampons on the bottom of your snowshoes. Without them you'd slip hopelessly back on steeper grades. But let the temperature warm up unseasonably and the snow takes on a wet, heavy consistency that introduces you to the experience of balling.

No, balling isn't what you think it is, and not nearly as much fun. It refers to the tendency of warm snow to gather in great lumps between the points of your snowshoe crampons. As some snow adheres to the metal, more snow adheres to *that* snow, and presently you pick up a "ball" of nearly a cubic foot of heavy, packed snow with every step. Keeping your balance becomes difficult, your equanimity impossible. It's a bit like trying to walk with a large and irregular basketball strapped to each foot.

But warm temperatures that produce balling are rare. More likely, you'll be lucky enough to have it colder...and colder...and colder...

Step out of the car at trailhead when it's -15° below, and in the many minutes it takes to get under way you're getting so cold that you put on all your warm clothing. Five minutes up the steep trail and you're suddenly aware that you're so warm with the exercise of breaking trail through soft snow with a heavy pack that you're starting to sweat. A danger sign: sweating into your clothes is a basic no-no in winter, since wet clothes (from whatever source of moisture) lose much of their insulating value.

So you stop, off comes that 50-pound pack, off comes the parka or a couple of sweaters, on goes the pack (with no car to prop it against this time). But every time the trail turns downhill your exercise may be so much less that you start to get cold and need one of those sweaters. So again, the tussle with getting pack on and off.

Then the trail turns uphill, and you run into the inexorable operation of Fye's Law—that for every 500 feet of uphill trail the pack increases in perceived weight by 10 pounds—and you start to sweat again. Off comes the pack, off the sweater, on the pack...

See what we mean about the "attractions" of winter on the backwoods trails? As for us, we love every minute of it.

It's critically important to keep your body temperature just right in winter. Overheat and you sweat into your clothes—a potentially disastrous mistake. Lose too much body heat and it may be hard to get warm again. For this reason, most winter hikers use the Layer System in clothing. First developed by Lester L. Layer, an avid winter climber and manufacturer of sweaters, the Layer System consists of carrying several different shirts, sweaters, and a windproof nylon outer shell, rather than just one great big down parka. Then you can wear just what you need, not more. It's a prudent approach, but it sure means a lot of stops and starts some-times—plus a lot of taking that pack off and on.

That's not counting the times you have to take it off because an uncooperative snowshoe binding keeps sliding off your toe or heel.

If you head for the challenging above-treeline terrain of Katahdin, the White Mountains' Presidential Range, Franconia Ridge, Vermont's Mount Mansfield, or the highest summits in the Adirondacks, not to mention the higher reaches of the western mountains, you'll encounter a special world. There's nothing like the raw bone-blasting power of the above-treeline tandem of low temperatures, hurricane-force winds, and no place to hide. Some-times that alpine world is far more benign—just often enough to lull the novice into thinking it's not so tough up there after all. But the weather can deteriorate with terrible rapidity.

Don't test this world till you're thoroughly at home below treeline in winter. When your experience has progressed and your common sense has deteriorated far enough, you'll find the alpine zone an experience without parallel in the outdoor world.

But be ready. Here the price of foolishness runs high: frostbite, hypothermia, even death. But even when the weather spares you from its worst, travel will be slower than in summer, every simple operation maddeningly time consuming.

Fortunately, though, daylight hours are so much shorter in winter that you have to curtail your carefree stroll. The short days of January and February seem to end right after lunch, and you've made only about half the distance you'd planned on. But no matter: now you get to the joys of winter camping.

Mushing around on skis or snowshoes, you catch yourself gazing at that quiet glade surrounded by drooping hemlocks. What a lovely spot to camp! How still and peaceful the night! How comforting the rich mounds of snow all around your snug tent!

The reality of winter camping is indeed a special paradise— but it may not turn out to be quite the idyllic scene you pictured.

First, when you stop moving those skis or snowshoes and start standing around doing camping chores, you find that you're getting cold. Your body isn't the efficient furnace generating heat the way it was when you were exerting yourself on the trail. So you put on every stitch of clothing in the pack and end up as rotund as Santa Claus. Warm (maybe), but hardly as mobile as you'd like to be for bending over, reaching around, and so on.

Now set up the tent. At 0°F you have to keep your mittens or gloves on for this process. Recall how easily the tent went up in summer? Now cold changes all. Tent stakes won't hold in the soft snow. Drop one and it disappears in the bottomless fluffy whiteness. Tent poles won't obey mittened hands. Take off the mittens and the metal sticks to your skin. Your hands are soon numb, as metal conducts heat away even through mittens. Leave your snowshoes on and you can't maneuver; take them off and you plunge to the hips at every step. Tent lines are ticklish to get around stakes or trees. Knots take forever to tie. In fact, every little process takes two or three times as long. Meanwhile, light is fading fast, temperature's dropping, maybe the wind's picking up and changing direction from what you had in mind when you oriented the tent.

At last you're inside, safe from the elements. But what's happened to the tent? Great gremlins, it's shrunk! No, it's just all that winter gear—puffy, voluminous down sleeping bags, myriad articles of clothing, cooking gear, big winter boots, not to mention an enlarged you (you're not wearing just T-shirt and shorts, re-member)—all taking up a lot of space in a not-so-spacious accom-modation. But if you think it's crowded now, just wait until morn-ing when a foot of fresh-fallen snow presses against sides and roof. No place for claustrophobics.

Now to get dinner! Somehow you have to spread out the cooking gear, stove, pots, and food, light the stove, melt great quantities of snow for water, get some of it into your canteen, get a pot of it boiling, cook dinner and wash up—all without spilling a drop or burning down the tent. Obviously impossible.

Many winter campers frown on cooking in a tent. They claim that unsafe amounts of carbon monoxide from white-gas stoves are dangerous in a closed tent. Carbon monoxide? Out here in this frozen wasteland? Sad, but true. Well, you'll just risk it and make sure the tent is ventilated because at 0°F and a strong breeze getting up you know you are not going to cook anyplace else. You're flying in the face of the conservative practitioners of the art, but you rationalize that there are times when you couldn't keep a stove going if you were cooking outside the tent—above treeline in a howling gale, for instance—so you feel that it's only right that you "practice" cooking in a tent (well ventilated, of course) now and then.

You want to be inside that sleeping bag, that beautiful buffer between you and the darkening winter world, with just your nose, eyes, and mouth showing, and two hands sticking out so you can get dinner.

Oh yes, dinner. You need food. The bag isn't really warming you and that's because you're cold—from the inside. You burned up those lunch calories long ago. Well, you've already filled the snow bag—a garbage bag–size obstacle at your right elbow filled with snow to melt for water. It takes up a lot of room, of course. With faultless dexterity you've managed to light the stove, get the snow melted, even boiling, and now you're having a warming cup of bouillon while you stir the pot. Things are looking a little less desperate.

But what's this? Good grief! It's snowing inside the tent! Impossible. This tent's in perfect condition. You're right twice— the tent's fine, and it is snowing. Condensation from the boiling water vapor has, at 0°F, built a lovely layer of icy crystals on the inside of the tent—roof, walls and all. Now you know another reason why the conservative faction cooks outside. You open the tent door a crack and mutter incantations designed to direct the steam from the pot out the small hole in the tent door.

Whenever you brush against the tent wall a delicate shower descends, covering clothing, sleeping bag, and you in a white blanket that rapidly proceeds to melt. You're horrified: water permeating your down sleeping bag! Wet down loses its insulating value—you'll freeze. So with infinite care you avoid touching tent sides and roof, brush every bit of snow or frost off the bag. Not easy. The tent has shrunk still further.

Still having a good time? Oddly enough, some of us couldn't be happier. It has been said that winter camping doesn't build character, it reveals it. Sometimes, it may reveal that you're out of your mind.

Finally you've finished dinner. Even made a pass at washing up. Mixing last night's dinner with breakfast oatmeal never did appeal to you. How could it have taken two hours? In summer you eat in less than half that. All the melting of snow for every drop of water takes time, and every tiny task takes twice as long with cold hands as it does in summer.

You sink luxuriantly into your sleeping bag, savoring the last bit of light from the two candle stubs that had lighted the process of getting dinner. You are full. You are warm. What a nice secure place to be! Let the elements rage outside! What was it Miriam

Underhill, America's greatest woman mountaineer, said? "I don't mind hardship, as long as I'm perfectly comfortable."

There is something overwhelmingly satisfying in lying there warm in a good sleeping bag, knowing that every square inch of air outside your bag (and those of your neighboring companions) for miles around is unrelentingly cold, cold, cold. As Herman Melville said in another context: "There you lie like the one warm spot in the heart of an arctic crystal."

Oh dear. A tiny thought struggles within you. You try to ignore it. But there it is. From the depth of your sleeping bag you know that that stew and all that liquid you drank are not going to let you sleep through the night. What time is it? 7:30 P.M. Seems later. It's been dark for hours. You'll never make it until seven the next morning. You resign yourself to the inevitable and struggle upward out of downy warmth. Boots go back on, then gaiters. Then sweaters. You search for your flashlight. Finally you're plunging through the snow into the trees, toilet paper in hand. Well, you think, you're just glad you're not camped above treeline someplace with the wind howling down on you. You painfully recall such a time when, at the crucial moments, the toilet paper was whisked away in a blast that nearly flattened you.

You're back in your sleeping bag again, thoroughly chilled from being out. You feel slightly disgruntled as you wait for the bag to warm you. Let's see. Boots are in the bottom of the sleeping bag (wrapped in a stuff sack) so they won't freeze. Canteen is under your left knee, so you'll have water. (You *did* get that cap on tight, didn't you? Better check…a process inducing a gymnastic tour de force that Nadia Comaneci would envy.) The breakfast is sticking you in the side, but you don't dare leave it out for forest beasties to rob. A few bulky items like sweaters squeeze you on the other side. You have to keep clothing in your bag or the condensation might fall on it if a wind comes up during the night. You try to find a spot for your feet. You don't want them lying on your cold boots. No room. Oh well.

Morning. How difficult it is to stick a nose out of that womblike bag. Oops. Ice crystals falling on your face. The top of your bag is covered with rime ice where you breathed out of it all night. You inch yourself toward the laborious task of preparing breakfast. At least you have daylight to work in now. A good two and a half hours later you're trying to stuff an ice-coated tent into its stuff sack. You lay it out, brush off the ice and roll it up again. Tighter. It barely fits in a sack it floundered around in all summer.

Your fingers are freezing now. In fact, you've got to get moving. All this inactivity of packing up camp has really cooled you down. Snowshoe bindings are stiff, awkward to get on. You hoist a heavy load—that water-soaked tent and sleeping bag have increased your weight—and mush on.

Idyllic winter camping? You bet it is. You can grow to love it. Wait till you try it above treeline…in freezing rain…two more nights to go and all your down gear wet…stove getting cranky about starting…ah, winter wonderland.

Appendix: Thratchett's Axioms on Winter Camping and Hiking

Back in the first chapter we mentioned our old hiking buddy Winslow Thratchett. We've been on many a winter trip with old Thratchett, sometimes just the three of us. From the accumulated wisdom of these years of winter camping—wisdom being the general category into which we place 30 years of mistakes, wrong guesses, stupid blunders, miscalculations, epics, fiascoes, and other instructive experiences—Win Thratchett has distilled the following 50 axioms of winter camping and hiking.

1. For a trip of more than one overnight, the volume of equipment and supplies required is equal to the carrying capacity of the pack plus 30 percent.

2. After the pack is finally filled and there is no more room, the most essential item of all will be found underneath the sheet of paper on which you listed "essential items."

3. The importance of a forgotten item of equipment is directly proportional to the distance from the trailhead at the moment of its being remembered.

4. The weight of the pack increases by 10 pounds for every 1,000 feet of elevation to be ascended.

5. The attractiveness of an itinerary times its feasibility equals a constant.

6. If a trip requires n hours, there will be $n-1$ hours of daylight available.

7. If, on a hike of eight hours' duration, you keep your parka hood up for seven hours and fifty-five minutes, the exact moment at which a tree branch laden with snow will drop its load from a point directly above the back of your neck can be determined to within five minutes.

8. After you have decided to don rain gear, stopped, taken off pack, unpacked rain gear, put on rain gear, put pack on again, and resumed walking—rain ceases.

9. After you have stopped, taken off pack, removed rain gear, stowed rain gear in pack, put pack on again, and resumed walking—rain resumes.

10. Precipitation probabilities expressed in public weather forecasts should be subtracted from 100 percent to determine the actual probability.

11. Waterproof stuff sacks aren't.

12. Changes in wind direction occur after tent site has been selected, tent erected, and occupants have entered and removed boots.

13. The probability of an error in the guidebook is directly proportional to the trouble it can cause.

14. Topographical maps will be found accurate for every terrain feature except those lying along your itinerary.

15. The compass never lies; it merely confuses.

16. Those fancy compass cases that open up to display a mirror on a vertical surface and the compass on the horizontal? The horizontal surface shows you *where* you're

lost; the vertical surface shows you *who* is lost.

17. To set a compass course, first walk where you want to go, then plot your course.

18. When you don't know where you're going, use good snowshoe technique.

19. When you are totally lost, it will be possible to make good time.

20. The prudence of making a major change in itinerary increases as the original destination is approached.

21. Speed of travel in winter is best estimated in less-familiar units—for example, furlongs per fortnight.

22. To determine the remaining daylight hours available, compute the number of hours needed to reach your destination and subtract one.

23. In January, darkness falls one hour after lunch.

24. The probability of a snowshoe breaking 10 miles from the road is directly proportional to the probability of a heavy snowfall that night.

25. Indestructible metal snowshoes aren't.

26. The component of your pack frame that breaks is (a) the one component not carried in your repair kit, and (b) the one component without which the frame cannot function.

27. When partially open streams must be crossed, ice will be selectively found on those stone surfaces most useful in summer as stepping-stones.

28. Ice will give way only after repeated testing has demonstrated that it will support body weight.

29. Trips on which someone falls into a stream are those on which spare socks were not brought along.

30. After the most difficult stream crossing has been negotiated at considerable peril and loss of time, it will be discovered that the trail goes back across the stream 100 yards later.

31. The time at which an emergency takes place is that moment when the time required to reach your destination and the number of daylight hours are equal.

32. The size of an object is inversely proportional to its

likelihood of falling into deep powder snow when you are unpacking.

33. White objects are most likely to be dropped into snow; black objects are most likely to be dropped onto mud; green objects are most likely to be dropped into thick vegetation.

34. The item first needed is the one at the bottom of the pack.

35. When one member of a party is unable to make the trip, he was the one to have brought the tent.

36. (Corollary to No. 35) That trip is the one on which it rains.

37. The life of headlamp batteries is equal to the number of darkness hours in which you need to operate minus one.

38. The spare batteries will be among the items discarded in order to get pack weight down.

39. If a stove functions perfectly on a tryout in your basement, it will malfunction completely at high camp five miles from the road.

40. When a stove malfunctions, the defective component will be the most difficult to reach and repair.

41. The replacement component will be dropped into deep powder snow.

42. The stove will malfunction just before the stew is ready.

43. In repairing the stove, the stew will be spilled.

44. When cooking in a tent, the likelihood of spilling liquid on a down sleeping bag is inversely proportional to the temperature that night.

45. When cooking in a tent, the likelihood of spilling liquid on a person is directly proportional to the temperature of the liquid.

46. Any absolute rules of safety in the mountains should be treated as variables.

47. A party of four is the minimum number acceptable in winter climbing, so that blame for major errors in decision making may be distributed evenly among three people, excluding the person assigning blame.

48. If you can keep your head while all about you are panicking, then you obviously don't appreciate the gravity of the situation.
49. When all else fails, abort the trip.
50. Bad trips make good stories.

6

The Greatest Walkers
of Them All

They were swifter than eagles, they were stronger than lions.

2 SAMUEL 1:23

WE'VE ALWAYS BEEN INTRIGUED with those year-end "ten best" lists that you read in the papers—the ten best-dressed celebrities, ten best college football teams, ten best movies, and so forth. Here we've compiled a few such lists of our own.

New England's Greatest Hikers

We'd like to salute the ten greatest hikers in New England's history. Why not? Here's our list:

1. *Chocorua.* This name evokes a legend and a curse. Chocorua was an Indian, whom we list as representative of what must have been a great many outstanding Indian hikers of pre-European settler days. For Chocorua New

Hampshire's rock-turreted mountain now climbed by thousands each summer is named. Legend has it that the chief's beloved son was accidentally poisoned by a settler's family named Campbell. Chocorua took vengeance by slaying Campbell's wife and children. In his turn, Campbell tracked the Indian to the top of the rock-spired mountain and shot him down. The dying Chocorua pronounced a terrible curse on the white man as he fell, the effects of which have plagued New England ever since—as evidenced by the hard, rocky infertility of her soil, the great storms that wrack her coast, and the results of many American League pennant races.

2. *Darby Field.* Mount Washington's first European conqueror, in 1642. Field made the ascent with one or two Indians, and was the first European to tramp for pleasure and exploration in the White Mountains. Even in those days, Field experienced typical Mount Washington weather—cloud, wind, and cold. It's been like that ever since.

3. *Abel Crawford.* Back in 1792 this gigantic figure strode into New Hampshire's most spectacular mountain "notch"—the one that today bears his name—and hacked out a homestead. For over 50 years he lived a robust mountain life there, becoming the first innkeeper to exploit tourist interest in New England's mountain scenery. A vigorous woodsman and climber himself, he and his son Ethan cut the very first hiking trail to the summit of Mount Washington. Still heavily used by hikers today, the Crawford Path is the oldest continuously used footpath in North America. Crawford was the first and possibly the most impressive of the true mountain men of New England.

4. *Alden Partridge.* Back in chapter 3 we mentioned this fellow as the first peakbagger of the region. His lifelong devotion to walking and to mountains was astonishing. In a day when transportation around New England was primitive, Partridge repeatedly climbed in the White Mountains *and* the Green Mountains *and* the Hudson

Highlands *and* southern New England *and* even border peaks way up in the dense forests between Maine and Canada. At the age of 45 he walked 220 miles in four days from his home in Vermont to Massachusetts and back, in order to climb a few little hills in the Holyoke Range. Later in the same year he walked to Massachusetts and back again, this time covering 300 miles, with 64 miles on the last day. If New England has always had stout walkers, surely the archetype and progenitor of the pure pedestrian was this ever-restless Partridge.

5. *Thomas Starr King.* In the middle of the nineteenth century, New Englanders were smitten with their first head-over-ears love affair with their mountains. This was the era when poets rhapsodized about mountains (William Cullen Bryant, for example); artists painted lavish mountain landscapes (the Hudson River School, they called it, but mountains were far more conspicuous than rivers on their canvases); Thoreau went off to live in the woods; Hawthorne wrote short stories about the Great Stone Face and other mountain themes. In the midst of all this romantic ardor for the heights, no one extolled the mountain's glory more than the Reverend Thomas Starr King. A preacher from Boston, he summered in New Hampshire and wrote a gushing flow of essays on the "White Hills," as he called them. He was a walker too, getting out all summer long for close personal inspection of the idyllic landscapes he loved.

6. *George Witherle.* In the nineteenth century, Maine's north woods were overrun with loggers, but few others. During this era George Witherle began trekking all over the forests looking for mountains to climb. The country north of Katahdin became his playground. It is doubtful whether anyone since (float planes and government maps notwithstanding) has ever known or loved those small but ruggedly fierce mountains any better than Witherle.

7. *Eugene Beauharnais Cook.* Violinist, chess expert, connoisseur of fine wines and good living, inexcusable

punster, this Hoboken, New Jersey, native adopted the White Mountains as his summer home. He was the leading mountain explorer and trail builder in the first generation of hikers who began building trails in that range. A man of stupendous appetites and energies, Cook reflected an age of vitality and exuberant love of the mountains. As a walker, he was amazing. Today only the most vigorous of New England's hikers attempt to traverse the Presidential Range in a single day. Cook did that in 1882, covering 24 miles and about 19,000 feet of elevation, winding up with supper at an inn in Crawford Notch—then walked back home 18½ miles over Jefferson Notch after supper.

    While we're mentioning fabulous one-day Presidential traverses, let us slip in a word on the first one-day winter traverse, by Willard Helburn and Henry Chamberlain in 1918. They went up Mount Madison via the Osgood Trail from the Glen House, encountered a full-scale snowstorm with high winds and low visibility, yet persevered across all the high summits and down to Crawford Notch, doing in a single day what most parties seventy-five years later take three days to do.

8. *Roy Buchanan.* A native Vermonter, Buchanan embodies the best of the twentieth-century trail workers who, like Abel Crawford in the early 1800s and Eugene Cook in the late 1800s, labored so hard for the benefit of others' enjoyment of the woods for years to come. Buchanan was one of those handful of fellows with the indefatigable vitality, organizational skill, and follow-through to build the Long Trail from one end of Vermont to the other. He laid out and cut the final 10 miles through to Canada, built the water bars and steps necessary to check erosion, and constructed camps where they were needed so that some shelter is available to the Long Trail hiker at intervals of never much more than 7 miles. A small man of enormous energy, strength, and humor, Roy is reported to have lived on strong black coffee and homemade

doughnuts. The diet worked—he headed the Long Trail Patrol for 36 years and was still vigorous when he died at 95 in 1977.

9. *Earl V. Shaffer.* For years after the 2,000-mile-plus Appalachian Trail was completed, no one thought of walking it all in one continuous trip. Shaffer was the first to do so, finishing at Katahdin on August 5, 1948. Some hikers of that day reacted with skepticism (was it really possible to do that?) or sneers ("a stunt," merely). But Shaffer had a vision of the future, and his accomplishment lit the way for all those happy through-hikers we told you about in chapter 4.

10. *Tom Sawyer.* No, we're not referring to Mark Twain's adolescent scamp. The other Tom Sawyer is a computer programmer from Portsmouth, New Hampshire, who was the first peakbagger to climb all 445 (!) 3,000-footers of New England. As we write, Sawyer is closing in on the even more ambitious goal of climbing all 445 of these alps in winter. Most of these peaks lack trails, so many are twelve- or fifteen-hour days required to bushwhack on snowshoes through miles of unfriendly woods, to reach low wooded summits with no views, often at temperatures at or below zero. We have had the privilege and poor judgment to follow Sawyer through some of the densest thickets on his outlandish odyssey. We can attest that no one knows how to move through dense underbrush more skillfully and swiftly than he—a truly meritorious heir to the mantle of Chocorua, Darby Field, Abel Crawford, and Alden Partridge.

New England's Finest Female Footers

But wait a minute. Our list thus far has been all male. In this day of equal opportunity, that will never do. In fact, when you consider the extraordinary handicaps that beset women walkers for so many years, the accomplishments of the "weaker" (ha!) sex are in many ways more astonishing. Consider the dress codes that required

women to wear long skirts in the woods all through the nineteenth
century. Consider too that women were brought up under psychological restraints that were perhaps even more restricting. Women
simply were not supposed to undertake physically strenuous activities. Consider finally that, with those obstacles at every hand, each
new generation lacked female role models to follow. Yet, despite
these penalties, some remarkable women came through as great
walkers. Here's our list:

1. *Granny Stalbird.* This hardy woman pioneered in the
   White Mountains in the early 1800s, when there were
   few people in those untamed woods, let alone women.
   She was said to be the first female of European descent to
   come through Crawford Notch, then a wild trace of a
   track with many rough stream crossings. Granny Stalbird
   had learned "doctoring" with herbs and roots from the
   Indians and tramped around the mountains visiting those
   who needed her skill. One famous patient was Ethan
   Allen Crawford, Abel's son, who ran his inn in the heart
   of Crawford Notch.
2. *The Austin sisters.* In 1821 these three sisters, Eliza,
   Harriet, and Abigail, were the first women to reach the
   top of Mount Washington. At the time, they were living
   in Jefferson, New Hampshire, and made the climb
   accompanied by several men, one of whom (Eliza's
   fiancé) had ascended the mountain the summer before.
   The group spent a few nights out at Ethan Allen
   Crawford's rustic camp, waiting for the rain to stop. Then
   they were escorted to the summit by Crawford himself.
   These three sisters were surely pathbreakers, since climbing for women was discouraged in those days and camping
   out in cramped quarters with men was not to be thought
   of.
3. *Lizzie Bourne.* This heroine of tragedy became famous
   because of the relentless drama and pathos of her death
   on September 14, 1855. Lizzie was not the first person to
   die on Mount Washington, but it is her death, over all
   deaths on that mountain, that has captured and held our

collective imagination. She was 23, she was engaged soon
to be married, she perished within sight of the summit
buildings she never knew were so near. Lizzie's hapless
last day contains many lessons for us hikers. The party—
Lizzie, her uncle, and her uncle's daughter—had not
started on their climb until two o'clock. They would not
be dissuaded from continuing by the caretaker at the
Halfway House, and so they were caught by darkness,
struggling with a merciless wind high on the mountain.
Lizzie collapsed and died that dark and stormy night as
guests at the Summit House—literally just a stone's throw
away—had a cozy dinner before the blazing fire.

4. *Lucia Pychowska.* This great mountain lady was Eugene
   Cook's sister and his flamboyant equal in enthusiasm for
   exploration of the New Hampshire mountains they held
   so dear. An ardent bushwhacker of the 1880s, Madame
   Pychowska (she was married to a Polish chevalier, a
   concert musician) dedicated herself to dress reform for
   women bent on climbing mountains. Recognizing that
   their restrictive dresses could keep women out of the
   woods and away from the mountain heights, she wrote an
   article published in the Appalachian Mountain Club's
   journal *Appalachia* on how to modify one's long skirts, yet
   not appear too shockingly immodest. Lucia and her
   daughter, Marian, her equal in effervescent spirit, delivered papers on their investigations of the rugged
   Mahoosucs, built trails on the high peaks that encircled
   their Randolph, New Hampshire home, and were full
   participants in the joyous life of mountain climbing that
   took place in the northern Presidentials more than a
   century ago.

5. *Two unknown women.* In 1882 two women made a week-
   long traverse of New Hampshire's Pemigewasset peaks,
   crossing through densely wooded country and climbing
   trailless mountains. They wore long skirts, which got
   ripped—actually, shredded—during the day's bushwhack,
   and which they sewed up at night sitting around their
   campfire. These women were accompanying the AMC's

new councillor of improvements, A.E. Scott, to scout
where to put a trail across the rugged and nearly unex-
plored country wherein lie such White Mountain summits as North and South Twin, Guyot, and Bond. Who
were these women who fought through this notoriously
dense spruce scrub and maintained an excellent sense of
humor? Their names, alas, have been lost to history, but
their bold, unquenchable spirit inspires all of us who've
ever tussled in a spruce thicket high up at 4,000 feet.

6. *Miriam Underhill.* An alpinist of rare ability, she was the
   first person to claim title to three coveted New England
   mountaineering feats: (a) she climbed all 46 of New
   Hampshire's 4,000-footers—in winter—many when she
   was over 60; (b) she went on to conquer New England's
   sixty-three 4,000-footers; and (c) she climbed the 100
   Highest of New England. A knowledgeable enthusiast of
   alpine flowers, Miriam was the organizer of the Appalachian Mountain Club's guidebook *Mountain Flowers of
   New England,* for which she took the photographs. Her
   autobiography, *Give Me the Hills,* tells of her pioneering
   all-women climbs in the Alps, her adventures out West
   with her husband, Robert, as well as her story of how they
   climbed the 4,000-footers in winter for the first time.

7. *Emily Klug.* A transplanted German who was a nurse in
   Brooklyn, New York, Emily Klug spent up to a month
   during the year more or less wandering, meandering
   among mountains, mainly the Presidentials. Her wandering was, in part, due to Emily's extreme near-sightedness,
   and not being exactly sure where she was headed. These
   trips took place from 1914 or so until she returned to her
   homeland just before World War II (possibly not a wise
   time to go home). Emily climbed alone, shunned crowds,
   and avoided shelters, plunking down to camp wherever
   night caught up with her, rain or clear. She used a half
   sleeping bag reaching her waist and a cape. Emily was
   devoted to the hutboys of those quieter years, and they to
   her, always giving her a hot meal in return for which
   she'd darn their socks, mend their shirts and pants, and

nurse them if they had a cold. Emily was "the best friend a hutman ever had," reported one. Emily's outfit was practical, if picturesque to the point of eccentric. She wore hobnailed boots and carried a small pack. She wore a wide woolen skirt with breeches underneath. While climbing she belted up the skirt around her waist so as to turn it into a pack, and in its folds she carried most of her belongings. She hung off of hooks on her wide belt a knife, a camera held together with rubber bands and tape, a saucepan, and a pendulous bag of food. Emily kept most of her supplies in an ice-filled cave in Huntington Ravine that was a base for her mountain tramps.

8. *Laura Cowles*. She lived in Burlington, Vermont, and was active in the earliest days of the Green Mountain Club and the beginnings of the Long Trail. This was around 1910. Her husband, Judge Clarence Cowles, built the earliest sections of the Long Trail on Mount Mansfield. Laura was an active snowshoer in those early days, climbing Mansfield many times. She was an early president of the Burlington Section. A trail on Mansfield is named for her.

9. *The Three Musketeers*. This colorful feminine trio traversed the entire Long Trail from Massachusetts to the Canadian line, and so became the toast of the Green Mountain Club. The three were Kathleen Norris and her gym teacher, Hilda Kurth, both of Schenectady, New York, and Catherine Robbins, a schoolteacher from Brandon, Vermont. In 1927 the northern part of the trail was not yet cut, merely blazed, and the women once went six days without seeing another hiker. Their walk, taking thirty-two days, was one of the earliest through-hikes of the entire Long Trail and had a quality of pioneering adventure unobtainable today. It became a public relations coup for the Long Trail and the GMC. The threesome were hailed as the "Three Musketeers," and their story hit the newspapers from coast to coast, with photos in the rotogravure sections of the New York *Herald Tribune* and in the San Francisco *Sunday Examiner*.

10. *Diane Sawyer*. We first met Diane Sawyer for a weekend
trip on the Long Trail in January, during which we
snowshoed through a drenching all-day rain and through
deep snow that was speedily turning into the consistency
of mashed potatoes. Diane and her husband, Tom (mentioned earlier), went on to complete their adventure of
hiking the entire Long Trail in winter. Although Diane
claims that Tom is the prime mover, planner, and captain
in their peakbagging odysseys, we know that she is the
cheerful, unflappable, stalwart, ever-ready, and dependable crew without which the Good Ship Sawyer could
never leave port. Diane is the quintessential first mate.
She has probably climbed as many of the Northeast's
mountains in winter as anyone we know. That is, Diane
and Tom together.

These two sets of ten great walkers are the celebrities of the
hiking fraternity. We concede that history has not recorded the
walking feats of many unsung striders along New England's rocky
footpaths. The early pioneers moving north and west into the hills;
the logging scouts seeking the virgin white pines of Maine's north
woods; later, the Yankee peddlers and itinerant preachers roaming
the rough paths between isolated settlements; still later, that hardy
twentieth-century breed, the Maine guide and his counterpart in
the Adirondacks; still more recently, the tough hut people who
stocked the high White Mountain huts, lugging 200-pound loads
up steep mountain trails before the helicopter took over—all these
must have been walkers of prodigious strength and energy.

The United States' Greatest Hikers

Let's expand our horizons from New England to the whole wide
country—plenty of space to walk in. Here's our list of the ten
greatest backcountry walkers this country's ever seen:

1. *Daniel Boone*. Representative of those many prodigious
walkers who pioneered the first footpaths off the eastern
seaboard, Boone drew his pay as an advance agent for the

Transylvania Company. He blazed the Wilderness Road, the first main artery used by settlers into the "southwest" (what is now eastern Tennessee) and on into Kentucky. Boone walked all over the previously unopened hills of that region, eventually reaching Missouri, suffering many hair-raising adventures along the way, which subsequent legends have doubtless greatly enlarged.

2. *Meriwether Lewis.* Lewis and Clark have found their names as inextricably linked as Gilbert and Sullivan, Sacco and Venzetti, and Ben and Jerry. We don't know who walked and who rode the canoe more, but we pick Lewis to represent the first great western walk, the expedition from Saint Louis to the Pacific—and back. Much of the trek was taken afloat on the Missouri River, but enough of it was on foot to make either Lewis or Clark qualify.

3. *Brigham Young.* Quite possibly the greatest hike in the history of America was the incredible trek by the Mormons across the prairies and mountains of the uncivilized West in 1846–47. The man who led that excursion was Brigham Young, a brilliant leader, stern moralist, and astonishing husband (he married 27 wives under the then-prevailing Mormon custom of polygamy).

4. *Johnny Appleseed.* Most people seem to think this character was a myth created by Hans Christian Andersen or Walt Disney, or perhaps the public relations agency for the Apple Growers' Association. In fact, he really existed, as John Chapman, born in 1774, a pioneer who walked all over Pennsylvania, Ohio, and Indiana in the first half of the nineteenth century, earning the celebrated nickname by promoting apple orchards wherever he went.

5. *John Muir.* The archetypal walker. Walks of 500 to 1,000 miles were his delight. His quests took him from Niagara Falls to Florida, from Cuba and South America to California and Alaska. Always full of inquiry, he studied botany, geology, and glaciology ("the inventions of God," he called them) as he walked along, filling notebooks that were later to become such books as *Studies in the Sierra*, *Mountains of California*, *Travels in Alaska*, and many

others. In 1892 he helped to found the Sierra Club, creating through his influence and writing a great sentiment for conservation at the turn of the century.

6. *Norman Clyde.* Quoting Emerson, he shouldered his pack and walked into the mountains in 1928, saying: "Goodbye, proud world, I'm going home." He spent the next 40 years living in the High Sierras and climbing countless peaks, many previously unclimbed, and many by new routes of surprising difficulty for a man climbing alone. His strength was incredible, and so were the enormous packs he carried. His load often weighed over 100 pounds, because Clyde took everything an unusual man might need: iron frying pan, several large kettles, cameras, rope, ice ax, several pistols, fishing rod, cups and dishes, cans of food, and a library of books in Latin, French, German, and Italian.

7. *John Burroughs.* Perhaps this country's best-known and best-loved naturalist. Patriarchal with his long, white, flowing beard, with a head that Hamlin Garland noted "had the rugged quality of a granite crag," he tramped the Catskill Mountains. Burroughs wrote 25 books, all on some aspect of nature, many while in residence at "Slabsides," his simple country log hut. In later years his stature was legendary. The public imagination responded to his trip to Yellowstone with Roosevelt, his mountain walks with John Muir, his camping trips with Edison, Ford, and Harvey Firestone. Burroughs was not a ground coverer like Muir. He saw walking as a state of mind. He wrote: "You are eligible to any good fortune when you are in the condition to enjoy a walk."

8. *Robert Marshall.* His Adirondack exploits, his long walks over Alaskan wilderness and in many areas of the Rockies, not to mention his leadership in conservation as an assistant secretary of the Interior and cofounder of the Wilderness Society, all rank him as a national figure in hiking circles. He also was just plain a wonderful guy. Of all the historical heros we've read about, this is the one we most wish we could have known and hiked with.

9. *Colin Fletcher*. The men we've listed so far were mostly hiking with an explicit goal in mind—usually one of exploration. Muir, Burroughs, and Clyde sought inspiration in the mountains, but they were also seeking to find new places or reach hitherto unattainable goals. We list Colin Fletcher as the man whose name is perhaps most associated with that post–World War II development, purely recreational noncompetitive backpacking. Both as walker and writer, Fletcher has touched a responsive chord in a generation of for-pleasure-only backcountry walkers.

10. *Grandma Gatewood*. Three-time end-to-ender on the Appalachian Trail, she started hiking at the age of 65. An Ohio farm woman, Grandma raised 11 children and *then* took up long-distance hiking. She broke all the rules, wearing sneakers and carrying her duffel slung over one shoulder. Not content with her AT notoriety, she walked, alone and in her 70s, across most of the US along the route of the pioneers, the Oregon Trail.

Worldwide Walkers

Not to stop at our national borders and a paltry few hundred years of recorded history, who are the ten greatest walkers of all time? May we have the next envelope, please. Here are our nominations:

1. *Moses*. Trip leader for that hike from Egypt to the Promised Land, and the only person to lead a hike through the bottom of the Red Sea, others having been unable to work out the arrangements. The Exodus was undoubtedly one of history's most significant walks.

2. *Po Chü-i*. A Chinese poet of the ninth century who makes our list because he was the first person who recorded climbing mountains purely for recreational reasons. Some of his climbs sound technically difficult:

    Grasping the creepers, I clung to dangerous rocks;
    My hands and feet—weary with groping for holds.

Even Po Chü-i, however, faced those Monday morning blues when, like most of us, he had to return from a great weekend in the mountains to go back to the office, as he wrote:

> Then with lowered head,
> Came back to the Ant's Nest.

3. *Marco Polo.* Maybe history's most famous traveler, he went from Venice to Beijing and back in the thirteenth century. That sure beats the Long Trail.
4. *David Livingstone.* Probably best known as the subject of Henry Stanley's presumption, this Scottish missionary crossed the breadth of Africa, including the Kalahari Desert, discovered Victoria Falls and the Zambesi River, and made a prolonged search for the sources of the Nile. He probably did more to fill in European knowledge of African geography than any other single individual.
5. *Sven Hedin.* What Livingstone did in Africa, the Swedish explorer did on the grander scale of the world's largest continent. Hedin crossed the great central regions of Asia, including the Takla Makan Desert and the Kunlun Mountains, eventually reaching Lhasa, the forbidden capital of Tibet. A fair hike from Stockholm.
6. *Hernando De Soto.* As Livingstone in Africa and Hedin in Asia, so De Soto in what is now the southern United States. Landing in Tampa Bay in 1539, the doughty Spaniard proceeded to walk across Florida, Georgia, Alabama, Mississippi, and Louisiana, touching base in Tennessee—all of it wild, Indian-populated backcountry at the time. He was the first white man to cross the Mississippi River, whereupon he continued his hike as far as present-day Oklahoma. All told, his hike was almost as long as the modern Appalachian Trail, but with no shelters, no trail signs—for that matter, no trail. With all that walking, it seems ironic that the poor man wound up with a car named after him.

7. *John Muir.* We mentioned him in the American list, but he ranks among the greatest of all time too, as the man who most walked over and celebrated the great American West.

8. *Roald Amundsen.* Beyond a shadow of a doubt, the toughest hiking in the world is polar exploration. Week after week of way-below-zero temperatures, howling blizzards, and brutal sled hauling (those dogs need help) put this kind of walking in a class by itself. Several extraordinary men have walked across arctic and antarctic wastes to a place in history—giants like Scott, Shackleton, and Peary—but we give the nod here to the man who first reached the South Pole, the greatest post-Viking Norwegian explorer, Roald Amundsen. As Wilfred Noyce wrote of another of the great antarctic walkers: "He was tough, and he enjoyed being tough."

9. *Tenzing Norgay.* In the annals of history's great walkers a place surely must be reserved for one of the two men who first walked to the top of the world, the summit of Mount Everest. Without wishing to limit the credit due to that great New Zealander, Sir Edmund Hillary, we award this spot to his partner in the Everest climb, the redoubtable Sherpa Tenzing. Nepal is a land of few motorized vehicles; people still walk wherever they go, even between cities a hundred miles apart, over ground that might fairly be described as hilly (the Himalayas). Tenzing is a worthy representative of the earth's greatest walking people, the Sherpas of Nepal.

10. *Some nameless Buddhist pilgrim,* inchworming his way from the plains of India over the mountain passes and across the Tibetan plateau to Lhasa. The approved system apparently involves a procedure as follows: (a) stand facing Lhasa, (b) utter a prayer (you'll see why in a moment), (c) throw yourself prostrate on your chest, (d) regain your feet, now one body-length nearer to Lhasa. Repeat this procedure as often as necessary to cover 1,000 miles or so. As you cross the higher mountain passes, it becomes tricky to keep snow off your tie. In the lower

valleys, check for cobras before step (c). You think the Appalachian Trail is tough!

We can't help observing the strikingly cosmopolitan character of this list—almost as varied nationally as an "all-American" soccer team. It shows how worldwide is the impulse to walk, to explore, to discover, to find out what is on the other side of that mountain pass. Our list includes:

one Jew	one Spaniard
one Chinaman	one American
one Italian	one Norwegian
one Scot	one Nepalese
one Swede	one Indian

If any country deserves more credit for its walkers, it would be England. Besides those great antarctic heroes we mentioned, Scott and Shackleton, and their men, we could have included such others as Sir Richard Burton, the disguised explorer of then-unknown Arabia (and translator of *The Arabian Nights*); Sir Francis Younghusband, who walked from Beijing to India over the Mustagh Pass in the Karakoram; or the late H. W. Tilman, the mountaineer and intrepid walker who once bicycled across Africa, despite few roads, broad rivers, and hostile beasts and tribes—to mention a few impediments not encountered daily by most ten-speed aficionados today.

Walkers one and all: from Chocorua to Miriam Underhill, from Moses to the out-of-shape weekend backpacker on Mount Chocorua today, they all heed the mandate of Isaiah:

"This is the way, walk ye in it!"

II

THE NEW ETHIC

And this our life, exempt from public haunt,
Finds tongues in trees, books in the running brooks,
Sermons in stones, and good in everything.
WILLIAM SHAKESPEARE,
AS YOU LIKE IT

FOR THE FIRST HALF of the twentieth century, those who
went off for adventure in the backwoods were a small band of
uncommon people. After World War II a number of factors began
to conspire to change all that: higher incomes, increased leisure,
what we call "improved" transportation (by which we mean
"faster"). When the 1960s came along, bringing widespread alienation from urban and technological values, the backpacking boom
began. In the 1970s it reached staggering proportions. In the 1980s
the pressure on the backcountry eased: the numbers of
recreationists leveled off, but they certainly did not decline. There
are different views of the prospects for the 1990s and beyond: some
say the boom will level, some say it will again grow. But no one
says there will be fewer people out there.

We watched this boom hit our New England woods and hills
and we winced at the changes it wrought. The caribou were gone
from the windswept heights of Katahdin, but the people had
come—by the hundreds and thousands. The shelters on Vermont's
Long Trail were crowded, carved up, and occasionally burned by

hordes of inexperienced hikers. On Slide Mountain, the Catskills' highest summit, near a rock where John Burroughs once bivouacked alone under the stars, the landscape grew blighted, trampled, and scarred in an ever-widening ring of hacked stumps as up to 100 campers per weekend sought that elusive summit solitude which Burroughs had enjoyed. Last time we were there, a dull-witted porcupine sat impassively in a fireplace, feeding on his accustomed fare, the trash of the previous weekend's campers.

These were some of the changes we watched in our New England since 1960. Across the country, the scene is similar. The Rockies and the Sierra and the Cascades have a little more room, but the popular magnets—the Tetons, Whitney, Rainier—are under the same kind of pressure as Katahdin, Slide, and the Long Trail. Deserts in the Southwest cringe under the impact of recreationists heedless of the consequences of their fun. Glaciers on Alaska's highest peaks stink with the accumulated wastes of climbing parties. In Wyoming's Wind River Range, where some of our friends used to go to avoid the Tetons crowd, the once-pristine waters of Lonesome Lake became polluted and the still meadows were pocked with tent sites.

Even the Himalayas feel the crunch. Tenzing viewed the destruction of trees for tourists' firewood along the popular trek routes and warned in his autobiography: "The tourists who come to Nepal to see the wilderness are actually destroying it as they go along."

The changes are not all measured in numbers of hikers and their impact. In response to the lug-soled army, restrictions and regulations have descended on the long-prized freedom of the hills; once-rough trails have been tamed with bridges and steps; "facilities" have been provided and upgraded where campers were once on their own, the entire experience has been softened, the rough edges smoothed, the challenge finessed.

Gradually, though, at first almost imperceptibly, but then with mounting force, a further change spread across the land of the backcountry. Backpackers began to recognize the consequences of their own actions. A conscience awoke. Concerned about both the

physical destruction of the natural environment and the degradation of the spirit of wildness that numbers, restrictions, and facilities imply, many hikers and campers began to grope their way
toward a new backwoods ethic. Thoughtful managers of wild lands,
who are daily involved with the problems of the backcountry,
helped guide opinion in constructive channels, wisely recognizing
that regulations are but a small if sometimes essential part of the
answer. The newer guidebooks and such magazines as *Backpacker*,
Wilderness Camping, and *New England Outdoors* promoted more
environmentally conscious practices in how we use the woods in
which we hike. The large hiking clubs, such as New England's
Appalachian Mountain Club and Green Mountain Club, embraced
the new concerns. Especially noteworthy was the admirable
reformation of the Adirondack Forty-Sixers. Not surprisingly, the
Sierra Club was at the forefront in this campaign, and published
the first how-to-do-it book that placed emphasis squarely on
environmental concerns: John Hart's *Walking Softly in the Wilderness*. More recently two leaders of the National Outdoor Leadership School brought the procedures of minimum-impact camping
up-to-date with their excellent manual *Soft Paths*. Their subtitle
says it all: *How to Enjoy the Wilderness without Harming It*.

Here, in this second part of our book, we talk about this new
backwoods ethic, as it implies changes primarily in the habits and
attitudes of the individual hiker, but also in the policies and
procedures of those who manage the wildlands in which we hike.

The new ethic has two equally important facets. One is the
physical impact, which we can inflict or withhold, on the land.
The other is harder to express: call it the psychological or experien-
tial or subjective or spiritual impact—the effect of our own actions
on the experience that we and others enjoy (or fail to enjoy) in the
backcountry. When we wrote the first edition of this book we tried
to cram both into the same set of pages. Fourteen years later either
the problems have grown or our perceptions of them are clarified
and intensified, because now we think both sets of problems are so
vital that we need two separate books. So in these pages we want to
focus primarily on our physical effects on wildlands. If we do not

preserve the physical environment out there—the real world of plants and soils, of trees and tundra, of pure waters and the good earth—if we do not protect those priceless resources, there won't be much point in brooding over the spiritual. First things first. So let's talk about brute physical impact.

We don't mean to belittle the importance of the subjective experience. If that interests you too, as we hope it does, please take a look at our companion volume, *Wilderness Ethics: Preserving the Spirit of Wildness.*

But for now we speak of cookstoves and sneakers and hammocks…and some new ways of looking at the same old woods and hills with an awakened environmental concern.

7

The Coming of the
Lug-Soled Army

A rabble in arms, flushed with success and insolence.

BRITISH GENERAL IN 1776, DESCRIBING THE NEWLY FORMED
ARMY OF THE UNITED STATES

COME WITH US up into mountains near where we live and let us
show you a small patch of ground that tells a story about the
impact of us hikers. In the end, it's an encouraging story, one with
a happy ending. But it didn't start out that way.

The Clearing in the Krummholz: Impact on Wildness

In the dwarfed, twisted, wind-racked, deep-green forest near
treeline on New Hampshire's Mount Lafayette, right next to the
lone hiking trail that cuts through to the alpine zone, there is a
clearing. It is surprisingly big, perhaps 40 by 60 feet. A few paces
farther, on the other side of the trail, is another clearing almost as

large. Both of these clearings lie in a sheltered depression just
below the Appalachian Mountain Club's Greenleaf Hut.

What are these clearings doing here? How did they open up,
amid a stunted forest that otherwise crowds in to the edge of the
maintained trail so dense and close that a person finds it almost
impossible to penetrate, even a few feet? Krummholz is German for
twisted wood. Twisted indeed! It's not easy to open any space at all
in this twisted wood, this shrunken, tangled forest of prickly spruce
and scrubby balsam fir. So how did the clearing in the Krummholz
get here?

We've tried that question on hut visitors and passing hikers
many times. The answers are varied, some ingenious, some enigmatic. A plane crashed here? Fire? Acid Rain? The hut crew grows
potatoes here? A helicopter pad? Moose? Indians?

Those who remember the boisterous backpacking boom of
1965–75 often guess the correct answer. Campers.

During those boom years, a swelling throng of backpackers
invaded the woods. All over the country, a nature-loving generation sought escape and inspiration in mountains, along murmuring
streams, on alpine meadows, in deep coniferous glades. The statistics on backcountry recreation tell a tale of manifold increase in
"use," but the land itself told a more vivid story, a tragedy of
overuse and abuse, eroded trails, flattened vegetation, polluted
waters, and loss of solitude and many of the very values that that
generation went to the woods to seek. Indeed, it was as if we
brought civilization with us, through our numbers and our manners. "We go to the woods in part to escape," lamented one sage
observer, Bill McKibben. "But now there is nothing except us and
so there is no escaping other people."

The impact on the wilderness environment was partly due to
the increased numbers alone. But it was also a function of the style
of camping. The backpacking boom was based on practices that our
predecessors of the 1930s had found perfectly satisfactory. They
took an ax, hacked down the trees needed for a blazing campfire,
carved out balsam fir boughs to make a springy mattress, washed
their dishes and themselves in the nearest stream, trenched their

tents, buried trash or tossed it in a communal trash pit at popular campsites.

These standard practices worked well when the number of wilderness recreationists was small. Nature has remarkable recuperative powers and shrugged off the impact of these early campers. But when the backpacking boom began, the backcountry could no longer absorb the impact. Where there had been one tent perhaps one weekend a month, there were now three tents competing for space every weekend, enlarging the tent site. The occupants hacked at more trees in a relentless search for firewood. That's how those clearings in the Krummholz were born, not just on Mount Lafayette but throughout the mountains. Perhaps there had been a solitary tent site during the 1950s. But with the boom more tenters crowded in and pushed back the forest until a 40 by 60 foot space was cleared. Not just cleared of trees: between boot traffic and constant tenting, the ground vegetation was completely worn off. The earth became so compacted that water could scarcely penetrate. Rain sheeted off, further depriving the vegetation of any chance for survival.

By 1970 we had a pretty ghastly sight: a 40 by 60 foot hole in the Krummholz, nothing but trampled, rammed-earth hardpan, a mud wallow during exceptionally rainy spells, punctuated by whacked-off tree stumps to a general height of 18 inches. Nothing growing under foot.

This clearing was characteristic of many others, products of the backpacking boom. The hordes especially liked to camp where a stream crossed the trail; most anywhere along a trail, particularly near water; around backcountry shelters; and above treeline on that mattresslike (but extremely sensitive) alpine vegetation. On a good weekend brightly colored tents could be seen stretching up from pristine alpine lakes toward the upper slopes of rocky summits.

Things couldn't go on like this. The mountains couldn't take it any more. Worse, the boom was projected to keep on rising. Backcountry managers were distraught: if it's this bad now and getting worse geometrically, where are we going to be in the year 2000?

The Old Ways

It wasn't just numbers, of course; it was bad habits. Or, to be more precise, as well as more fair to an innocent earlier generation, it was habits that had once been perfectly appropriate, but that numbers transmogrified.

Back in the 1930s Doc Waterman guided canoe parties down the Allagash every summer, and the camping way of life of the Maine north woods in those days was the pattern that his son Guy first learned. On Girl Scout trips just a few years later, Laura was schooled in the same equipment and techniques, which she practiced faithfully over Vermont and New Hampshire hills in the 1950s.

Tents were larger and much heavier, with no sewn-in floors, and the color was invariably a kind of monotone somewhere between brown, green, and gray. Sleeping bags alone weighed about as much as an entire overnight pack does today.

Camping without a campfire would have been unthinkable. We all carried an ax or hatchet or both (depending on the trip), and one of the first jobs on reaching camp was to scout the area for a judicious mixture of the right hardwoods plus a little softwood for kindling.

Thirsty? Drink out of any stream.

Dirty? Grab the soap, strip, and plunge into the nearest stream—yes, the same one you drank out of, but maybe down-stream a little.

For a comfortable night's sleep, we learned to cut fir branches and arrange them just right. In case of rain, we'd dig a small ditch around the uphill side of the tent.

In today's environmentally concerned world, we shudder to recall some of those camping habits. Yet for their time, there was nothing wrong with this way of living in the woods. We want to emphasize that point: in that quieter time the backcountry was so big and resilient that a handful of campers could live according to the old ethic without scarring the land permanently. It was the right way to do things in its time. It is not that we have become

more virtuous—rather, we have become more numerous, by
manifold, and so we have been forced to change.

In those old days you could run the Allagash and the lakes
around it for six weeks and see maybe two or three other parties,
together with the lonely fire warden on Allagash Mountain, who
talked to himself unless you were there to talk to, and old Frank,
whose team toted your gear across the carry between Mud Pond
and Umbazooksus on mud-rutted roads. There were miles of true
wilderness with no one else around, so it really was OK to take
deadwood and even some live, wash in the streams, cut bough beds.
It was sound woodsmanship. But in the wake of the backpacking
boom of the 1960s and 1970s, it was a way of life that could not
continue.

Consider an incident that we often recall when we think
about the changing camping scene.

July 7, 1966. One of us and two teenage sons were climbing
Mount Moosilauke. This is a big slumbering giant of a mountain
with a massive rounded top, not at all a picture-book summit like
Chocorua or the Matterhorn. Though among the ten highest in
New Hampshire's White Mountains, it stands way off by itself to
the southwest, as if dropped there after all the other peaks were
finished.

The three of us had been hiking for two weeks straight and
were feeling in fine shape as we raced up the rough trail to the
summit in late afternoon. On our way down, just below the summit, we passed two Boy Scouts. Exchanging the usual trailside
courtesies, we asked where they were headed.

"Beaver Brook Shelter," said one of them.

Now this news was of passing interest, since we too planned
to spend the night at that shelter, which lay at the foot of the trail,
almost 3,000 feet below.

Gingerly we asked: "How many in your party?"

"Fourteen."

Well, there's about room for six in that shelter, crowding it
some, and it looked like rain. So we decided we'd better pour it on
if we wanted a place under the roof. Being in the shape we were in,

and large Scout groups traveling at the pace they do, we had no trouble passing them in bunches of twos and threes until, well before the end of the trail, we had counted 14 and could let up our pace a little.

When the first Scouts got down to Beaver Brook Shelter, they found our three sleeping bags rolled out. We were models of woods manners in offering them what was left of the shelter space. However, their leader cheerfully assured us: "That's OK, we'll go camp a little way off toward the pond."

So we had a nice quiet evening alone in the shelter after all. But just before dark it began to rain, and conscience began to prod us into wondering how the Scouts were making out. What we found is a scene that sticks in memory: a beehive of activity, centering around an enormous jerry-built lean-to, large enough to sleep 14 underneath, with long fresh-cut poles (some up to six inches in diameter) lashed together and covered over with a thick matting of fresh-cut evergreen branches. The Scouts had it almost completed when we got there, and had a roaring campfire stocked with plenty of wood. The entire area was trampled thoroughly with the milling and scuffling of 13 eager Scouts. The crowning touch was that their leader was idly sitting by the fire whittling—a sure sign that the troop had performed this ritual many times before, thus requiring no direction.

Just multiply that troop of 14 by several hundred other Scouting outfits, summer camps, outdoor clubs, and college outing clubs—then multiply by the number of years that has passed since 1966—and then try to imagine what would be left of the woods, had that pattern continued unchecked.

Formidable Philosophical Underpinnings

In the next chapter we'll get to the happy ending, but let's pause first to consider the array of formidable and diverse allies that supported the worst tactics of this lug-soled army. Camping reform was up against some entrenched philosophical underpinnings that

it's a miracle were ever overcome. These antagonists included—
and to a degree still include—the frontier tradition, democratic
ideals, modern education theories, urban renewal, ideas of personal
freedom, motherhood, the sociability of clubs, the mystique of the
old campfire, the lug sole, and the black fly. That's an opposing
lineup powerful enough to awe the most dedicated reformer.

1. The frontier tradition. Too many hikers had, and still
   have, an image of going out to "conquer" the wilderness
   rather than live with it or as a part of it. David Langlois, a
   Vermont camp director whom we'll be talking more
   about later, cautions: "We try to remember that we're
   spending a night, not founding a settlement."
2. Democratic ideals. A lot of people think that if the woods
   are good for some of us, then everyone should have an
   opportunity to experience this blessing. You can be
   labeled an elitist if you see anything wrong with getting
   everybody in the entire city of Boston to tramp through
   the most beautiful sections of New England's woods.
   What would be left of the beauty when this had come to
   pass?
3. Modern education theories. Spearheaded by the highly
   successful Outward Bound program, many camps and
   school courses now see it as their mission to get every kid
   in the region to experience "survival" and "challenge"
   (ever-popular fad words) in the remote backcountry.
4. Urban renewal. The warm-hearted theory is abroad that
   every ghetto kid can gain a new lease on life if exposed to
   the great outdoors.
5. Ideas of personal freedom. We are strongly in favor of as
   much freedom in the hills as can possibly be maintained
   in this day and age. But we sense that many hikers use
   personal freedom as a license for irresponsible habits in
   the backcountry. Of what value is the freedom to take a
   bath (with soap) in any mountain cascade you come to, if
   the result is a polluted water supply for the party that's
   camping downstream?
6. Motherhood. How's that again? We're simply referring to

the underlying fact of the population growth. That is, after all, what got us into this mess to begin with. Fundamentally it's a problem of simply too many people.

7. The sociability of clubs. Nothing destroys the illusion of wilderness faster than running into a party of 20 or 30 people traveling together. Camp groups are among the worst offenders. Most clean-camping advocates urge limiting group size, many clubs have at least put an end to group discounts on club facilities, and others request that parties be limited to 10. Yet club traditions die hard, and many hiking clubs, schools, and camp groups still schedule mass ventures, with large mobs of sociable hikers blasting along the trail, making a mockery of everyone's hopes for a feeling of wilderness solitude.

8. The mystique of the old campfire. One of the most deeply entrenched camping notions is that you're just not doing it right unless you build a blazing fire. This emotional subject deserves separate discussion (see chapter 11). Suffice it to raise here a question that the Appalachian Mountain Club posed once in a poster: "What if we *all* built fires?"

9. The lug sole. Actually one of the biggest impacts of the backpacking boom is in the scuffling up of groundcover by that obsolescent status symbol the lug sole. That's why many clean-camping advocates urge everybody either to wear lighter shoes or at least to take a pair of moccasins or sneakers to change into after reaching campsite.

10. The black fly. Even this pesky insect has its impact. How's that? Because camping in hammocks does far less damage to the woods than tenting—but if you tried to sleep in the early hammocks during black fly season, you came to realize that your dedication to clean camping had its price. We understand camping hammocks now come equipped with built-in netting.

All of these obstacles to camping reform made it hard for the last generation to reform, and they still linger on today. But if we all go on abusing the wilds, we're going to bring environmental havoc to the mountains and, with it, restrictions and rules that will spoil it for everyone.

We don't greet the reform attitudes and practices as unmixed blessings. Sometimes we're sad to see the change from those old days. Often we yearn for the yesterday when you could hike all day and never see another person. Our personal tastes run to the drab old canvas wall tents, rather than the sleek nylon international orange lightweights. We love to wield an ax—and do so plenty, but at home in our own woodlot, on a carefully planned sustained-yield basis, not on overrun, overused hiking country. Who is there that does not respond to the warm conviviality of the campfire? Sometimes we truly feel we were born too late—the golden age of camping lies buried in the good old days.

Sometimes we're more optimistic and feel good about the new era—to see that people are capable of adapting their exploitive ways, of trying to soften the weight of their impact, of conserving a natural world that renews and enriches the human spirit.

They say that an optimist thinks that this is the best of all possible worlds, and a pessimist fears that's the case. This dichotomy applies to attitudes about the changing camping scene. Pessimist or optimist, we have to acknowledge that it is changing.

In the 1840s and 1850s, Henry David Thoreau visited the Maine woods. As we read his narratives, we recognize many of the spots he visited. He too walked the carry from Umbazooksus to Mud Pond, and it was just as mud-rutted then as it was when we were there in 1946. The interesting point is that in many ways there was less change in Maine's north woods during the entire century from Thoreau's first trip in 1846 to ours in 1946 than there was in the 30 years from 1946 to 1976. The opening of the Allagash Waterway to vacationers, the new roads, the seaplanes, the big camp groups—all have completely altered the scene. Well, not completely. Some things don't change. The loon still sounds his enigmatic laugh. You can still experience today what Thoreau wrote about:

It is a country full of evergreen trees, of mossy silver birches and watery maples, the ground dotted with insipid small red berries, and strewn with damp and moss-grown rocks—a forest resounding at rare intervals with the note of the chickadee, the blue jay, and the woodpecker, the scream of the fish-hawk and the eagle, the laugh of the loon, and the whistle of ducks along the solitary streams.

Years ago, when the onslaught of the tourists began hitting the Alps and the English hills, the great Scottish climber Norman Collie wrote:

Civilization has stretched out its hand and changed it all, and though those who knew the old days are somewhat sad that the old order has changed, yielding place to new, yet the new order is good, and the land of the great woods, lakes, mountains, and rushing rivers is still mysterious enough to please anyone who has eyes to see, and can understand.

8

Cleaning Up Our Act

There is, nevertheless a certain respect, and duty of
humanity, that ties us, not only to beasts that have life
and sense, but even to trees and plants.

MICHEL DE MONTAIGNE

WE THINK OF the woods and hills as eternal, and most of the time, from man's puny perspective, they are. And yet what a change is going on under those trees! Our camping fathers and mothers of pre–World War II would be astonished if they could come along on a modern backpack. And herein lies the solution to the problem posed by the coming of the lug-soled army.

On a recent three-day camping trip in New Hampshire's Pemigewasset Wilderness, we were struck with how different it all was from when we got started camping years ago. We were with a large group of campers in the "Pemi," a sizable chunk of rolling forest surrounded by peaks of the White Mountains. There were 14 of us altogether. The seven two-person tents were the latest sleek nylon lightweight models, the brilliant colors ranging all over the rainbow (except purple). Each pair of campers reached into aluminum pack frames and pulled out portable cookstoves fueled with white gas. No one ever suggested we build a crackling warm campfire. Had anyone started to cut a bough bed for extra comfort, this person would have been attacked with an ax—except that none of us carried an ax or even a hatchet. Though we camped near the banks of Lincoln Brook one night—nearer than we should have—no one washed in the waters, and when nature called, each person went well back into the woods away from stream and trail to answer.

Our group violated some canons of the new ethic. We were too many, to begin with. In just about every section of the country, responsible managers are trying to discourage groups of more than 10. Those brightly colored tents are more of an intrusion on the woods scene than they need be ("like a light you can never turn off," says conservationist and author John Hart). And we should have gone further from the banks of Lincoln Brook.

Still, if you went back to the places we camped on that trip, you'd find no sign of our having been there. Indeed, it might be hard to find the sites at all. Where the tents were, no tent has subsequently been, and the forest floor is well on its way back. You'd find no blackened fire ring, no stripped branches or bark, no cut boughs, no dug latrine, no litter or can pit unearthed by animals.

When we were on that trip, we couldn't help thinking back with a smile to what it was like when we were learning how to live in the woods in the years just after the war, but before prewar camping technology and habits had changed the old ways we described in the last chapter.

As was learned by all of us who were around when the lug-soled army invaded the woods in the 1960s and 1970s, the old ways couldn't continue. With increasing numbers projected to rise through the 1980s and 1990s, backwoods managers were bracing for the onslaught and prepared to introduce restrictions and permits and quotas, maybe to macadamize the trails, or make them one-way, or something...anything!

Backwoods Ethics: The Low-Impact Principle

What happened? How did we escape that Orwellian scenario?

For one thing, the backpacking boom slacked off. By the end

of the 1970s it was clear that, if the numbers hadn't exactly dropped, they certainly were not rising anymore. That piece of arithmetic was crucial: with continuing population explosion in the backcountry, there is no telling where we'd be now. The slackened backcountry boom was not the only story, however, not even the main story. Two other things happened: regulations and education.

Land managers implemented the regulations. Backpackers were warned not to camp in the vulnerable spots, such as along heavily used trails; where any trails crossed streams; within a quarter mile of backcountry facilities like shelters or huts. Shelter sites were made over with innovative platforms on which you were to place your tent, thus getting it off the ground. No camping at all was permitted above treeline.

Big change! That generation was the first to find out that the freedom of the hills had its limits. If we were not going to destroy our own resource, we all had to accept restraints on our actions.

But in the long run an even more important requirement was a change not just in our behavior but in our attitudes, our perception of our role in the backcountry.

You couldn't write regulations to cover every conceivable situation, and even if you could, you couldn't enforce them. One US Forest Service researcher, David N. Cole, pointed out the problem in regulations standing alone:

> For example, visitors are commonly asked not to camp close to lakes; however, defensible reasons for this request are seldom offered. Without a rationale, visitors may not understand why the action is important and may decide that it is *not* important. They are more likely to interpret recommendations incorrectly, and they are less likely to think of additional means of mitigating the problem.

Another way of putting it was expressed by the Izaak Walton League's newsletter, in a message to fishermen about responsible behavior in their realm:

> Every time the legislation of ethics comes up, it shows the

failure of education. The sad thing is that we increasingly turn matters of conscience over to cops.

You had to reach people's minds and get them to understand the underlying rationale for change. You had to help people to see the fragility of the apparently rugged terrain they were visiting, and the consequences for that terrain of their own actions as visitors. You had to change people's perceptions of their own place in wilderness.

The mentality of the frontier had to close down, as the frontier did long ago. The frontiersmen's children needed to move into new frontiers of consciousness, to explore new ground in understanding their relationship to the land. Frederick Jackson Turner's thesis needed a replacement suitable for our time. A new generation needed a new ethic through education, not just regulation.

A regulated camper begrudges what you tell him he must do (or must not do). He'll be tempted to cheat when you're not looking. An educated camper is intrigued with what he can do, recoils from what he should not do, and takes pride in finding an appropriate place for himself in the mountain environment. As forester Cole concluded:

> Low-impact wilderness education must be an ethic and a way of thinking if it is to realize its full potential. It is more a matter of attitude and awareness than of rules and regulations.

And so began the process of thinking about our own actions, of helping to educate the whole backcountry population, and especially of reaching the new generation of enthusiastic recreationists. Backcountry managers developed communications arts they'd never needed before. Hiking clubs played a major role in reaching their members and the public. Both the managers and the clubs reached out to leaders of large youth groups, summer camps, Boy and Girl Scouts, school groups. Some of these youth leaders became zealous prophets of "clean camping" or "no-trace" wilderness travel. Their teachings were especially valuable, because they addressed the next generation of hikers.

Education took many forms. Every shelter and hut, every trailhead and information point in the forest had signs and leaflets advising visitors how to camp and hike responsibly. Magazines such as *Backpacker* and *Wilderness Camping* and *New England Outdoors* carried frequent articles on the new ethic. Outfitting stores responsibly preached the message to their customers. Some manufacturers of outdoors equipment prepared educational leaflets on the proper use of their own gear. The hikers themselves, as they began to soak in the word, felt the missionary's zeal to spread the word to fellow travelers.

Elements of the New Ethic

What was this new backwoods gospel?

1. Carry a lightweight backpacking stove. No fires. Leave the ax at home. In areas where campfires are still appropriate, there are a lot of sensible practices that fire builders can use to minimize their impact, both physical and visual.
2. Those who do insist on a fire, and are in an area where it is both legally and environmentally feasible to have one, have an obligation to take special pains to keep it safe and small, and to destroy all evidence of its having been there when they leave.
3. Use a lightweight foam pad. No more cutting bough beds for mattresses. (At least one camping manual of the old days had advised taking one entire balsam fir tree per bed!)
4. Wash away from streams, both dishes and yourself, using biodegradable soap, and not much of it.
5. Choose a low-impact tent site so that you don't need to provide drainage by digging a trench around your tent. This one is a bit tricky, and it illustrates the need for campers to understand the subtleties of the problem and the underlying objective, rather than just memorizing a rule or regulation. If you are in an area already heavily

impacted, it is better to use the site that everyone else already has, rather than create a new one. But if you come on a lightly used site that is just beginning to show wear, it is better to disperse and find another place, preferably one that others are unlikely to find or reuse. No pat instruction can be handed out, but if you understand what the objective is, you can choose the right place to camp.

6. As a general rule, camp at least 150 feet from water and from hiking trails.

7. These days it's increasingly possible to purchase tents and packs of softer colors—green or brown—rather than the flaming reds and oranges that stand out so blatantly from far away and trumpet your presence to every other passing hiker.

8. Some conscientious campers carry hammocks to sleep entirely off the ground. More on this in chapter 10.

9. From wherever you camp, take a different route between there and the trail and the stream when you go for water. That way you won't wear a path. Take a large water carrier with you so you can get ample water on the first trip.

10. Choose a different campsite every time. Most important: never camp where someone else has (but also see rule 5 above). It's repeated use of the same site that causes the damage. Limit use of any one site to two or at most three nights. (Some would say just one night.) It's rather difficult to stay longer in one place and not have it look—and *be*—well worn.

11. Wear soft-soled shoes around your campsite. Take off the heavy lug-soled boots while in camp, so as to take it easy on the ground cover. For that matter, many hikers feel that running shoes or similar lighter footwear are entirely adequate for most day hikes at least. Automatically strapping on the big lug soles is not necessarily the way to go.

12. No litter, of course. Carry out everything you bring in. Go one step farther and pick up trash left by those who haven't got the message yet.

13. Dispose of human wastes with discretion and some understanding of what pollutes and how decomposition acts
fastest. Where toilets are conceivably available, use them. In
remoter locations, dig a very shallow cat hole, maximizing
the speed with which nature can compost what you leave—
well away from streams and trails, of course.

14. Don't pick the wildflowers or forage indiscriminately for
what some nature writer told you was edible wild foods.
And will this generation at last be the one to leave all the
birchbark on the white birches? Nothing symbolized
careless irresponsibility in the woods more than stripping
birchbark.

15. Limit group size. One of the primary findings of the 1977
report of the Adirondacks' High Peaks Wilderness
Advisory Committee was that groups of more than 10
hikers have "a greater pressure on the resource than
would the same number of users as individual day hikers
or backpackers." All over the country now, officials frown
on groups of over 10.

16. Keep voices down near other parties, and especially keep
quiet after dark. As for radios—?!?!

17. Remember, it's low-impact hiking as well as low-impact
camping. As you hike along, stick to the existing trail
rather than skirt its edge and widen it. Resist the temptation to walk alongside the person you're conversing with,
if that requires you to walk outside the existing track.

18. When hiking off-trail, fan out through the untrammeled
woods, rather than tramping single file, thereby starting a
herd path that could become a trail.

19. On trails, if you see drainage that's clogged, scrape it out
with your boot or a stick. Trails would survive so much
better if every hiker had a sense of stewardship. We
should stop thinking of ourselves as trail users, and think
of ourselves as trail stewards.

20. Have consideration for the local regulations when pack
animals are used. Nothing tears up mountain meadows
and trails or pollutes watersheds quite so much as a string
of horses, mules, burros, or llamas.

21. Even on human feet, think about your impact. Notice the season of the year when the snows first thaw and reveal the land for the first time. Then is the earth uniquely vulnerable. The mud that churning hiking boots create at such time goes deep fast. It is not like mud in a midsummer rainstorm. It is much deeper, much more disturbing to the integrity of the soil. Therefore, many hikers seek to stay out of the hills in mud season. It's not a great time for hiking anyway. In the 1970s Vermont's Green Mountain Club began urging its members to stay off popular mountains in May, and Vermonters bought the idea. Now state government officials take to the television screen every spring to exhort the good citizens not to hike on vulnerable trails at that critical point of the seasonal cycle.

22. Above treeline, exercise special care to protect alpine vegetation. This means sticking to designated trails where there is one, and where there isn't, walking carefully on rocks only. It certainly means not camping on the tundra vegetation. The tent above treeline has to be a luxury lost, save in winter on a protective snow cover or in remote areas where a site may never be found and used again by other parties. But beyond camping, the aware hiker has developed an instinctive concern for where to put each footstep.

23. Cooperate with the sometimes onerous restrictions that backcountry managers install to cope with the impact of people.

24. Contribute constructive thinking to the problem. Those in charge are looking for ideas, and "public involvement" is a byword in the lexicon of modern backcountry management.

25. Remember, every time you're walking up a trail or camping in the backcountry, that the *mountain environment is fragile*.

That was the basic agenda of the new backwoods ethic. What was the result? A good answer is to go back and look at that clearing in the Krummholz near Greenleaf Hut that we described at the start of the previous chapter. It is now fifteen years since the regulations and (more important) the education began, and since hikers started to live by the new ethic. What do we see?

The change is perfectly extraordinary for anyone who can recall what it looked like in 1970. It is tremendously heartening. Now we see a clearing still, but it is grass green. It may not remain a clearing long. Bushy shrubs and young balsams to a height of several feet grow in around the edges and cluster in the middle. Look for those bludgeoned-off stumps we mentioned. The new growth of fir overwhelms them—scarcely a stump visible! As you gaze, a snowshoe hare hops out from the dense edge and begins to nibble on that tempting thick grass. (Or is it sedge? The hare doesn't seem to care.) On a young balsam a white-throated sparrow sings.

Implications for the Future

What do we learn from the backpacking boom and its aftermath? The first two lessons are these:

1. When people come to the mountains in large numbers, they can, wittingly or no, do great damage.
2. But if we back away, see the error of our ways and try to correct them, try to respect the land, become stewards of wilderness, then nature has magnificent restorative powers. The forest, at least in our Northeast and to a degree everywhere, can come back.

Nature has an irresistible urge to *grow*, to regenerate, to rebuild. Fortunately for us in the Northeast, nature does this growing with surprising speed and ease. She is helped by a wet climate. (Backpackers know all too well that wet climate!) Some call it the asbestos forest: it is so wet it is hard to burn. In the West the land recovers more slowly, but there you also have wider expanses over which to disperse. Above treeline, East or West, recovery is also slower, so restraint and respect is especially needed in alpine areas. But in any place where we can reform our ways and walk quietly over the land, nature can restore itself.

...But only if we do the right things. The optimistic message is valid only so long as we correct our abuses and give nature a chance. A sense of stewardship is vital to the future of the backcountry.

9

Low-Impact Hiking: Of Boots, Mud, and Grandmothers

Even in the land of Goshen
Hard lug soles cause erosion.
WINSLOW THRATCHETT

THE TALISMAN OF today's hiker-backpacker is his boots. The hiker without his boots is like the hunter without his gun, the fisherman without his rod, Heifetz without his violin, Babe Ruth without his bat. And yet the image of the traditional hiking boot is changing, partly as a result of the new way we look at our hiking surroundings.

Throughout most of our early hiking years, virtually every experienced hiker we met on the trail was shod in a heavy, stiff-soled boot. The things make a terrific racket tiptoeing across a mountain cabin floor, and they track in dirt and mud every time they step inside. But no self-respecting backpacker dared be seen without his or her mammoth boots. We had ours—it was a badge of the tribe.

In fact, during the early days of the 1960s and 1970s boom in outdoor recreation, the heavy, lug-soled hiking boot became a kind of status symbol. Everyone who coveted an outdoorsy reputation had to clomp around on big, stiff wafflestompers. College coeds, newly signed up for the outing club, stomped from class to class in their hiking boots with ⅜-inch raised cleats.

Arguments against Lug Soles

Then a minor revolution took place. Two points began to dawn on a lot of outdoors walkers. The first was an environmental consciousness. The second was the question of whether the heavy boots are really necessary.

The environmental conscience beset backwoods hikers in a big way. Many backpackers advocated environmental-saving measures such as those we described in the last chapter.

When this environmental conscience took a look at the mud tracked in on the cabin floor, it began to ask some embarrassing questions. Questions like, Where did all that mud come from? Lug-soled boots were picking up a little bit of every trail they passed over and were carrying it out to shelters, cars, and homes. The impact of heavy, cleated boots on trail erosion began to be noticed.

A hiker named William Harlow determined experimentally that those little raised-earth footprints left by a cleated sole tend to wash away in rainstorms. Harlow found that the amount of earth left so exposed by one cleated sole weighs close to an ounce. Figuring a 2½ foot stride, he computed that one hiker traveling one mile leaves 120 pounds of raised earth in his footprints, ready to be eroded down the trail at the first rain.

Carry that logic out and you'll find that a party of four lug-soled hikers walking up a five-mile trail just before a rain just might be responsible for a ton of earth washing down. That's a lot of backcountry being washed down into frontcountry.

Harlow wrote up his results for *Backpacker* magazine, arguing strenuously for hikers to use smooth-soled boots or lightweight footgear for any kind of travel except the most demanding moun-taineering. "Millions of backpackers," proclaimed Harlow, "wear lug soles in country where such footing contributes little to hikers' safety, yet claws at trails and smashes vegetation in cross-country rambles."

In western high country, some of those lovely high alpine meadows are especially vulnerable to boot impact. One national park estimates that as few as 15 lug-soled hikers crossing the same meadow in the same place can cause significant damage to the soils and plant life. Divide 15 into the kind of visitor totals some of these parks get and you can imagine the impact.

Thus all over the country wildland managers and concerned hikers began to question the last generation's love affair with the lug. (A lug affair?)

A first step was to begin taking lighter footgear along to change into when you camped in the woods. Maybe you want the big lug sole to hike in, but once in camp, change to something that won't scuff up every inch of turf you walk on. Counciled one Vermont camp director: "Sneakers, moccasins, or even bare feet, have far less impact on the ground cover."

In springtime especially, there's no question that lug soles are tough on a wet trail. As we mentioned, Vermont's Green Moun-tain Club has officially urged its members not to hike during the early spring mud season because of the damage hiking boots can do when trails are wet. More recently others, like the Adirondack Mountain Club and New Hampshire's White Mountain National Forest, have asked hikers to reconsider mud season hiking, and the Society of America Foresters raised this issue in a 1989 booklet called *Wilderness Management.*

We agree 100 percent about mud season. We are involved in volunteer trail maintenance, some of which absolutely must be done in May, so we see what the trails look like at that time of year when the snow pack and the frost have just left the high country for the first time. The mud you see then is not like the mud you see during a summer's all-day rain. It's much deeper, much squishier, the soil far more vulnerable. We cringe at our own impact and wish there were some way to reconcile that needed trail clearing with a moratorium on trail workers, or anyone else, tramping on those vulnerable soils at that time of year. For pure recreation, we—and increasingly lots of others—stay off the trails during mud season.

The environmentalist antilug reaction is strong enough to have engaged the attention of the Quabaug Rubber Company of Massachusetts, the American manufacturer of Vibram soles. This company has issued a public-spirited booklet on how to minimize hiker impact on the backcountry and has produced a variety of alternative soles that cause less damage to trails. Three cheers for Quabaug.

If it were just an environmental conscience that argued against heavy lug-soled boots, the move to other footgear probably wouldn't get very far. However, while relatively few hikers seriously ask, "What are we doing to the environment?" quite a few began to ask, "What are we doing to ourselves?" A lot of walkers we know wondered whether it's really necessary to carry all that weight around at the end of each leg. Might it not be a lot more practical to wear something light and more comfortable? Are heavy hiking boots really necessary?

Grandma Gatewood, the fabulous woman who hiked the entire 2,000-mile Appalachian Trail three times—the first time at age 67— wore sneakers. If Grandma Gatewood could hike 2,000 miles in sneakers, does Joe Athlete really need heavy boots with lug soles?

Another grandmother, the Adirondacks' super hill walker, Trudy Healy—who climbed all 46 of the 4,000-foot mountains in the Adirondacks at least six times and wrote the first guide to rock climbing in that region—originally climbed those 46 peaks in sneakers. So did her six children.

We've noticed that some of the young people who work in the high mountain huts of the Appalachian Mountain Club have discarded their big black hiking boots—formerly so much a symbol of their hiking prowess that many hut guests wondered whether the boots were surgically appended to their feet. Now we occasionally see hut people clad in sneakers or running shoes.

In the summer of 1977 two of those hut boys traversed all eight high huts in a single 16-hour day—racing up and down 49 miles of rough mountain trail with elevation changes of over 1,000 feet at many points along the way. The two chose to wear running shoes rather than hiking or mountaineering boots for the incredible jaunt. Their achievement struck a body blow to the conventional wisdom that rugged hiking requires big heavy boots.

One American friend who now lives and hikes in Switzerland is a devotee of running shoes. "From the store shelf to an eight-hour walk and never a hint of a blister," she writes. "Dear me, when I think of all those Band-Aids and moleskin consumed! To say nothing of the weight."

Another friend recently traveled to the Andes to climb several high peaks, one over 20,000 feet. For the upper snowfields he took mountaineering boots, but as high as 16,000 feet he wore simple running shoes.

The idea is that hiking boots are simply a lot heavier than they need to be.

One friend of ours, embarking on a long hike involving major ascents and descents through the mountains, carried both hiking boots and sneakers. On the uphills he wore the sneakers and carried the hiking boots, feeling much lighter afoot that way. Then on each summit he'd switch to the hiking boots and carry the sneakers for the jarring descents on those rocky trails.

Those superwalkers the Sherpas of Nepal have not traditionally enjoyed the questionable benefits of big heavy boots. Many walk their rugged trails barefoot, even crossing snow passes unshod. These days, we're told, the Sherpas that escort visiting hill walkers on treks through Nepal's hill country wear a colorful variety of sandals, sneakers, work boots—whatever westerners' largesse may have brought them—and still occasionally bare feet.

The Other Side of the Question

Now, having said all this, we must say a word on the other side of the question. At least three good arguments on behalf of the old lug sole deserve attention.

First is the matter of safety. When you are dealing with slippery footing, rain-slicked rocks, frozen ground, or any terra that is less than completely firma, the lug sole has undeniable advantages. We must report that more than one person we know who is involved with search-and-rescue work tells us that the victims are disproportionately clad in softer hiking footgear. Unquestionably the lug sole grips slippery surfaces better.

We would hate to be responsible for a rash of accidents by people indiscriminately switching away from old-fashioned hiking boots as a result of reading this chapter.

Second, we've heard at least one respected source argue that lug soles are in some ways easier on the mud than sneakers. C. Peter Fish, Adirondacks ranger extraordinaire, contends that he sees sneaker-clad people slip on slanting mud where a good lug sole would grip that same spot without slipping. Thus, Fish argues, the mud takes a worse beating from the slipping and sliding of the soft-soled hikers, while the lug-soled denizens plant each foot just once and securely.

Third, if you have any weak ankle or knee problems, you're probably well advised to stick with a good solid, substantial hiking boot. As both of us have grown older and our limbs less dependable, particularly following ankle and knee injuries, we must concede we've gone back to our good old Limmer boots, with their strong ankle support—and their tough lug soles.

Where does this bring us out? Not to any simplistic answer, apparently. Each individual hiker must consider what kind of hiking he or she wants to do, on what kind of terrain, and even in what kind of weather. For the extreme mud of April (at low elevations) and May (at high) maybe we should all give the trails a respite from any kind of foot traffic. For the rest of the summer and fall, if you think lighter footgear is right for you, you may be helping the mountain environment in the bargain. But judge each case on its merits.

What comes out of reflections like this, however, is maybe the most important point of all: *think*. Consider our environmental impact as recreationists. Question the old ways—not necessarily to reject them, but to evaluate them in light of new concerns. The mountains and forests and deserts and wetlands and tundra and grasslands are under a lot more people pressure than they were 50 or 100 years ago, and what worked fine in Dad's and Mom's youth may not be fine today. Think about what we do.

If you think, and still decide "I think I'll wear my good old monster hiking boots," that's fine with us. But if we all are conscious of the issue, maybe it will help us to modify not only exactly how and where we choose to walk, so as to reduce the worst of our footprints' mischief, but especially when we choose to walk at all—maybe mud season is a time for reading about the mountains and environmental problems, rather than hurting the former and becoming the latter.

Throughout this book, that point is the most important message—not so much a set of convenient and inflexible rules as an invitation to think about our actions and try to be a little less of the problem and more of the solution.

10

Low-Impact Camping: Swinging in the Woods

That fellow's got to swing.

OSCAR WILDE

EVERYONE KNOWS THAT summer camps of inexperienced youths are the most destructive of campers, hacking up the woods, peeling birchbark, littering, destroying others' solitude by their presence—right?

In one case at least—wrong! During the very height of the backpacking boom, an outfit called Killington Adventure in Vermont set out a program of low-impact camping that had far-reaching implications for today's overcrowded backwoods.

Killington's camp director, David Langlois, was an innovator who threw away the heavy groundcloth, tent, foam pad, and air mattress. He raised camping off the ground, where most of the impact occurs, and into the air. His campers, a couple of hundred scattered in two- or three-week sessions throughout the summer, swung from hammocks to get a good night's sleep. Furthermore,

129

they got off-trail and away from shelters and streams to set up
camp, so their presence didn't bother others. Because of their
airborne tactics, they could go into the most fragile fern bed or the
most rock-strewn sloping mountainside and set up camp quite
comfortably—and with minimum impact. Langlois claimed that
with his method he could camp a large group for several days in
one spot and the next party wouldn't know that anyone had been
there since the Indians left.

The implications for the problems of the crowded backwoods
are tremendous. The effect of campers repeatedly tenting on the
same sites is devastating: Soil compacts, ground cover dies, trees
get hacked and peeled in the voracious search for firewood. Then
come official restrictions on camping, caretakers telling you what
you can't do, and the dead hand of "permits"—all taking away
what was once the freedom of the hills.

Langlois seems to have charted the most pleasant way out of
this vicious cycle that we have seen yet. His "clean camping"
methods go far toward reducing the impact of even a large group's
passing, as well as removing the justification for stifling restrictions.

Hammocks

A symbol of the new trend in low-impact camping is the lowly
hammock.

Centuries ago, Duke Alexander J. Hammock grew tired of
sharing the four-poster with Lady Hammock, who snored violently.
The duke came up with a marvelous invention. For years the hammock has been perceived as a place for a backyard siesta for the tired
housewife or husband who just finished cutting the lawn. Now imaginative backwoodspeople are realizing that Duke Hammock's invention
is a great way to spend the night in the woods. It sure beats air mattresses, foam pads, heavy "lightweight" tents, roots or stones sticking
into your back, rainwater running under the floor, condensation on
the ceiling, and all the other disadvantages of being grounded. Go
airborne and you enter a whole new world.

One thing that may have attracted the attention of backpackers was the hammock's utility in big-wall rock climbing. Out in Yosemite, where climbers may take several days to work their way up the sheer 3,000-foot walls of El Capitan or Half Dome, the best and sometimes the only way to bivouac is to string a hammock between two pitons. Many hikers gaped in awe at heart-stopping photos of climbers snoozing contentedly with 2,000 feet of empty air between them and the rock talus below. But eventually the image of these admired hard men using hammocks began to sink in.

The move to the hammock was not confined to Killington and the East. In fact, western outdoors writer Russ Mohney soon reported that "the light-weight nylon hammock caught on strongly with western backpackers last season." Out in the Cascades, apparently, people used them not only for spending the night but also for an occasional trailside siesta in midafternoon.

Some campers have used hammocks for years, even in such noninnovative establishments as the army. Sailors used them to offset the roll and pitch of the sea. But their widespread adoption among backpackers is relatively new.

There are risks, to be sure. Langlois reports that one night he strung his hammock with 16 inches of clearance off the ground, only to be awakened when a 17-inch-high porcupine chose to pass under the bridge. In cold weather or winter conditions, hammocks may not be practical, and on a night when the bugs are out in full strength, you're in for trouble. Nevertheless, from our experience in making the switch from tent to hammock for summer backpacking, we pronounce it well worth the risks.

Duke Hammock's original model was built of hemp and flax, with brass fixtures, and most backyard hammocks for years were luxurious cloth and rope jobs, far too heavy and bulky to carry any distance. For modern backpacking, however, the hammock has made great strides. During the 1970s, when we first became interested, there was beginning to appear a new version, made of lightweight nylon mesh, incredibly light and so small you could stuff it into your pocket.

If you wanted to go with those early backpacking hammocks, you put together a jerry-built system that included:

Hammock. A few equipment stores and mail order catalogs offered hammocks at prices ranging from $3.50 to a little over $10—a minor investment when you compared it with purchasing a tent!

Tarp. 8 by 10 feet, either coated nylon (expensive) or 6 mil poly (cheap).

Nylon cord. About 20 feet.

Tent stakes. Four.

Armed with this equipment, you then followed a quaint set of procedures, roughly as follows:

To set up your hammock, choose two trees about 12 feet apart. Suspend your hammock 3 feet off the ground. Make sure it is tight as a bowstring—otherwise excessive sag will place you in a "jackknife" position.

Next, tie your nylon cord about 2 feet, or at nose level, over the hammock. Now you have two parallel lines, the hammock below, the cord above.

Then throw your tarp over the cord and stake it out at the four corners. The tarp should be well away from the sides of the sleeping bag and, if properly staked, will act as an effective waterproof cover in case you're cooking dinner in the rain.

Getting into the old hammock could be a little tricky at first. If you weren't careful, you could get dumped faster than a Presidential candidate coming in last in New Hampshire. Once mastered, though, the technique became routine. Here was the Rube Goldberg–approved version, which we followed:

1. Unstuff sleeping bag.
2. Stand beside the hammock near the middle.
3. Place stuff sack on the ground and stand on it (with boots off!).
4. Step into sleeping bag and pull it up around you. Zip it about two-thirds shut. Pull top well around your shoulders and hold in place with chin or teeth.
5. Find one edge of the hammock and pull it down past your thighs to just above the back of your knees. Sit down,

being careful to position yourself in the center of the hammock. Keep the sleeping bag around your shoulders.

6. Swing legs (and foot of sleeping bag, of course) into hammock.
7. Adjust sleeping bag around back and head.
8. Lie back and sleep!

If that sounds too intricate, here's a method that required fewer acrobatics:

1. Unstuff sleeping bag and spread it out in the hammock. That sounds easier than it is, but with patience and about five arms, you can eventually get it centered.
2. Partially unzip bag.
3. Sit down carefully and precisely in the middle of the sleeping bag, legs dangling over the side. The consequences of not being precisely centered are probably too obvious to require mention. If you weren't right in the middle, pick yourself up, shake out the sleeping bag, and repeat step 1. Then try again.
4. Raising one leg at a time, maneuver yourself into the bag. Again—carefully.

No, really, with practice it wasn't all that difficult. The resulting sleep was beautiful. And there was never a root in the small of your back.

Some of the gymnastic pyrotechnics of those early hammock arrangements have been overcome by modern camping-hammock designs. Now you can buy fancy models (unfortunately with fancy prices) that deploy mosquito netting and an easy-on-easy-off rain fly, together with lightweight "spreader bars" for greater stability and to elevate the netting and fly. People who have tried them tell us that new hammocks make it easy and more comfortable to be swinging off the ground.

Dispersed Camping

Switching from tent to hammock is one giant step toward leave-no-trace camping. An equally important step is to make a clean

break from the old habit of heading for a shelter or known campsite. This is a good idea whether you're in hammock or tent.

Be sure to find out what the regulations are in your area. In
our New England, customs and requirements vary. Along the
northern end of Vermont's Long Trail, for example, hikers are
asked to stay only at the closed cabins ("camps" or "lodges" in local
parlance) specifically provided for overnight camping; this was
historically private land, and the landowners were friendly to
hikers largely on the assurance that indiscriminate camping along
their land would not take place. In Maine's Baxter State Park as
well, camping is limited to designated sites, on reservation. However, elsewhere in New England, for the most part, camping spots
are virtually unlimited and perfectly "legal" as long as you stay 200
feet away from trail or stream. Pick a spot where water is not too far
away, naturally, and do *not* camp on the stream bank, the way
everyone used to, causing so much blighted "bootleg" sites.

Under a truly dispersed camping approach, no one will ever
wind up in the same spot twice, and that's what will save the land
from degradation. Part of your strategy should be to go back and
forth to the trail by a different route each time you make the trip.
Similarly, pick different paths to the water. That way you won't
start a recognizable trail, one that might attract others to your site.
(This precaution will have the added advantage of protecting you
from theft if you leave your gear set up during the day when you are
off hiking.)

Take your bearings carefully when you leave the trail, with a
compass if necessary. If you don't find your way back to your gear,
it could be a long cold night.

The advent of lightweight backpacking stoves also helps
protect the environment. The age of indiscriminate campfires all
over the woods is past.

When you break camp, make sure every scrap of litter is
picked up. Brush in areas that look heavily trodden; this will help
them to regenerate, as well as conceal your passing. If you do set up
a tent, drag some dead branches over the ground you flattened.

Camp in your chosen spot only once. Repeated use will turn

it into a "bootleg" campsite that will quickly be discovered by other backpackers, and progressive degeneration will set in.

If you're interested in an excellent summary of the clean-camping ethic, look up the profile of National Outdoor Leadership School instructor Del Smith in the April 1992 *Outside* magazine. It's both interesting and instructive. Kudos to *Outside*, to NOLS, and to Del Smith for a superb presentation of the full array of low-impact camping techniques in a vividly readable style.

Advantages of Low-Impact Camping

The advantages of the combined innovations of hammock plus dispersing into the woods are legion:

1. Loads are lighter to carry, by several pounds.
2. Camp is easier and quicker to set up.
3. Camp can be set up anywhere (except above treeline, of course)—the weary search for level, smooth tent sites is over.
4. No roots will stick into your back all night.
5. No other people will be around (ah, solitude!), since it's so easy to set up off-trail, out of sight.
6. There is no risk of theft when you're gone, since only you know where your "camp" is.
7. No well-trained "wild" animals will be waiting to raid your pack at night, like those that inevitably take up residence at shelters (though you still have to guard food against chance passerby squirrels and other potential marauders).
8. You won't have to deal with caretakers, restrictions, fees, crowds, and other hassles.
9. You will help reduce the pressure for more regulations, sure to come about if we all continue to squeeze into already overcrowded campsites.
10. You will be part of the solution, not the problem.

Perhaps the most satisfying thing about practicing low-impact camping is the experience of opening your mind to trying a new approach. Once again, a major theme of this book is to open our minds, to take a fresh look at problems and solutions, to *think*.

It's easy to fall into a rut of maintaining the same camping patterns—head for the same good old shelters, build that heart-warming campfire. But once these routines are thoroughly mastered, they can become dull, and you can become set in your ways. "Powerful indeed is the empire of habit," wrote the Roman Publilius Syrus. Trying new camping habits can be a satisfying and rewarding experience.

11

Low-Impact Cooking: The Fire Goes Out

A little fire is quickly trodden out;
Which, being suffered, rivers cannot quench.
WILLIAM SHAKESPEARE, *HENRY VI, PART 3*

HEAVY RAINS continued to pour from the wild mountain clouds on our forlorn little tent all day. A little past noon we began to reach that elevated state of boredom known only by those who have been cooped up in a five-by-seven-foot space for 20 hours and have just about exhausted the eight basic ways of trying to sit or lie comfortably for long hours in a sleeping bag.

So we were delighted when the monotonous sound of descending water on the tent fly was suddenly and most unexpectedly supplemented by a barely discernible human voice crying to us from somewhere out there.

Now, many backpackers love to hike in the rain. In New England's summers, you *have* to love hiking in the rain, because the good Lord of our hills sees to it that you get plenty of opportunity all summer long. The theory that the Almighty is practicing up for a new 40-day flood has its strongest empirical support in New England's weather trends. We hear it can be wet in the Cascades too, and on the coastlines of Alaska and Washington State.

However, this was not summer. This was mid-March: temperatures in the mid-30s, six hours' slog from the nearest road, every possibility that the chilling winter rain could be followed by temperatures plunging to 0°F or below—a situation, in short, where survival depends on keeping dry. Mad dogs and Englishmen may go out in India's noonday sun, but they have sense enough to stay inside for New England's winter rain, an invitation to hypothermia. We were holing up in our tent, prepared to sit it out and be alive to enjoy some more climbing when good weather returned.

But what was that voice out there?

Two bedraggled backpackers stumbled up to our tent, obvious candidates for an emergency. Blue jeans and summer boots, all soaking wet, betrayed their inexperience at winter camping. When they discovered that the shelter that they had hoped to find had been torn down two years earlier, they managed to string up a sagging tent and crawl inside.

The last communication we had with them before settling down for a long wet night was when one of them asked us how we were cooking. It developed that they had counted on starting a fire—a patently impossible achievement in their situation—and that all they had for dinner was two enormous steaks, destined to remain as raw as the day the poor cow died.

Here is the point of our story: those two hikers, who so badly needed nourishment, went hungry (except for what we cooked them on our portable gas stove) because they had not brought food suitable for a backpacking trip under adverse conditions.

The predicament of those two was extreme, but it illustrates the modern backpacker's paramount need for simple meals, lightweight and compact equipment, and complete self-sufficiency.

Fire Building: Pro and Con

First off, reliance on fire building in the backwoods has become a highly questionable policy in light of the new environmental concerns. If we could be sure that everyone going into the backcountry would disperse to a different spot every night, knew how to construct a small fire and then leave no trace when they were through, maybe fires would be OK. But the deadwood supply has long been used up at the most commonly visited campsites, and the devastation wrought by irresponsible hatchet wielders is an ugly sore.

As long ago as 1893 the Appalachian Mountain Club was urging a halt to the cutting of firewood in the fragile area of the Presidential Range. Asking club members not to cut the scrub growth around newly constructed Madison Spring Hut, AMC's Councillor of Improvements warned that "the growth is disappearing too rapidly." If it looked bad in 1893, that worthy councillor should see some popular campsites today!

More than any other piece of the clean-camping mosaic, the discouragement of fires encounters a hard core of deep-felt resistance. The good old campfire dies hard; its emotional embers won't go out. It has a deep meaning to many woodspeople, evoking time-hallowed (almost primeval) associations of warmth, light, security, and good fellowship. Ernest Thompson Seton, one of the patron saints of woodcraft, argued: "What is a camp without the evening campfire? It's nothing but a place in the woods where some people have some things."

It must be conceded that a good woodsman knows how to have his fire and leave the site without a trace. But when hundreds of novices get out their hatchets, the result is scenes like that of so many backwoods shelters during the backpacking boom: miles from the road, yet surrounded by a wasteland of hacked stumps. Even 20 years ago, when you camped at Chimney Pond in Maine's Baxter Park, you had to walk about a half a mile to find any deadwood on the forest floor. Deadwood performs important ecological functions as it decays back into the soil, and when armies of campers burn it all as it falls, the forest is deprived. Also, many inexperienced fire builders don't appreciate the risks of underground fires that smolder for days under the duff and may spring to conflagration long after the fire builder has left, thinking he has put out all his embers.

Harry Roberts, editor of *Wilderness Camping*, labeled camp-fires as "ethically indefensible in heavily used areas." In high dudgeon, Roberts cried in his excellent treatise, *Movin' Out*:

> Look at the trees! They're scalped up to eight feet off the ground. And those saplings. My God, they're chewed off a foot above ground! The poor, spindly stumps catch your boots and send you sprawling. Every twenty feet there's the curdled, half-charred remnant of somebody's cooking fire, adorned with unburnt poly bags and unburnable aluminum foil. The place looks like the morning after Shiloh; all because a large number of jackasses didn't give a damn about the environ-ment or what the next guy would find.

A subtle and sensitive argument against fires concerns their effect on the relationship between the camper and the night. Fires have a hypnotic effect—that's part of their attraction. They draw your eyes inward and you sit gazing into the flickering flame and glowing embers. Meanwhile, you lost contact with the woods around you, the stars above you, the wildlife (which gives your fire a wide berth), and the silence and sounds of nocturnal nature. The campfire is its own uniquely satisfying world—but it tends to isolate you from the larger natural world around you.

We'd like to see this antifire ethic spread more generally. For example, many public campgrounds are doing the cause no good by making firewood available to the public. People should be encour-aged to make the transition to gas cookstoves, not indulged in the phony fantasy of building obsolete fires from trucked-in wood, sometimes procured from local lumberyards.

Some groups that bill themselves as educational still use a completely unacceptable volume of fire in the backcountry. We hear of schools that send out gangs of high-school-age kids to "experience" the backwoods life, complete with wood fires night

after night, year after year, usually in the same backwoods locations. The impact on the backcountry must be tragic. But worse
than that is the "educational" effect, the message sent to all those
kids that it's OK to burn every scrap of deadwood in the area, that
the modern way to camp necessarily means fires. What an inexcusable lesson to give the rising generation, a generation that should
be developing a careful sense of stewardship and personal responsibility for reducing our impact on the overcrowded and overused
backcountry.

The Green Mountain Club of Vermont has largely taken the
wood stoves out of its shelters on the Long Trail, after a bitter
history of fires burning down some of the fine old shelters, and after
observing the widening circle of destruction to the surrounding
trees. It is interesting to note that the club encountered almost no
resistance to or resentment of this policy. Most of today's backpackers understand.

A sophisticated argument against stoves and for fires is that
stoves are not environmental saints either: they run on various
derivatives of petroleum, which must be painfully plundered from
the earth's dwindling resources to the accompaniment of pipelines
bisecting caribou migration routes, oil spills on coastal marine life,
and Gulf Wars.

This is a legitimate argument, worth heeding. Wood is a
renewable resource. At our home, on a 27-acre woodlot, we cook
and heat and sugar entirely on our own wood, and 27 acres proves
sufficient to support such activity indefinitely on a self-sustaining
basis. That is, the forest produces deadwood, through normal
turnover, at almost precisely the rate at which we burn it to
support our low-consumption life-style. This marvelous balance,
however, is never going to be achieved at popular camping areas in
the backcountry, not in the post–backpacking boom era. But it is
also true, and disturbing, that almost all portable stoves add to the
demand for fossil fuels, which we are all collectively using up at an
unacceptable rate.

What it comes down to is a choice between making a minor
contribution to the support of faraway oil markets versus a major,

immediate, and disastrous impact on the backcountry in a place that is here and now, the essential backdrop to our wilderness experience. So we vote for the portable stove. Let's cure a problem that the backpacking community can single-handedly solve. Then, as voters and citizens, perhaps we can support those who are seeking a rational public policy on the much larger question of depletion of limited resources on this beleaguered planet.

Emergency Fires

Among those who concede the undesirability of backwoods-campfires as a regular way of life, there are still those who believe that everyone should practice how to build a campfire in case of emergency. We demur even here. The emergency use of fire is highly questionable for a variety of reasons.

There are rare circumstances in which an emergency fire could save a life, no question about that. So it's probably desirable for backpackers to know how to build one. But practice isn't necessary. Building an emergency fire falls roughly into the same category as treating a snakebite or performing an emergency tracheotomy on the trail. Furthermore, like performing a tracheotomy with a penknife, it has been done but should be undertaken only as a last resort.

Why is fire building of so little use in emergencies?

1. If getting warm is essential, starting a fire will be little help. An outdoor fire is an extremely inefficient heat source, even for the one side of you that gets any warmth. Great quantities of fuel are required to produce a negligible amount of useful BTUs.
2. The modern backpacker usually carries a good sleeping bag, and he's much better off inside that bag than out. Inside, the considerable heat his own body generates is retained.
3. If the backpacker gets a fire going, he should then get into his bag anyway. Once inside, how can he tend a fire effectively?

4. If hot food or drink is his greatest need, it is much more efficient to use his cookstove.
5. If he is above treeline, fire building is a useless art because there will be insufficient burnable material at hand.
6. Most emergencies in which a fire is alleged to be needed occur in winter. If the novice starts a fire on a six-foot snow cover, he'll soon have a pit several feet deep with the fire at the bottom, where it will furnish no heat but plenty of smoke. It's not easy to cook anything way down there either.
7. If a backpacker has the energy, tools, and daylight to amass many large logs to construct a fire platform on the snow, he should probably use his time and energy instead to do something of more lasting benefit—like walking out.

If you should be caught in a wintertime emergency without tent, sleeping bag, or stove, you *might* want to get a fire going. But you would probably be better off using the natural protection of deep snow by digging a snow cave or trench, if conditions permit, or burrowing under a blowdown, where natural caves can occur.

Often you hear people cite Jack London's marvelous short story "To Build a Fire," recalling how a backwoodsman died because he couldn't keep a fire going, despite great effort. We like to point out that while the man wasted his time on futile fire-building efforts, the dog in the story very sensibly devoted his energies to walking out. The man died; the dog lived. Where's the moral there?

One of the authors was once caught in a somewhat desperate situation at −35°F with winds strong enough to knock him over. When camp was finally established, there was a difficult struggle to keep a Svea stove going long enough to melt snow to supply badly needed hot liquids. The idea of getting out of his down bag long enough to start a fire would have been patently absurd.

So why burn down the woods practicing fires that aren't really needed, won't keep you warm, and are out of step with today's environmental concerns? Read up on how to build an emergency fire, because you just might need to, just as you might

need to perform an emergency tracheotomy. But as for practicing—
keep the penknife away from our throats, and leave the trees alone
too.

In making the transition to the compact, portable gas stove,
we've found we don't really miss that old campfire—in fact, we
wouldn't want one now. We prefer to get along with no smoke in
our eyes, no soot on our pots, no scouring the forest for deadwood,
no setup and breakdown time, no nighttime beacon of blazing light
that makes the stars hard to see and scares off animal life. It's a
matter of what you grow accustomed to.

12

The Forty-Sixers

*Virtue, by the bare statement of its actions, can affect
men's minds so as to create at once both admiration of
the things done and desire to imitate the doers of them.*

PLUTARCH

ONE OF THE northeastern peakbagging clubs, the Adirondack
Forty-Sixers, has taken a long hard look at its own role in the
mountains, sensitive to the critics described back in chapter 3.
What they have done is an uplifting sample of how the new ethic
can shape our actions.

About twenty years ago the Forty-Sixers held a meeting at which
they seriously considered disbanding. Just to hold such a meeting in
itself was a serious violation of Parkinson's Law and sound bureaucratic
tradition. However, the group decided instead to reorient the focus
toward one of responsible action to help preserve the environment of
the Adirondacks' High Peaks. In the years since the meeting, they
have moved forward on at least six major programs that deserve
attention and commendation. Critics of peakbagging should consider
whether any other group can show such a record of responsible
stewardship, as demonstrated in these six programs.

Antilitter Campaign

The original Forty-Sixer litter bag program was the brainchild and personal cause célèbre of Glenn Fish, a large authority figure of a man who served a term as president of the Forty-Sixers. The objective of the program is to get hikers to carry out all of their own trash, along with any other they may find in the Adirondacks.

After meditating long on the litter problem, Mr. Fish reasoned: "I have a deep conviction that many hikers are induced to 'litter' simply because they are unsophisticated enough to leave home without making any provision for carrying out their litter generated while they are in the woods." Hence, the solution: Give them each a bag and they'll lug it out.

The original Glenn Fish system was based on a two-bag principle: the outer bag (to be reused) was made of plastic and displayed the Forty-Sixers' emblem; the inner bag was biodegradable paper to be thrown away, with the accumulated litter, at home or in trash baskets at trailheads.

The energetic and exuberant Mr. Fish, who sometimes lurked at trailheads to see how his program was working, reported with pride that "I have witnessed hikers emptying litter from a Forty-Sixer bag into a trash can, and then carefully folding the outer bag and stuffing it in a pack for reuse." He then would surface and approach these surprised hikers to thank them "for joining with the Forty-Sixers in cleaning up our recreational areas."

Since this program started there have been a couple of interesting changes. The first outer bags carried a picture of a pot of dinner cooking over a fire of fresh-cut branches. That was a surefire (sorry!) way to endorse wood fires in an age when many outdoors people were trying to discourage fires in favor of portable cookstoves. So in 1979 the club issued new outer bags, depicting an innocent scene of mountains and lakes, with the message, "If you pack it in, pack it out!" Eventually it was found that the inner bag was unnecessary and was therefore discontinued.

In 20 years the Forty-Sixers have distributed more than 60,000 litter bags at key points around the Adirondacks. And the club can proudly say that "not one single report was received relative to misuse of the plastic bags. They were not scattered in the woods, stuffed down privies, tucked in corners of lean-tos."

Because of programs like that the woods are getting cleaned up and staying cleaned up.

In New Hampshire the White Mountain National Forest and the Appalachian Mountain Club have their own "Carry In–Carry Out" programs. They have been going on for many years now, and White Mountain hikers are (we hope) all familiar with the Carry In–Carry Out poster tacked inside shelters, at trailheads, or displayed at the AMC huts. It must be working, for one doesn't see half as many freeze-dried food packets at campsites, or gum wrappers on the trail, as before.

A wonderful hiker we knew from Connecticut, Ned Greist, used to speak of a rampant disease that he called "hiker's pocket." Those afflicted with the disease suffered from an incurable urge to pick up every piece of litter left by others in the woods and jam such litter into one pocket. The afflicted litter picker can bend and scoop up the offending object without even breaking stride. At the end of the hike, the stuffed pocket can then be emptied into trash cans. In this day and age, we realize the problem doesn't end there: those trash cans have to go somewhere. But at least the litter is out of the woods and perhaps on its way to the best ultimate disposal site.

Virtue has its own reward. You'd be surprised at what valuable things you find when your subconscious is continually trained on noticing and seizing shiny objects. We've come across two handsome woodsman's knives, and even, over the years, a handful of nickels and dimes (once a quarter!) that wink beguilingly at you just like aluminum foil. Sometimes you find bottles or cans for which a reward is offered at local markets. Reimbursement in the pursuit of a just cause?

We hope the Forty-Sixers and others will keep on the pressure. Newcomers are taking to the woods daily, and they need to become initiated litter pickers too. It's a fine madness that can't have too many converts. To join the Litter Pickers Society, all a hiker need do is bend down at least once on a woods walk to pick

up a candy wrapper, a cigarette, a piece of tinfoil, perchance a
dime...

That Trowel Project

A slightly less happy project of the Forty-Sixers consisted of a
1984 campaign to cope with the problem of increasing human
wastes in the backcountry. This program attracted support on the
crest of a wave of giardiasis, an intestinal disorder created by bad
drinking water, some of it infected by improper disposal of human
wastes. (Animal wastes could infect water supplies too, notably
those of beavers—hence the popular name for giardiasis: beaver
fever.)

At the suggestion of a New York State ranger, and after
polling the membership, the Forty-Sixers launched a campaign to
give every hiker a small, sturdy plastic trowel, with a message about
digging a small pit for your human wastes when you had to go in
the woods. In the first year the enthusiastic members passed out
5,000 trowels. That's a lot of digging power.

Unfortunately, this project was considerably less than an
unqualified success. In the first place, many of the trowels managed
to get into circulation without the message, so there was some
confusion about just what their purpose was. Then a large number
of trowels began to show up behind lean-tos in popular camping
areas—obviously becoming a not-inconsiderable litter problem.

Furthermore, ideas began to change about what constituted
the best way to dispose of human wastes. Perhaps too deep a hole
(easy to dig with a handy trowel) would inhibit decomposition and
actually aggravate the problem. The revised theory is to scrape a
very shallow hole with the heel of your boot and cover it with the
lightest of forest duff (twigs, bark, moss, light soil). That way the
wastes will compost more rapidly and soon be harmlessly absorbed
into the forest ecosystem—as long as they're kept away from water
supplies during the decomposition process.

So the trowel project died an early and merciful death,
unlamented.

But all was not loss. The trowel project heightened public

awareness of the importance of backcountry sanitation; it helped people see not merely that giardiasis was a problem but also that their own careless actions were part of the cause; and it encouraged people to think about how to change their actions so as to become part of the solution to the problem. Even if the Forty-Sixers had to throw in the trowel on their project, they still helped to stir public thinking on a vital issue.

Trail Maintenance

The Forty-Sixers, being peakbaggers from way back, do a lot of walking on mountain trails that can't stand heavy foot traffic without showing wear and tear. This means erosion that turns trails into deep gullies, or pitiful widening around wet places that obliterates trailside vegetation.

A very significant program launched by the reformed peakbaggers was one of volunteer trail maintenance. Hordes of Forty-Sixer volunteers, having enjoyed the trails so extensively, agreed to "pay back" time spent hiking with time spent fixing up the trails for the next generation of hikers. The state rangers designated trails needing work, and gangs of Forty-Sixers began going to work on those trails.

This project was doubly blessed with leadership. The dean of Adirondack hikers and trailcutters, James A. Goodwin (Forty-Sixer number 24 on a list of over 3,000), who had hiked and worked on trails for almost 60 years, agreed to be the Forty-Sixers' first "trailmaster." With his enormous prestige and profound knowledge of trail making, Jim Goodwin got the program off to a flying start during the late 1970s. The second blessing arrived in 1982 when the Behr family took over the leadership from the retiring Goodwin. Chris G. Behr became trailmaster, ably supported by his wife, June T. Behr, and presently to be joined by his son, Chris M. Behr, as cochairman in 1986. The Behrs provided dynamic leadership to carry on the Goodwin tradition.

But leadership is just the tip of the iceberg. Scores of eager, energetic, physically indefatigable Forty-Sixers have contributed volunteer time to trail work. The club awarded honors to those who contributed 46 hours of hard labor. But in less than 10 years so many members had contributed far more than 46 hours that the club set up two further levels of awards: for 146 hours and for 346 hours (*sic*) of trail work. The last time we looked (1991), more than 100 hardworking trail maintainers had won these awards, and 11 of these had won the top award for 346 hours, which is the equivalent of just about a whole summer of full-time eight-hour days, five days a week.

That is putting your muscles where your heart is.

Alpine Areas Restoration

One special facet of trail work emerges where trails rise above treeline into that special world of alpine tundra, so beautiful, so fragile, so precious to the mountain experience.

The impact of hiker traffic is nowhere so damaging as it is on those few summits of the Northeast that are above the treeline. The alpine, tundralike ground cover on these peaks is astonishingly well equipped by nature to withstand the ferocity of arctic cold and hurricane winds. But when a large volume of hikers tramps over, it's in deep trouble. A quarter century ago, under the direction of scientist and peakbagger Ed Ketchledge from Syracuse University, an experiment began to see if humans could reintroduce vegetation in areas where boot traffic had seriously damaged both plant life and soils on above-treeline summits.

The full story of this interesting project and the interesting man who launched it belongs to a later chapter (16). Suffice it to mention here that, as alpine restoration began to be taken seriously, the bulk of the human labor to make it work was provided by the Forty-Sixers. This has meant not only packing up hundreds of pounds of seed, fertilizer, and lime, but also considerable work in defining a stabilized trail through the tundra, so that human visitors can use a single track to the summits, leaving the rest of the alpine area for the native vegetation to enjoy.

Wilderness Leadership Workshop

Recognizing that their own good deeds alone would never save the mountains in this era of the outdoor recreation boom, the

Forty-Sixers have attempted to spread the message to other major groups of recreationists.

The club decided to aim at children's camps, Scout troops, YMCAs, college outing clubs, and any other sources of large groups coming to the Adirondacks. Reach these people, they reasoned, and you get the message to perhaps the principal causes of impact on the mountain environment.

Since 1972 the Forty-Sixers have staged an annual Wilderness Leadership Workshop—an intensive 2½-day course covering all aspects of taking groups through the mountains. The workshops are well and attentively attended. In fact, the leaders turn away half again as many applicants as they can accept, to keep the seminars small enough to allow for full participation by everyone.

Much of the advice deals with just plain practical problems of how you steer a bunch of energetic and hungry kids through the backcountry without losing any. But in between the nuts and bolts, the Forty-Sixers weave the message of the new environmental ethic: walk softly, don't cut bough beds, think about using campstoves instead of burning up every stick of firewood, carry out your litter, don't let the kids discard shredded plastic.

The entire "faculty" at these workshops is composed of peakbagging Forty-Sixers—people who have long worked with summer camps or school groups. They are brimming with practical tips on how to run a successful trip, and they are also sensitive to the need to soften the impact of recreation in the mountains.

The state Department of Environmental Conservation cooperates with the club; in fact, the opening session has often been conducted by Interior Ranger Pete Fish, whose presentation is a cornucopia of sensible and useful advice on all aspects of leading groups in the northeastern mountains, laced with an underlying message: "The responsibility for environmental quality rests with every single person every moment of his life."

We wish the critics of peakbaggers could attend one of those workshops and see the personal dedication of these people to making life better for the mountains they climb.

...And Still Counting

Not that the Forty-Sixers have lost their original love of climbing mountains. Far from it! They still bag peaks with the best of them, and aren't a bit ashamed of it. More than 3,000 individuals have now climbed them all. About 100 have done them all in winter. Several have climbed them all a dozen or more times. One hardy soul has done them all via bushwhack routes. Another has done them all by moonlight. Some self-righteous souls swear at this sort of thing as insufficiently sensitive to the mountain environment. We say, let each enjoy the mountains in his or her own way, so long as they are damaging neither the mountains nor the experience of others. As for the Forty-Sixers, are any of their critics doing as much for the benefit of the mountains? We love 'em all.

We especially love the two old-timers who, as of when this book went to press, do so much to keep this organization rolling. Grace Hudowalski, first Forty-Sixer president in 1948, is now well over 80, but she still answers all the mail, more than 1,000 letters per year, and sends out the patches, with encouraging notes and responses to a variety of questions. A. G. Dittmar, another octogenarian, still serves as executive secretary/treasurer of the group, keeping tabs on the finances. Ditt's annual dues reminder always takes the form of some outrageously funny piece that he's composed or unearthed somewhere during the past year—followed by his hitting us up for this year's dues.

And do you know what the dues are? Here is a group that does effective trail work, works on summit restoration, holds workshops and other activities to educate others, and puts out a truly outstanding quarterly publication—and do you want to guess what the dues are? Bear in mind that other northeastern hiking clubs are charging $20 or $30 per year, and one gilt-edged group holds up its membership for something like $50. Do you know what the Forty-Sixers dues are (as of 1992)? Two dollars. Well, they ask everyone for another buck to cover mailing costs, so it's really three dollars. *Three dollars!* Here is a group with no hidden agenda, no bureaucracy, no padded costs—just dedication to their beloved mountains and the experience of being among them.

Dr. Ketchledge speaks for many of the Forty-Sixers when he expresses his own deep-felt sense of stewardship for the High Peak region that has given him and others so much enjoyment: "For 29 years I've climbed in this country," he told one workshop, in a talk delivered while standing on the very summit of Mount Jo, the panorama of the High Peaks circling around him and his listeners. "In a pantheistic sense, all of this," he said, sweeping his arm over the breathtaking landscape, "is part of me." It's that kind of sense of personal involvement and obligation that has sparked so much good work to help preserve the mountain environment.

Next time you hear someone criticize a peakbagger, think about these men and women in the Adirondacks, tirelessly passing out litter bags, tugging branches around to brush in an eroding trail, toting grass seed and fertilizer up a mountain, or giving up a splendid May weekend to help spread the message of stewardship to others.

These are the peakbaggers.

III

TOWARD A SENSE OF STEWARDSHIP

One generation passeth away,
and another generation cometh:
but the earth abideth forever.
ECCLESIASTES 1:4

"TO EVERY THING there is a season, and a time to every purpose under the heaven." In the narrow, limitless world of the hiker, we pass through stages. Have we not all known the mountains as different places at one time or another? Are we going to the same hills now that we saw when we made our first climb? Do we not perceive a different backcountry at age 40 from that we saw at age 20 and that we will see at age 60? Do we climb this weekend for the same reasons we climbed last weekend?

Sometimes we wish we could reclaim and hold forever that bloom of excitement when we saw Tuckerman Ravine for the first time; the first time we tied on to a rope and followed up a cliff; the mix of fear and joy when first we stood on a steep snow slope and watched the kicked-off clumps cascade endlessly down into the void beneath our feet. Remember the strange new exhilaration as darkness fell on those first nights camped out? The first loon heard? The first experience of a wind-wracked whiteout above treeline? That first long bushwhack, separated from trail and any other link to humanity's tools of security, committed to the compass and the map and the patience to keep moving through those dense thickets?

156

Yes, there was an edge to those initial exposures that we can never recapture for ourselves, though we can recognize that blend of ecstasy and apprehension in others when we're with them on their maiden flights into the mountain world.

Does this mean it's all metaphorically downhill after the first ascent? Not at all. By no means! Those to whom the mountains hold most meaning keep coming back to find satisfactions of a different order. When we're lucky, those satisfactions grow rather than diminish. That's why we return to the mountains, why we come back forever, why we lift up our eyes unto the hills, from whence cometh our help.

Excitement and wonder remain. But to these surface delights are added many other satisfactions. Perhaps they may differ from one person to another, or from one trip to another for the same person.

Consider the variety of compelling attractions that draw people to the backcountry. Some grow fascinated with detailed knowledge of the flora and fauna; others wax zealous in pursuit of as many different summits as they can climb; others like to return over and over to the same familiar crags or glens; still others gain great joy from increasing speed afoot on mountain trails, or increasing difficulty on rock or ice faces. For some, those rare days of dazzling sun and clear, windless, deep-blue sky are priceless times to be high; others emphatically prefer to be blown about in a sightless whirlwind of winter storm, tested to the limit.

How many people pass from the stage of first seeing the big-name peaks of their region, to a second stage of pursuing the list of local 4,000-footers or 14,000-footers or whatever, to a third stage of returning over and over to some special favorite peak or camping spot? Or maybe to a stage of introducing others to the world we've come to love, or leading beginners and teaching the arts of the backcountry?

As with each of us in our personal hiking or climbing lives, so with the hiking community as a whole: in every region we can trace historical phases in the hiking life of the region. In our New England, we can look back through history at the excitement of

the first people to explore the mountain heights—or, more accu-
rately, the first whose ascents were recorded:

- The illiterate pair who walked together to the top of the
  region's highest peak, Mount Washington, in 1642, one of
  them a Native American whose name is lost to history, the
  other a wide-eyed colonist named Darby Field, from one of
  those earliest coastal settlements in the region of what is
  now Portsmouth, New Hampshire.
- A much later generation of curious botanists, in the early
  years of the nineteenth century, learned gentlemen who
  clambered all over the more rugged and hitherto inacces-
  sible corners of Mount Washington and its neighboring
  peaks, primarily to discover and study and record the
  diversity of alpine vegetation in that strange new world of
  mountain tundra.
- Early land surveyors poking through the endless maze of
  rivers and forests until at length they emerged on the high
  open plateau of Katahdin and walked to its highest point,
  to gaze with sudden rapture down the eastern precipice to
  tiny Chimney Pond.
- George Witherle and his patient wife, who hired two woods
  guides (a father and son), and as a party of four tramped yet
  further north to explore and climb dozens of smaller mountains in the northernmost ranges of Maine.
- The Swiss scientist Arnold Guyot, who pushed to the tops
  of many peaks hitherto unknown to the early settlers who
  had seen them only from afar.

Following on the footsteps of the explorers came those who
sought to make the glories of the heights more accessible to others.
New England entered a period of trail building and even an abun-
dance of bridle paths and carriage roads up the gentler slopes.
Mountaintop buildings were erected with names like TipTop
House or Peak House or Summit House. At a slightly later stage
came a spectacular flurry of trail building to open up every mountain summit and, on the more famous peaks, every ridge and valley
approach.

Then there came a backlash of concern for preserving the mountain world from overexploitation. People realized we might destroy the wild quality that had attracted us to the hills in the first place. The first phase of this concern was directed against overconsumption of mountain resources, such as the timber of the surrounding forests. So national forests and state parks and private reserves were set up to control indiscriminate logging and other economic uses of the land. The second phase of this concern was to restrain our own friends from overdeveloping mountain recreation: so some ridges were left trailless, some trails allowed to revert to nature, and summit houses either torn down or burned, and not replaced.

A few years ago, on the heels of that unprecedented backpacking boom of the 1960s and 1970s, our New England entered still another phase of its centuries-old love affair with the mountain world. In this, our region was joining a new movement that spread nationwide. This was the age of awakening environmental concerns, of a new backwoods ethic.

These were the years when our generation began by picking up every scrap of litter in the backcountry, cleaning up the can pits and trash piles behind every backcountry shelter, keeping the soap and wastes out of water supplies. Then we moved on to combating trail erosion, building drainage ditches and water bars, placing heavy stepping-stones, erecting scree barriers to direct hiking traffic where it would do least harm to the fragile mountain environment. This was the age when most of us stopped building campfires and began carrying camping stoves. This is the age we described in the preceding part of this book.

All of which we review in order to ask the vital question: What's next? Where do we go from here? What new phase lies in store for backcountry recreationists?

Our crystal ball is no less cloudy than anyone else's, so we look for the answer in what we think we see beginning to happen already around us. What we see is clear and present, and very encouraging. It is a growing sense of stewardship, a spreading feeling of commitment to a role of stewards for the mountains.

Both among individuals we know and broadly throughout the hiking community of our region, we see people moving on from just hiking, or even just being responsible and careful environmentally clean hikers and climbers, to a new phase. That phase is one of personal involvement in protecting and enhancing the mountain environment. At the core of this new consciousness is a concern about what kind of backcountry we are leaving to the next generation. And what gives vitality to this new concern is that it is linked to a resolve for practical action.

This is the new sense of stewardship that we describe in the next few chapters.

It is our observation and prediction, and also our fervent hope, that this generation of backcountry recreationists is entering a new phase of protective caring for the land. Sure, there will always be people coming into the hills for the first time, and others taking on the heady pursuit of the 4,000-footers or 14,000-footers or other personal goals. We see nothing wrong with that. But more and more we see people turning with pleasure to that next phase— of giving something back to the hills, which give us so much.

Join us in these next few pages—and then join all of us out on the trails and up on the heights. We are delighted with the spirit we find abroad in the backcountry today, and with the people who are putting their backs where their hearts are (hmmm, that sounds awkward) to try to preserve and strengthen the mountain heritage that we have been blessed with and that we wish to pass along to the next generation. It's a brave new world that has such people in it. Come on along.

13

A Day in the Life of the NUTS

Whatsoever thy hands find to do, do it with all thy might.
ARRAM DAVIDSON, "THE MAN WHO SAW THE ELEPHANT"

LET'S LOOK AT an example of what we mean by stewardship, as revealed by a day in the life of some people we know.

Tempest on the Barbarossa Ridge

Wind-driven rain sweeps the ridge leading to Yellowbush Lodge all Friday afternoon as we hike up. If you have been on an exposed ridge in a driving rain, you know how thoroughly the wet penetrates, breaks through every defense, infiltrating to the very marrow, systematically soaking everything you have on. The only effective strategy is to keep enough clothes inside the pack thoroughly dry—triple-bagged in plastic, we say—and otherwise be prepared to get just plain wet.

Regardless, the nine members of the Northern Uphill Trail Society slog up the trail in groups of twos and threes, starting as work schedules and driving times permit, each succeeding party being wetter than the preceding one. When we all arrive and shed damp clothes for dry, we warm ourselves with hot cocoa, cook up our communal supper. The conversation runs to black humor as we exchange trail tales with each other and with the score or so of other wet guests at wet Yellowbush Lodge. Otherwise conflicting weather forecasts agree that the storm is to get worse for a few hours, then blow clear. What stage will it be in tomorrow morning?

The night is unbelievable, if you have not been in a small building perched atop an exposed knoll at treeline in the teeth of a full-scale storm. Apparently the mountain gods have lost their tempers. They are yelling and throwing things. The noise outside is a confused shout of primal elements, the building palpably shaken; rain slashes by the windows, penetrates the glazing; the floor runs water beneath each windward window. Having brought clothes and sleeping gear appropriate for June, not January, we have to commandeer everything we can lay our hands on to stay warm through the night, sleeping as much as one is inclined to sleep when accosted all night by mountain gods in high rage on the Barbarossa Ridge.

The Barbarossa Ridge is an impressive alpine upthrust of high peaks, beautiful in summer sunshine, wild and terrible in storm. As this weekend has begun as a violent storm, our group, the Northern Uphill Trail Society (NUTS), is more than happy to enjoy the primitive luxury of the American Mountaineering Club's hostel, Yellowbush Lodge, a simple four-room closed cabin right at treeline on the western flank of the Barbarossa Range.

The Northern Uphill Trail Society consists of nine volunteers (the NUTS) who have agreed to maintain the hiking trails on the Barbarossa Ridge and its satellites. We are mostly members of the American Mountaineering Club (AMC), but we work independently. Each of us maintains one trail on our own all year long, but twice in the spring and once in the fall we get together to work as a group, so we can blitz any outstanding problems with all nine of us in force.

It is the spring of the year, and time to clear all the winter blowdown and scrape clean all the drainage ditches. On this particular weekend the plan is to stay Friday night at the AMC hostel; to clear the trail over the north end of the Barbarossa Ridge and northeast along the connecting Arthur Ridge to Mount Arthur; then return to the hostel building for Saturday night.

The tradition in NUTS is that whoever's trail we happen to be working on at any particular time, that person is The Boss. The Arthur Ridge Trail is officially the responsibility of Tom and Betty Alkuk, so Tom and Betty were to be in charge of our work on Saturday.

The Alkuks are a couple of contrasts. Tom is big (6 feet 3 inches, 220 pounds), bearded, in his late 30s, his hair and beard prematurely silver, a very impressive figure on the trail, especially moving large rocks or blowdowns. Of Russian descent, his taciturn and almost dour exterior conceals a wry sense of humor never at rest. He is the sort who, if told that nuclear bombs had just destroyed Washington and New York, would respond with a slight widening of the eyes. At his office job, he's an innovative social engineer, making waves within his company and the industry. In his community he wins awards for organizing community volunteer effort. But your first impression meeting him in the mountains is of the strong, silent type. An earlier generation of Hollywood directors would have wrangled over whether to cast Burl Ives or Sydney Greenstreet in the role.

Betty Alkuk is the perfect contrast to her mate. The smallest of the NUTS, she is a miniature dynamo of energy, voluble and unquenchably cheerful, quick to laugh and to spark conversation. Where Tom might brood over a half-empty canteen, Betty would beam on seeing a half-full one. A keen observer of people, she has gradually but unobtrusively become the chief organizer of the schedule of NUTS work weekends, the scribe who sends us all reminders of upcoming assignments.

The Alkuks' plan on Saturday morning is to divide the nine of us into two groups. Tom and three others of us will arise in the dark, eat a quick cold breakfast, and leave at first faint light to hike directly all the way to Mount Arthur, four and a half miles of rugged mountain trail distant. Those four should then be in position to start working back from Mount Arthur at just about the time (about eight o'clock) that the other five, led by Betty, will start working from the hostel toward Mount Arthur, having slept a bit later and eaten a leisurely breakfast. Of the two of us (your authors), one is to go with Tom's group, the other with Betty's.

It Was a Dark and Stormy Night...

All night long the hostel building is pummeled by mountain winds, slashed by relentless rains. The noise is impressive: some of the guests genuinely fear that the hostel building may be blown off its moorings. No one is as warm as he or she would like to be, not having brought winter sleeping bags.

Next morning the glimpsed view out the fogged-up windows is unworldly. (Tom's eyes widen slightly.) The stunted treetops resemble the waves of a stormy sea, in a state of continual agitation, the upper branches torn and whipped about. As far as you can see—but you can't see very far—all is violent motion and hubbub, clouds scudding by, rain nearly horizontal. The whole world up there is wet, but it also seems in a state of high energy and of instability verging on disintegration. This is our view from inside a building at 4,000 feet, on a bare knoll still within the realm of spruce and fir trees. We can only conjecture what lies upward of treeline, in the land of rocks and dwarfed alpine vegetation, where no protection lies between you and the arctic wastes from whence originate all these violent assault forces.

Tom, ever the imperturbable, inscrutable Russian, has no words to say as he silently drinks tea, dons rain gear, assembles trail tools in the dim dawn light of the lodge. The other three of us whisper and giggle about what madness this is to venture into such a world. More than a mile of our trip across the roofline of the Barbarossa Ridge and over to Mount Arthur will be above treeline. Is Sydney Greenstreet really suggesting that we go out into *that*? Apparently he is. Somewhere on the far side of that crazy violent mountain ridge are blowdowns to be cleared, water bars to be scraped, a job to be done, a work ethic to be fulfilled. Cowed by the wall of silence from our leader, the rest of us don our gear, divide our tools. Fortunately all four of us have training in winter climbing above treeline. This is, of course, not winter but summer, not snow but rain—but just barely on both counts: the temperature, we later learn, is in the mid-30s.

That first hour—roughly 5:30 to 6:30—is a grim struggle to make first upward, then lateral, then downward progress in the face of the storm. We are unceasingly staggered by winds, blown against rocks, yelled at by angry mountain gods, unable to talk to each other in the roar and confusion and sense of urgent haste about our itinerary. By the time we are into the trees on the Arthur Ridge, we are, needless to say, once again totally and thoroughly soaked. We stop for water and conversation now that we are out of the wind. When we stop moving, we get cold quickly. Still, we note, the rain seems less punishing—is it letting up? Spirits pick up as we derive some pride from having crossed such a wild high ridge under such demanding conditions. Jokes flow freely. We wonder how many of the other guests at Yellowbush Lodge will attempt the crossing—even the other NUTS.

On we slosh down a trail that is mostly running water. We withstand temptation to clean water bars on the way; that would deprive the other half of the NUTS their assigned task. Our first goal is to get to Mount Arthur, then work back toward the Barbarossa. Soon we encounter blowdowns, the residue of winter's cruelty. We climb over their slimy trunks, dive through their water-soaked branches. Sure this is wet, but we are already wet to the skin. Wet is the word for this day. We reach the top of Mount Arthur about 8:30, just about the time the other group might be starting out from the hostel.

At this point we notice a pleasant surprise. The rain has definitely stopped. Though the wind is still stiff, it appears to be dispersing, not gathering, rain clouds. We have something to eat, shiver every time we stop moving, clammy in our wet clothes. Then Tom silently rises, grips his hoe, hoists his pack. We turn back down the trail we just ascended. Two of our group wield cutoff garden hoes, scraping each water bar, leapfrogging each other down the trail. The other two go ahead with ax and saw. The first blowdown is simple, a single dead and largely branchless trunk. One saw cut and a two-person heave of the upper section, and the trail is clear. One down, about 59 to go. The second is not much worse, a leaning live spruce, with thickly clustered branches. A few ax blows to clear a space for the saw to work, then tumbling the sawn top, end over end, to the downhill side of the trail. The third blowdown is a mass of half a dozen trunks that came down together, their upper branches a chaos of interwoven circuitry. When the water bar cleaners arrive here, they discard their hoes and join in the common effort to deal with this obstruction. Half an hour of hard labor ensues, with spirited cooperation in the teamwork of seeing what is needed, each person leaping to do the little piece of work necessary to support the other's effort. One by one the trunks are driven from the trail. Unsmilingly Tom nods his approval of our accomplishment, picks up his hoe, hoists his pack and moves down the trail. We follow immediately—we would follow him to clear the good intentions from that famous path to Gehenna. Leadership by example.

Meanwhile, Back at the Lodge

At this point, step back to Yellowbush Lodge and see an entirely different wake-up and breakfast, almost as though it were on a different mountain. When the other five of us, awakened by Betty, rise at 7:00, we see the last of the rain dispersing, clouds driven off by the wind, patches of blue appearing above, glimpses far down into the pastoral valley below. While we leisurely breakfast and pack, the wind continues strong, but it sends a different message. It is clear to everyone that the storm is over, the mountain gods appeased for now. A cheerful buzz of anticipation enlivens not only our group but the others at Yellowbush Lodge. This will be a splendid, exciting morning on the Barbarossa Ridge, windy but exhilarating, not threatening. True, we wonder if Tom's group might have got a bit wet perhaps, but not our problem. So we dress in shorts and light tops, donning wind parkas only at treeline, kept warm by the exertion of the climb. We make speedy work of crossing the Barbarossa Ridge, and soon turn east and down along the Arthur Ridge.

Right at treeline we encounter our first water bar, one that is not functioning as it ought. Water from the storm is escaping down the trail. Betty looks on the escaping water with mild reproach, like a schoolteacher at her first-graders who have strayed once again into a long-suffering neighbor's backyard. This water must be brought back where it belongs. I don't want to have to speak to it again. All five of us pitch in, first with a babel of suggestions how to fix; then, once Betty has pronounced the decision, with labor— hoeing a deeper trench, breaking down a barrier of earth and stones on the downhill side, repositioning some rocks on the trail. As our work nears completion, bubbling gales of approval burst from Betty's cheerful soprano. Never has such a small piece of work been more lavishly praised or more proudly admired.

Then we move on, deploying ourselves as follows: one with hoe on the water bars, two with ax and saw on the blowdowns, and two with the humble clippers. Betty and Tom had observed that the first part of that trail was growing in too much and needed brushing back. Clipping is slow, but it is the bread and butter of trail work. The sign of an effective trail maintainer is one who takes pleasure in the slow, meticulous job of clipping brush, and who does it well, thoroughly, and thoughtfully. So the two who are clipping lag behind, while the other three make rapid progress through the water bars and blowdowns, propelled by Betty's infectious chatter and humor.

The work of cleaning blowdowns and scraping water bars, when described on the printed page, sounds like a tedious and repetitious task. To be out there doing it is to discover that each downed tree and each drainage ditch is unique, presenting initially a mental challenge of deciding how to approach it, then a satisfy-ing physical effort, enriched by the pleasures of teamwork, re-warded for the one group by little Betty's bubbling enthusiasms,

and for the other by an unsmiling grunt of approbation from big
Tom.

Gradually the trail opens up and drains properly, and at about
12:30, in a low col somewhere on the Arthur Ridge, the two groups
meet. Here is an extraordinary contrast. Tom's group had begun
the day in that spin-rinse cycle gone mad, and our bodies had
geared down to being soaked wet at 35°F. We had worked hard
now for several hours, but we still felt cold, still wore our wet wool
balaclavas, our wet polypro underclothes, wet wind pants, wet rain
parkas. To us it is still a wet, cold day even if the rain had stopped.
It is accordingly like meeting visitors from another planet to
encounter our three friends (three, because the two clippers were
back a ways) dressed in shorts and T-shirts and pleasantly warm
from their exertions. Tom's group is at first reluctant to believe the
story of strolling comfortably across the Barbarossa Ridge from 8:30
to 9:30. Betty's group, on the other hand, is genuinely concerned
that some of Tom's workers appear borderline hypothermic. Tom's
group is urged to return now to the warm hostel, having put in
seven hours of hard exertion already.

So while Betty's group remains in the trees of the Arthur
Ridge to finish some detail work and get the patch of clipping
completed, Tom's group ascends back to the top of the Barbarossa
Ridge. There Tom mentions some problems in defining the trail
better above treeline, with a view to deterring hikers from wandering indiscriminately over the alpine vegetation. Immediately
proposals blossom about where a new cairn could be placed, an
existing one moved, a piece of scree wall pushed back here or
angled in there, some loose rock meticulously removed from one
place and littered randomly over another. Busy hands fly at the
work. Forgotten is the warm hostel below. One of Tom's party,
Sara, has an artistic bent, an incurably creative impulse, and a
contagious imagination. Cairns built with Sara in charge are no
shapeless heaps of rocks; each becomes a unique artistic expression,
carefully shaped to fit its special niche in that mountain landscape.
Have you ever seen a cairn with soul? A cairn with a sense of
humor? Try one built by Sara. On this afternoon on the Barbarossa

Ridge, one cairn leads to another, and another. Other touches are added to channel hiker traffic unobtrusively but effectively, it is hoped. In a couple of hours, a 200-yard stretch of trail has been completely refashioned to provide a more easily discernible footway and to guide the traveler more helpfully and with less impact on the alpine surroundings.

Now, about 4:00 P.M. of an energetic day that began with a stiff tussle against the mountain elements and proceeded through jumbles of blowdowns and scrapings of water bars to elegant cairns and wrestling with large rocks, Tom's Gang of Four heads wearily back across the Barbarossa Ridge and down to Yellowbush Lodge. Betty's group too straps their clippers to their packs and heads back. The one of us who had been with Tom's morning group sits a long while on the summit of Barbarossa, warm at last, then realizes that Betty herself has not yet passed to descend to Yellowbush. By now it is well after five. So we turn back and, half a mile along the Ridge, encounter Betty cheerfully directing two of her co-workers on the reconstruction of a partially knocked-over cairn. The two good-humoredly chide Betty with not letting them go, the slave driver, mercilessly pointing out unfinished work. When that cairn is done, we all turn and head for Yellowbush—and dinner!

But we carry to this day a vivid image, in that late afternoon slant of sun on the Barbarossa Ridge, of Betty coming slowly along, well behind everyone else, her concentration riveted on every detail of her trail, using her hoe as a broom to remove every loose rock, stopping to replace a heavy stone in the scree wall, critically eyeing a cairn to judge if it was doing its job properly, never once looking up from the job at hand. That trail is going to be right before Betty goes down for dinner.

Thus ends a day in the life of the NUTS.

14

Trail Tending

So summer after summer, hot, dirty, redolent of dope,
we have struggled through blowdowns and
scrub....Always there was the odor of balsam, the song
of thrushes, the drift of cloud shadows.

NATHANIEL GOODRICH, *TRAIL LOCATION*

WHAT HAVE WE described in the preceding chapter? Well, a bunch of nuts, sure—trail nuts. Heading out in the teeth of a wild storm above treeline, because there was work to be done, coming down late at the end of a long day because the work was going to be done right. To our minds this illustrates the essence of stewardship in the mountains. In the Alkuks and people like them we see people who have loved the mountains for years, who divide their weekends and vacation leisure between hiking, backpacking, rock climbing, snowshoeing, skiing, and ice climbing, but who have in late years decided that they want to give something back to the mountains. The form of stewardship they've chosen is trail tending. Having elected that choice, they throw themselves into it—Tom silently, Betty volubly, both with a drive that makes the word *dedication* pale and inadequate.

170

Tom and Betty and those other NUTS are but a few of a growing legion of trail tenders who give something back to their beloved hills. The form varies. Some work in volunteer trail crews, always in a large crowd of coworkers. Some like to work alone, in solitary contentment clipping along their adopted path, meticulously deciding where to clip each branch, tossing the clippings carefully out of sight. Others work in small groups of friends, like the NUTS.

Hazardous it is to pass judgment on an era you're part of, but we just might be in a Golden Age of Trail Maintenance. Consider that, in our part of the world at least, the basic trail systems were built a long time ago. Whatever the situation elsewhere, there is plenty of trail mileage in place in the Northeast to accommodate the most voracious hiker. So the challenge now is not to build more trails but to keep what we've got.

This is no easy task. Trails don't take care of themselves. They need work; some of them need a lot of work. So we are fortunate that a new generation of trail workers has risen to take the places of the legendary giants who built them originally. Actually, we are already in at least the second generation of trail maintainers.

Some of the trail maintenance assignment is brutally hard, involving the delicate placement of rocks that weigh more than most trail workers. For such work special skills must be mastered. In recent years a number of expert trail crews have evolved all over our part of the country. Some are paid professionals, like the Appalachian Mountain Club's White Mountain Trail Crew. Most, however, are all volunteer, yet no less expert. Some of the best are fielded by (1) the New York–New Jersey Trail Conference in the area around New York City; (2) the Adirondack Forty-Sixers, working in a range where on the whole trail maintenance has lagged and is just beginning to cope with long-neglected problems; and (3) the Trailwrights, a lively volunteer squad operating mostly in New Hampshire. There are many more.

But the heavy-rock work is only the most visible and dramatic form of needed trail maintenance. Almost more important is the day-to-day preventive maintenance. This more pedestrian (appropriate word!) detailed work is vital for keeping trails from needing the heavy-duty measures of the big trail crews.

For this branch of the art, *trail tending* is a better term than *maintenance*. We like the word *tending* because it expresses the feeling of looking out for, which is the essence of the spirit of stewardship needed for today's trails. Here's how our Webster's defines *tend*: "To take care of; minister to; watch over; look after; attend to [to *tend* plants and animals]." My, yes: trail *tending* is just the right word here.

Just what's involved in trail tending? So many people, especially hikers, have asked us that question. Most trail tending in our part of the world takes place on paths primarily through woods, maybe with a few open ledgy areas, but not much really above treeline. Work above treeline, in the alpine areas, as described in later chapters, is not at all typical of most trail tending. Down there in the trees, the trail tender does five basic tasks, as described herein.

Keep Water off the Trail

You can't overstate the importance of keeping water from careening down the treadway. The combination of boot traffic, falling water, and grade (the steeper the grade, the worse the wear) can cause significant erosion. A couple of good hard summer thunderstorms or one ordinary spring thaw, unleashed over a heavily used, moderately steep trail, can gully it out so that all you have left are the big rocks and roots the rush of water couldn't dislodge. This gully, formerly a trail, may be three, four, or five feet below the surrounding landscape—sort of the inverse of a large surface vein on an old man's hand. Now it's a suitable walkway no longer, and hikers will take to the banks to find a way around the obstacle, wearing a new path, breaking down vegetation, and threatening to repeat the destructive process in a new bed. No one will call this environmentally acceptable.

You get water off the trail by digging and maintaining drainage ditches. The steeper the trail, the more drainage will be needed. These ditches are the plumbing of the mountain trail system. Sometimes the drain is literally just a ditch, cutting through the downhill bank. More often a log or a series of overlapping rocks—better yet, one big long rock if you can move it, or rather, if Tom Alkuk can move it—is set at a rakish downsloping angle. Such a device is called a water bar, and it is a very effective means of getting the water off. Most early water bars were logs, but wood is ultimately perishable, so trail tenders have found that rock water bars are the more lasting.

The first and most essential job of the trail tender is to check the plumbing: to keep these drainages clean. Essential! Rain washes dirt down the trail into the ditch, where it silts up. Autumn leaves and windblown twigs lodge in the ditch. The tender walks his trail several times a year and rakes or grubs out silt, leaves, sticks, small stones, and anything that is blocking the pipes. The critical time for water bars to be clear is during the spring runoff, when all that accumulated winter snow joins forces with spring showers to produce the year's wettest grounds. So clearing the water bars thoroughly just before winter and again first thing in the spring is vital.

To do this work, a trail tender may carry one of a variety of tools, either specialized mattocks or "hazel hoes," or simply a cutoff garden hoe—anything that has a five- or six-inch-wide metal surface perpendicular to a three-or four-foot handle. You may get some odd looks and puzzled questions as you walk your trail, garden hoe in hand. Are you raising potatoes in the mountains? Prospecting for the wild asparagus? But remember: every question is an opportunity to answer with the message of stewardship.

Also mark these words: if your water bars are not well cleaned, every other trail tender who walks your path, be sure, will note your lapse with disdain, perhaps mutter a disparaging word. (You, of course, may do likewise on his trail, if deserved.)

Remove Blowdowns
This work is done with ax and saw. Going after blowdowns (trees or parts of trees fallen across the path) is mostly done in

spring, because most trees come down owing to rough treatment by harsh winter. It is important to get blowdowns early, or hikers will find their way around, often forming a new path where there shouldn't be one.

Removing each blowdown is a skirmish with a new opponent, a fascinating exercise in studying each specific case. How to remove it with a minimum number of cuts? Can you drag or push it off? Ax or saw? Will a saw cut bind? When you cut it here, can you roll it there?

Using chainsaws for this kind of work is controversial. You might be able to guess which side we're on. At home, for the past 20 years, we've burned about seven cords a year for cooking, heating, and sugaring, and we've cut every stick of it by handsaw and ax. So you can't tell us chainsaws are essential in any nonprofessional sphere. And you *know* they are noisy, smelly, and cut an aural path that carries over acres of wild backcountry. Think of what the rasping, grating, whining noise does to other hikers' experience up and down the trail. Well, we're not crusading on that subject here, and we grant that some trail maintainers believe in chainsaws reverentially.

Small and even medium-size blowdowns can be handled easily with a light handsaw and a hefty ax, together with a little care. If you feel it's too time consuming or dangerous, save it for another day when you can get a friend or two to help. If a *very* large tree lies athwart your trail, you might want to leave it there as a new and interesting trail feature. Cut a flat step or two to make it easier for hikers to get across, sort of like an old-fashioned stile. Mountain trails aren't meant to be sidewalks.

Blaze

A good trail is well marked by ax or paint blazes. Ax blazing is frowned on these days as being environmentally too harsh. Instead the modern blazer lightly scrapes and smooths down the bark on a tree where the blaze is to go. Paint blazes must be freshened every few years. To do this properly, the artist first walks all the route, painting in one direction; he then reverses and paints the other

way on the return. It doesn't seem to work to do both directions at
once. You just don't see well where to put the backward blazes
when you're walking forward. The blazer always tries to make neat
rectangles of just the right size. While you don't need to be com-
pulsive about geometric proportions, sloppy drip marks or paint-
sprinkled vegetation are always noticed—especially by other trail
tenders.

Overblazing or excessively large blazes have long been held to
be the mark of a novice trailworker. Today overblazing is worse: it
is a blight on the wooded landscape, a completely needless intrusion of human excesses on what should be sacred confines. With
today's heightened awareness of environmental concerns,
overblazing is an unforgivable sin. It differs little from graffiti, and
is equally out of place in the woods. The same goes for plastic
ribbon as a way to mark trails—but more on that in the last part of
this book.

Keep the Growth Clipped Back along the Trail Edges

The trail tender's least glamorous job, and thus all too often
neglected, is to walk the trail with clippers, making sure the
summer's growth is not swatting hikers in the face. You'll want to
cut high enough so new growth is not interfering with high backpacks. You'll also want to get down low enough: knee- or ankle-
height growth, after rain storms, can soak everyone's socks. The
best trail clippers take the time and trouble to remove cuttings
from the trail and put them out of sight. As in that sophomore
English exam, neatness counts.

If water bars are the plumbing of the trail system, clipping is
its haircut. Most trails need a trim at least every couple of years.

For this lowly, painstaking, slow work, your primary tool is a
good stout pair of long-handled clippers. For lower-elevation
routes, or elsewhere where brambles, grass, or ferns invade the
footway, you need something akin to what we've always called a
swizzle stick—a Y-shaped metal frame with a double-edged saw
blade connecting the ends of the Y. You swing it with verve in
wide arcs, trying not to collide with rocks or solid logs on the

downswing, or with fellow trail tenders on the upswing or follow-through. Give someone a wide berth if they're warming up with a swizzle stick.

A trail kept clear of intrusive brush is the mark of a trail well tended. Too many trail workers love only the glory of swinging an ax or hazel hoe or moving herculean rocks. The fastidious clippers are the real heroes and heroines, the foot soldiers, of well-tended trails.

Catch Trouble Early

Like human health, good trails can best be preserved by spotting danger signals early. Erosion once underway is hard to stop. If you adopt a trail, keep an eye out for developing problems, ones that may become too big for a single trail tender or pair of trail tenders to manage unaided. Such situations may need the help of experienced or strong-armed trail crews. But if noted early enough, they may be taken care of a lot easier than if neglected too long. So the fifth job of the trail tender is to be the early warning system, on the lookout for bigger jobs before they're big.

The tasks of trail tending are oddly satisfying. A lot of hikers we meet on the trail seem never to have considered that trails need maintaining; they are surprised to learn the amount of work involved. At first it sounds prosaic or even tedious. But we've never seen someone who took up trail tending who didn't eventually get hooked on it. This low, grubbing, custodial work quietly absorbs, gradually moves into the realm of craftsmanship. Before long you can persuade yourself that this is a fine art you're dealing with. The work, the results—so invisible to most passing hikers, so vivid to the practiced trail tender—become their own reward. And of course you have the immense satisfaction of knowing you're giving back something to the mountain world, which has given you so much.

15

Seven Days in April

...in the spring,
When proud-pied April, dress'd in all his trim,
Hath put a spirit of youth in everything.

WILLIAM SHAKESPEARE, SONNET 98

BELOW TREELINE, TRAIL-TENDING presents one set of tasks,
as described in the last chapter. Above treeline, we confront an
entirely different challenge. Up there in the alpine zone lies a
unique and wonder-filled world of jagged crags and delicately
wrought tundra.

The northeastern alpine zone is a place of paradox. These
scattered acres—on Maine's Katahdin, New Hampshire's
Presidentials and Franconias, Vermont's Mansfield, New York's
highest half dozen peaks, and perhaps no more than a score of
much smaller sites elsewhere in those four states—exhibit some of
the qualities of arctic tundra hundreds of miles further north.
Northeastern alpine areas have been called "the last remaining
vignettes of our recent postglacial history." Here are found alpine
flowers that you'd have to go to Greenland or Baffin Island or
much, much higher mountains to see otherwise. Their habitat is

racked by some of the most ferocious weather to be found on the planet Earth.

The vegetation that fights to survive here is obviously tough. It regularly resides in a zone that humans find unapproachable on many days of the year. Winds we can't stand up in are common occurrences in the lives of those tiny plants. They must indeed be resilient, rugged, robust.

Yet that same alpine vegetation is also painfully fragile. A small disturbance is cataclysmic to its odds for survival. The tiny alpine flowers, so admired by botanists and passing hikers, can lose their precarious grip on life if subjected to unwonted force—such as, for example, a trampling boot from one of those botanists or passing hikers.

Recognition of the extreme vulnerability of the tundra landscape has generated a brisk concern among land managers, botanists, alpine ecologists, trail crews, and hikers themselves. This concern has spawned a tremendous volume of concentrated attention, study, thought, policy formulation, and just plain hard work.

During a single week in April recently, we were privileged and immeasurably pleased to watch a quick succession of gatherings focused on saving the alpine zone. In the space of seven days we watched a schedule of four separate events involving concerned alpine-zone experts or enthusiasts, each of the four occasions with a different focus, yet all zeroing in on the tundra world above the trees.

We'd like to tell you about these four happenings. Years ago we remember a best-selling book and popular movie called *Seven Days in May*. We herewith present our own "Seven Days in April." The former was an exciting but ultimately trivial entertainment about a fanciful takeover of the US government by a military junta. The message, if there was one, was it could happen here, and don't let it. Our story in this chapter is just the reverse: not quite as exciting perhaps, but neither is it as fanciful or trivial. Its message is that this *is* happening here, and we *must* do something about it— and a lot of good folk are getting together, in proud-pied April and year-round, to put a spirit of youth into the effort. The decidedly nontrivial result is a solid substantive movement among alpine managers.

Friday, April 10–Sunday, April 12

We had just wound up a poor season of making maple syrup at our homestead when we drove across Vermont to the start of a three-day "Alpine Managers Gathering," hosted by the Green Mountain Club. The purpose was to bring together, for the first time in one room, all of the land managers, trail workers, and concerned hikers who are working on the scattered alpine areas of the Northeast.

The first day's "reception" was held in a slightly shabby but very comfortable low-rent ski dorm below Mount Mansfield, as 20 or 30 people began to mill about and meet each other, most for the first time. Land managers, hiking clubs, trail crews, and individual concerned hikers have been working on alpine-area problems independently all over the Northeast for most of this century, especially since about 1970. But up until this Friday afternoon they had worked for the most part in isolation from one another, hearing only fragmentary rumors of techniques being tried elsewhere. Each group was learning some interesting lessons from its own experimental experiences, but no one had found the perfect solutions to alpine problems.

The theory behind the GMC-sponsored gathering was that we could all learn from each other. The gathering provided a forum for groups to tell what they'd been doing, to report what seemed to work, to warn about what didn't work, to provide some answers, to ask more questions, and to explore possibilities with others.

People came from all over. Every one of the significant alpine areas of the Northeast was represented. Participants ranged in age from mid-20s to late 60s—big people and little people, men and women, all with lessons learned and experiences to tell about, but all also eager to improve what they were doing and profit from others' ideas. Some were distinguished academic botanists with a string of degrees; others were down-to-earth (literally) trail workers unaccustomed to having clean hands. There was a wealth of experience in the room, yet one participant caught the spirit of the occasion when he described the gathering as having no experts, only beginners. There's much we don't know yet about wise stewardship of alpine areas, much we can gain from listening to what others are doing and pondering how to apply it with profit on our particular piece of alpine turf.

So at this "reception"—that word is much too grandiose for the humble setting or dramatis personae involved—you would have seen New England's top alpine ecologist, Dr. Charles Cogbill, exchanging insights with the Adirondacks' veteran forester Dr. Edwin Ketchledge, while a few feet away a pretty young woman from Maine's rocky coastal Mount Desert chatted eagerly with a professional-looking representative from the Mount Washington Observatory and a rugged, sunburnt ranger from the Adirondacks High Peaks Wilderness. A naturalist from New Hampshire's Sandwich Range Conservation Association recognized a former kindergarten classmate now managing the University of Vermont's alpine holdings on Mount Mansfield—both of them here reunited after 30 years by their common concern for saving alpine vegetation.

This diverse group reflected the interesting diversity of the Northeast's alpine areas. We all think of the Presidential Range, wherein lies the Northeast's largest alpine area by far, a sprawling, rambling uplands that measures about 10 miles in length of unrelieved tundra, the width of which varies jaggedly, following the splattered ridge lines radiating out from the summits of seven or more mountains (depending on how many subsidiary peaks you grant independent status to). A strong second in size is Maine's remote Katahdin, with its high windswept tableland. In the Adirondacks you can find seven or eight major summits with significant alpine acreage. Vermont has two major alpine areas, on Mansfield and Camel's Hump. New Hampshire has two major locales besides the Presidentials: the Franconia Ridge and Mount Moosilauke. Maine has several high summits well west of the

Katahdin group, the most notable being rugged Saddleback and the
Bigelow Range.

But besides these prominent alpine areas, there are a scatter-
ing of peaks that barely poke their tips above the spruce-fir-birch
forest. Each of these lesser giants has a small area where you find a
tiny zone of genuine alpine qualities, sometimes perhaps 100 feet
along a spiny ridge, or a little patch ringed around a rocky summit.
Good examples are New Hampshire's South Twin or Bondcliff, or
Vermont's Abraham. Because of their postage-stamp size, these
areas have received generally less attention than the Presidentials
or Katahdin. But in recent years, with the rise of interest in alpine
ecology, new attention is being directed toward preserving these
tiny gems.

Yet a third category of peaks attracts the interest of alpine
ecologists, managers, and trail workers. These are the distinctly
lower peaks that, for a variety of reasons, have evolved exposed
ledgy areas with tundralike attributes, plus a large number of
visitors whose impact creates problems not unlike those of the true
alpine areas. Mount Desert in Maine's Acadia National Park is a
good example: these "mountains" aren't even 2,000 feet high, but
because of their devegetated, weather-racked, seacoast perch, a few
choice summits have extensive zones of exposed rock interlarded
with islands of precarious vegetation. With a high volume of
visitors swarming all over the tops, these vegetative colonies are
frightfully vulnerable. Another good example here is Mount Welch
in New Hampshire's Sandwich Range—a low (2,605 feet) summit
with islands of fragile vegetation scattered across rocky ridges,
attracting a large number of hikers all summer long.

All day on Saturday and on to Sunday noon, these diverse
alpine areas were the center of attention in a series of panel
discussions, with full participation by the throng of alpine managers, a total of 50 now arrived. These discussions were held in a
converted barn where GMC hosts meetings of this sort—just the
right size for this group. The plain board floor and exposed old
wooden beams gave an aura of practical work, not theoretical
speculation.

Panels focused on threatened and endangered alpine plants, on trail design and maintenance, on meeting the public and educational efforts, and on cooperation between government agencies, hiking clubs, and individual volunteers.

A trail crew boss from Maine's Katahdin described an ingenious method for transporting rocks for trail work without trampling vegetation. Vermont and New York reported on their disparate programs for on-site education in the alpine zone. An ecologist from the University of Vermont reported the results of a just-completed study of Mount Mansfield and Camel's Hump. Participants brought up such varied sources of potential damage as large parties, dogs, and winter campers.

One striking feature of this alpine managers gathering was its studied neglect of hierarchies: everyone seemed as keenly interested in the problems of little Mount Abraham as those of lordly Katahdin; the large professional staff of the high-budget Appalachian Mountain Club was no more prominent than the moonlighting volunteers of the Adirondack Forty-Sixers, the academic expert was no more an expert than the fieldwise young trail worker. And throughout the weekend a frequent theme was the recognition that we were all part of the problem and must all be part of the solution; the need to avoid thinking in terms of those bad hikers and us good managers. Said one participant: "We want to share with our fellow hikers the stewardship of the mountains."

While formal sessions were lively, perhaps the most useful part of the weekend was the opportunity for meeting helpful new colleagues in this struggling art of tundra preservation. The group concluded the weekend with a discussion of what to do next year, how to continue this exchange of information, ideas, and inspiration.

One could not help wondering if, high on the snow-strewn slopes of the Northeast's alpine areas from Algonquin to Hamlin, the mountain gods nodded their approval of this struggling effort by 50 frail mortals to understand better and to work together more fruitfully.

Monday, April 13–Thursday Morning, April 16

After driving home across Vermont on Sunday afternoon, we immediately took off again on Monday morning in the opposite direction, to the town of Randolph, New Hampshire, at the foot of the Northern Presidentials. High on the slopes of Mount Adams, the Randolph Mountain Club maintains four small cabins for the use of hikers. Only one cabin has a stove for winter warmth, but that doesn't stop winter climbers from staying in all four. For the assistance of these guests, for the protection of RMC's property, and as a first line of search and rescue, RMC hires a caretaker to spend the winter in the heated cabin, to check in on the other three, and generally to provide a useful presence in the Northern Presidentials during the winter months. That caretaker takes a few vacation days from time to time, and one of us had agreed to serve as his substitute during days off.

So, after three days of indoor discussion of alpine problems, one of us now headed up for three days of practical application, one might say. During the next three days we handled a multitude of little chores, from dumping the slop bucket and replacing toilet paper in the outhouses to checking on avalanche conditions on the side of Mount Jefferson and answering questions about whether it was prudent to try for Mount Adams this afternoon. On this and several earlier stints for RMC, we had seen every kind of weather, from warm all-day rain to –28°F and one day that never got above –12°F; every kind of population density from 26 one night (in a cabin with a theoretical maximum of 18) to one train of three days without seeing another soul, day or night; and every kind of visitor from crack trained alpinists to novices in blue jeans and summer hiking boots.

Full moon rose on the 16th of this April, so on the last evening there, with no guests and after reporting in on the radio to RMC's valley-based authorities, we took off by moonlight to the top of Mount Adams, second-highest peak in the entire Northeast. Unusually heavy late-winter snows had carpeted the peaks in white, and quick thaws and refreezing had left a hard crust ideal for crampons. The moonlight glistened. The prospect from the subsidiary peak known as Adams 4—with mounts Madison, John Quincy Adams, Adams, and Sam Adams arrayed above—looked positively Himalayan. The relative calm at 4,500 feet gave way suddenly, above 5,500, to a chilling breeze on the final rise to 5,774-foot Adams's summit, with its cavernous drop to the low forests on the far side. The whole provided a stirring reminder of the values of the high alpine experience, the ultimate reason why 50 concerned managers had been meeting for the preceding three days to try to figure out how to preserve this incomparable landscape, this vitally important inspiration for the human spirit.

Thursday, April 16

Early the following morning, we rendezvoused at the base of the RMC's trail so as to whisk off to two further meetings that same day.

The first was the Alpine Study Committee, a small advisory group assembled by the staff of the White Mountain National Forest, at the staff headquarters in Laconia, New Hampshire. The purpose of this gathering is to advise on alpine-area problems within the forest, with primary focus on the Presidentials. This group brings together Forest Service personnel with representatives of the New Hampshire environmental agency, botanists from the Natural Heritage Inventory, staff members from the Appalachian Mountain Club and New Hampshire's Nature Conservancy, plus a couple of interested individuals. The agenda ranges over everything from how to reduce the impact of winter camping and how to clean up the mess left by an Air Force research program shortly after World War II, to how to word an educational sign for posting at treeline.

What we find impressive is that the Forest Service staff treats these meetings as vital to its managerial role. Top staff people regularly attend, and they take notes on which to base action. Clearly these public servants are listening to the public they serve and are keeping a sharp eye open for preserving the integrity of the land they're commissioned to manage.

At three o'clock sharp the meeting broke up, and five of us piled into a Forest Service van and headed for Boston. In an unseasonal snowstorm, we crawled through rush-hour traffic along the Tobin Bridge and Storrow Drive to a parking lot under the Boston Common, and eventually to the headquarters of the Appalachian Mountain Club, one block from the Massachusetts State House—and a long, long way, geographically and spiritually, from the moonlit windswept snows of Mount Adams just 24 hours before.

Here in the heart of Boston, at 7:30 that evening, a group of active winter campers from the AMC's Boston chapter had requested an opportunity to hear from and discuss with the Forest Service and others about the latest regulations affecting winter recreation in the alpine zone.

Until the winter of 1990 winter camping was unrestricted in the alpine zone. Then, responding to concerns of botanists for the safety of alpine vegetation, the Forest Service instituted a complete ban on all winter camping above treeline. In 1992, responding to the concerns of the winter campers, a compromise policy was reached: above-treeline camping only where there was a cover of at least two feet of snow. The theory behind this policy is that alpine vegetation is well protected from the effects of tenting when swathed in a protective coating of snow and ice. Earlier that winter we had conducted a hasty survey of where two feet of snow seems to form regularly in the Presidentials, and prepared a map of such places—hence our inclusion on this panel.

The resulting discussion was animated and frank, with many campers asking questions and voicing informed views on what they looked for from the Forest Service, and how the impact of their arcane sport might be held to acceptable limits. On both sides there seemed to be recognition of the importance of balancing the needs of a fragile physical environment with the legitimate opportunity for people to experience a night out in that incomparable alpine world. One of the Forest Service officers later wrote to one of the more articulate campers:

> There is a large pool of skills and knowledge "out there" which we often fail to fully recognize and use. There were many suggestions and ideas presented that consider the balance between a unique recreation opportunity and protection of an exemplary natural community. The meeting "set the seeds of developing an ethic for use of the alpine zone."

It was after midnight before that Forest Service van crawled home through the snowstorm and we got into our own car and headed for a night's sleep.

Thus ended our seven days in April.

In this one week it was our privilege and pleasure to see an intense focusing of a lot of able and involved individuals and groups on the special world of the alpine area. Much of the time we dwelt on specific and tangible issues, practical measures, here-and-now solutions to urgent problems. But underlying it all, for the entire week, we were conscious of a rising concern throughout the Northeast, a public conscience, a deep commitment to that special world above the trees.

At stake is a reconciliation of twin objectives: to preserve the threatened and endangered species of alpine vegetation or, more broadly, the fragile alpine ecosystem of which such vegetation is a natural part; and to preserve equally the opportunity for people to be up there on the mountain heights, to honor the great value to the human spirit of experiencing that realm of the mountain gods.

To reconcile and synthesize these vital objectives is why 50 managers gather in an old barn in Vermont for three days, why RMC stations a caretaker on the high slopes of Mount Adams, why a government agency convenes and harkens to an advisory group, and why Boston hikers meet with Forest Service managers during a snowy evening on Beacon Hill.

With such forces let loose, one cannot resist a fundamental optimism. During those seven days we were aware of differences of viewpoint about alpine-zone policy—at times distressingly aware. But with many people of good faith working together toward solutions, one must be hopeful. Above all, though, stands that bright vision of the pure alpine snows by moonlight on Mount Adams.

16

To Save a Mountain Flower:
Preserving Alpine Areas:
A Three-Part Saga

To see a World in a Grain of Sand
And a Heaven in a Wild Flower.
WILLIAM BLAKE

MOUNT FUJI, JAPAN'S graceful symbol of purity and spiritual-
ity, has become a mess from top to bottom. One quarter of a
million people ascend the sacred peak during summer months, and
they leave a preposterous volume of trash behind. Authorities have
installed automatic can crushers along the trampled path. The
great peak bears despondent testimony to the detrimental effects of
tourism run rampant.

Here in our backyard we witnessed a similar desecration of
(we'll concede) a considerably lesser mountain shrine, New
Hampshire's beautiful Franconia Ridge. We don't get nearly a

quarter of a million people here, but we get plenty enough to create an environmental impact that might be called, in technical terms, wicked awesome. Probably awesome and definitely wicked.

By 1977 the Franconia Ridge was in very bad shape as a result of heavy and indiscriminate hiking traffic. The struggle to find ways to save and restore the alpine vegetation on that ridge makes an interesting case study in humanity's efforts to undo its own mischief, to make amends to an abused and uncommonly pictur-esque crease on the earth's surface.

The Franconia Ridge is a narrow, elongated uplift running for almost 10 miles over such peaks as Osseo, Flume, Liberty, Little Haystack, Lincoln, Lafayette, and North Lafayette. For about two miles, from just south of Little Haystack to just north of North Lafayette, the ridge soars above treeline, with steep drops on both sides, spectacular rock formations, breathtaking vistas, and a lush display of alpine vegetation—rich swells of diapensia, fields of Labrador tea and of alpine cranberry, splashes of vivid mountain avens, with the ubiquitous mountain sandwort enlivening the lovely scene everywhere. The Franconia Ridge Trail had existed since the early nineteenth century with very informal markings, only a few cairns in scattered array.

By the 1970s, with the increasing traffic of that decade, the ridge was being loved to death. Between Lafayette and Little Haystack especially, vegetation had been kicked away in wide swaths, as hikers wandered indiscriminately over the ridge. On the shoulder just below Lafayette's summit, a strip as much as one hundred feet across was brown where it had once been green. On a subsidiary hump between Lafayette and Lincoln—known to Franconia Ridge insiders as Truman (though whether so named by Democrats to honor or Republicans to insult him is not known, it being just a little hump)—a rabbit warren of different paths etched scars in the vegetation. Just south of the top of Lincoln, another wide belt of flora had been lost by hikers covering a yards-wide path instead of a single footway.

As the authors Bruce and Doreen Bolnick have expressed it, "sometimes 'leaving nothing but footsteps' is leaving too much."

Saga 1:
The Physical Component

"Your feet's too big."

ADA BENSON AND FRED FISHER (TITLE OF A 1936 POPULAR
SONG MADE FAMOUS BY THOMAS "FATS" WALLER)

Beginning in 1977, officials of the White Mountain National
Forest and the Trail Crew of the Appalachian Mountain Club took
decisive action to do something about this crisis. Following directions indicated by WMNF, the AMC Trail Crew marked out a
three-foot-wide trail corridor all the way from Little Haystack to
Lafayette. This was the first place where extensive use was made of
"scree walls," low borders of rock on each side of the trail, normally
about one foot high.

This was a radical innovation. Controversy ensued: a few
hikers were highly critical of the artificial "Chinese Wall" that had
suddenly been imposed on the previously unmanaged landscape.
Those critics charged that the mountain experience was inexcusably degraded by the "sidewalk" look. If you've read the first edition
of this book, you'll recall we welcomed that original trail work
about the way Rome welcomed Attila the Hun. We were about
equally effective in stopping it. Well, we and most other critics
acknowledged that the environmental havoc could not have gone
ignored much longer. But the wild character of that magnificent
ridge seemed to have been violated.

The problem is the classic one of preservation versus use. Can
we save alpine flowers and still save also the spirit of wildness that
they symbolize? What is at stake on the Franconia Ridge is a
microcosm of the challenge for backcountry management everywhere. How can we preserve the physical resource and the wild
mountain experience at the same time?

Within three years—in 1980—the AMC launched its Adopt-a-Trail program. The authors were signed up right away to maintain the Franconia Ridge. From the role of critics, we were suddenly handed the responsibility of "doing something" ourselves. Our bluff was called.

As we go to press with this book, we have been working on that trail for 13 summers. It is not like most trail maintenance assignments, where you clear water bars and blowdown each spring and fall and get back maybe once or twice during the summer to clip brush, freshen paint blazes, or deal with some special problems. Our ridge trail needs constant attention. For 13 years we have made an effort to get up there at least once every three weeks between May and October, occasionally more often. One of us has climbed that ridge (as of July 4, 1992) 229 times since 1980, usually with the other of us, and sometimes with friends who generously help in the fascinating and demanding work.

It has been 13 years of education for us. We have much yet to learn. We set out to try what could be done to keep hikers on one trail for 1.7 miles between Little Haystack and Lafayette, while, if possible, minimizing the artificial visual blight of one long scree wall corridor. We have learned that this mission is a surprisingly complex and subtle one, that answers do not come easily or quickly, but must be earned by long observation, hard thinking about the problem, and consultation with anyone and everyone who might have ideas, including many passing hikers themselves.

Gradually, painfully, with much trial and much error, as well as much observation of hikers and discussion with friends, at least a dozen strategies have evolved and been implemented on the Franconia Ridge.

Step 1: Scree Walls

Scree walls remain the first step to traffic control in alpine areas. But where the scree comes from is of no little note. Until recently scree wall builders seized any rock lying around in the tundra and eagerly pried it up for use in their wall. Then alpine ecologists emitted a cry of dismay: often individual rocks form a key

part of the microhabitat that the alpine plants require to maintain
their precarious hold on life above treeline. So now wall builders
are asked to select rock with care: much better to bring them up
from jumbles of rocks or other more desolate places. Those tundra
rocks that shelter a minigrove of diapensia or mountain cranberry—leave them in place.

When we began work on the Franconia Ridge, one of the first
things we noticed was that, for all the sharp visual impact of those
long walls, they were not doing the job of keeping hikers on one
trail. Doubtless they helped. But we quickly noticed that hikers
were leaving the trail much too often all along the ridge.

Whatever you may read elsewhere about scree walls being
"effective in protecting alpine habitat from hiker trampling," we
can report unequivocally, based on 13 years of careful observation,
that on the Franconia Ridge at least, scree walls alone were not
solving the problem. Hikers were not staying within the walls
enough to allow the impacted flora to recover. Observed vegetative
recovery is due to the cumulative effect of a broad range of other
strategies. As long as scree walls were the sole reliance, significantly large and numerous areas of continuing unacceptable impact
were apparent.

What was wrong? If the scree walls were not working, what
could be done to make them more effective? How could the hiking
traffic be encouraged to stay on the designated trail, short of
building three-foot-high fences or arresting violators on sight—
both totally unacceptable for maintaining the mountain experience on that magnificent ridge?

Step 2: Cairns

The traditional marking for above-treeline trails, cairns, had
been sadly neglected on the Franconia Ridge. Except for the first
half mile north of Little Haystack, there were virtually none left.
Many had been dismantled to obtain rock for the scree walls. Some
that were left were as much as 10 or 20 feet outside the scree walls
and thus were counterproductive.

So, we began building cairns, trying to be careful about where we got rock. We started at the places where most people often left the trail. We've built perhaps half a dozen cairns every year since.

Soon, we found there is much more to proper cairning than just throwing a few rocks together at intervals. To be effective, a cairn must catch the hiker's eye at just the right moment, so as to direct his or her steps onto the trail. This means care for the visual background against which the cairn will be seen. Ideally it should stand out on the skyline at the critical moment you want it seen—sky, not more rocks, behind it. At the least, it definitely should not blend into a background of similarly colored rocks. It must be clearly on the trail, so as not to pull people off it. Yet if it is too much in the line of traffic, it will be knocked down as hikers stumble against it. Exact placement of cairns required far more thought than we had first realized.

Step 3: Paint
Paint blazes help channel traffic. But too liberal smearing of paint is a visual blot on natural scenery. Still, where other steps are not working, a strategically placed blaze or arrow can make a difference in steering traffic.

Step 4: Water Bar "Bridges"
We began to notice a lot of contributing problems that could be dealt with individually. Wherever there is a water bar, the ditch tends to look like the trail, and people may turn into the ditch and out on to the vegetation we're trying to protect. So, all along the ridge, wherever there are drainage ditches, we find long rocks that can be placed across the water bar at the edge of the trail, as a bridge. This breaks up the trail-like look of the ditch. Building bridges over water bars implies a commitment to tending them regularly: they tend to catch rubble and fill in, so one must clear under bridges often.

If the bridge has too flat a surface on top, it may look like an inviting stepping-stone. If too many hikers stomp on it, they may dislodge it. Also, they may use it as a stepping-stone that carries them in the wrong direction, out of the trail. Therefore, it has to be made unfit for stepping on. The remedy is to gather a few smaller, random-shaped rocks and pebbles and scatter them over the surface of the bridge rock. Someone has called these smaller stones our "barbed wire."

Step 5: Removing Loose Rock

We noticed that people don't like to tread on loose rock and do like to step on smooth surfaces. So we make a point of not letting three weeks go by without walking the trail and chucking each loose rock out of it and onto the area immediately adjacent to the trail. This is an exceedingly important step. During the course of a week or two there will be an inevitable accumulation of loose rock casually kicked into the trail. It must be removed, or people may start going off the trail to avoid it.

Step 6: Reducing High Steps

Hikers do not like high steps. They'll go out of their way— and out of the trail onto the tundra—to avoid stepping up more than about six to nine inches in one step. The 1977–78 trail work included many rock steps that exceeded that height, and each such step became a place where people were getting off trail. One remedy—still being worked on on a case-by-case basis—is to provide an intermediate step alongside each high one.

Step 7: Shoring Up Eroding Banks

One consequence of the worn trail bed is that wind and wind-driven rain now scour the exposed turf on the side of the trail. This appears as an undercutting of the turf and vegetation alongside the trail in many places. The remedy we've tried for this problem is to place rocks embedded into the turf where it is undercut. The hope is that such rocks will prevent further wind or water erosion and provide a point of stability for the gradual restoration of soil and turf in and around the rocks.

Step 8: Sufficiently Wide Paths

If the idea is to keep folks on trail, it is vital that the trail be wide enough for passing. If too narrow, it forces hikers out onto the vegetation just to get by each other. Slowly we work at widening the track at critical points, a little bit each year.

Step 9: "Room at the Top"

On the major summits, there is no way hikers will stay within a three-foot-wide track. When 50 or 80 people congregate on the top of Lafayette or Lincoln or Little Haystack—numbers that we often count on popular weekends with good weather—nothing will stop them from fanning out to sit down and have lunch or see the view.

This happens not only on summits; we have gradually observed that wherever there is a short rise in the ridge, hikers display a strong tendency to wander a bit. Where the ridge dips, they'll stay on trail, but where it climbs to a new height, they simply won't stay within a three-foot corridor in many instances. Perhaps they seek a rest after coming uphill, perhaps they stop to look at the view, perhaps they wait for slower friends—whatever the reason, the tops of rises are vulnerable points. Others have also found this to be true. In her landmark study of hiker patterns on Mount Mansfield and Camel's Hump, Vermont's Kathleen Reilly found that most visitors left the trail at high points where they thought a good view was obtainable.

So on both summits and intermediate rises we try to preserve the credibility of the scree walls by pushing them back and allowing hikers "room at the top." Yes, this sacrifices some vegetation, but that's happening anyway, since hikers won't abide by unrealistic constraints at such points. Our theory is that it is better to concede the space they require, and then work hard to save the vegetation beyond that point. When in doubt, we consult with the White Mountain National Forest rangers and abide by their instructions as to how wide an area to concede and where to draw the line.

Step 10: Scrub Obstacles

On Truman we found that nothing we did could stop a certain minority from leaving the trail to wander. A shortage of loose rock on that summit precluded higher scree walls or more prominent cairns. Yet the ugly blight of trampled vegetation was unacceptable. What to do?

Again we consulted with forest personnel and requested permission to go down into the krummholz and cut scattered dead trees, bring them up, and line the trail at critical points where people seemed to be leaving the trail. A gnarly, twisty, prickly, thorny piece of dead scrub is a spectacularly repellent obstacle to leaving the trail. Backcountry Ranger Roger Collins not only secured permission for this measure but personally helped us cut and drag up the dead scrub. It turned out to be a very effective deterrent to wandering hikers and went a long way toward solving that persistent problem on Truman.

Several precautions on the use of dead scrub: We exercise great care not to remove too many dead trees from the same place, because we don't want to give the wind a chance to punish the adjacent scrub too severely and open a wide belt of killed vegetation. Nor do we want to open up an inviting tent site! Also, it is important to secure the dead scrub in place effectively, remembering that terrific winds will do their best to rearrange the furniture. And, most important, cutting trees, dead or alive, should absolutely never be undertaken without the permission of the backcountry manager responsible for that area.

The scrub tactic has had a completely unforeseen side effect of fairly important significance. After two or three years we noticed that around the base of the scrub, the native vegetation leaps back much faster than elsewhere. Apparently the scrub provides protection from the wind, a catch basin for seed and organic matter, and a condensation point for moisture. These and perhaps other factors greatly accelerate the regrowth of vegetation. Since that's what the whole battle's about—restoring the vegetation—this is major good news.

Step 11: Yogi's Maxim
Dr. Lawrence Peter Berra, that eminent scholar of baseball and innovative linguistics, once stated: "You can observe a lot just by watching." This maxim applies to alpine trail work. We spend many hours unobtrusively watching our fellow hikers and trying to understand why they leave the trail at point X or stay on at point

Y. Human behavior is without question the most obscure subject in the field of knowledge, and we feel there's much yet to understand about human alpine-areas behavior. But close observation has been of great value in learning how to apply many of the preceding tactics.

Here is one interesting observation: Go *south* from the summit of Lafayette and you find scree walls, cairns, and a wide range of other measures to keep people on trail, but only imperfect success and wide areas of blighted vegetation as yet unrecovered. Go *north* from Lafayette and you find hardly any scree or other measures, except a positively regal line of stately cairns, fashioned in the past five years by the trail adopters, Barbara and Charles Kukla. But despite the relative dearth of scree walls, dead scrub, or other tactics, a single narrow hiker's track threads through lush beds of vegetation most of the way. Why the difference? You tell us. But here's one theory.

Consider the extremely heavy use by day hikers south of Lafayette and the virtual monopoly of overnight campers north of that summit. Day hikers have light packs or none, feel free to skip around, and include many inexperienced folk who are simply unaware that there is any problem up there. If you turn north from Lafayette, you're probably on an overnight trip, carry a large pack, and thus have business to attend to (getting that pack from here to there). Further, the chances are you've heard about the environmental concerns up there. It is an interesting contrast.

Step 12: Help!

Alpine zone management is a new art. There are no real experts yet. Some have learned a lot in the last few years, and we make every effort to learn from them. If they're willing to walk the Franconia Ridge with us, we go over all the problems we've identified and ask counsel on solutions. A lot of officials of the White Mountain National Forest have been extraordinarily helpful; so have Edwin H. Ketchledge, the preeminent alpine ecologist of the Adirondacks, and Brian T. Fitzgerald, a leader of the Green Mountain Club of Vermont, not to mention the West End Trail Tenders, a group of energetic and creative AMC volunteers who maintain adjacent trails in the Franconia area. Many other experienced hikers or even passing day-trippers come up with good ideas, shrewd observations, or innovative suggestions. We mine ideas wherever we can find them. Readers of this book: do you have any suggestions for us?

Help can also take a more direct physical form. Probably a score or more of our friends have spent a day or two on the ridge with us, building a cairn here, repairing a water bar there, placing scrub, picking up loose rubble, or watching the passing parade to see how a particular problem might be addressed. And not only friends: sometimes if we're working on a particular problem, passing hikers will drop their packs and join in. Surely another score of people we'd never met before and may never see again contributed significant labor to the work of the Franconia Ridge during the 1980s.

These are just a dozen measures we can think of; doubtless we're forgetting a dozen more. Perhaps others who have worked on other alpine zones could name two dozen more.

We wish we could report that the purely physical obstacles and inducements to keeping people on trail solved the problem. They don't. They're a good starting point, an essential step. But something more is needed, or people will still get out and wander over the fragile vegetation to an unacceptable degree. That additional need is the subject of the next saga.

Saga 2:
Education above the Trees

Soap and education are not as sudden as a massacre, but
they are more deadly in the long run.

MARK TWAIN

In the long quiet battle to preserve the alpine areas, these physical obstacles we've described are not completely effective, and we suspect they never could be. Even the best-placed array of scree, cairns, scrub, blazes, and other techniques is not sufficient. People still wander.

In the long run, education is the key to people's treating the alpine zone less destructively. You have to reach people's minds, not just their feet. What we need in the minute alpine zones of the northeastern United States is but an application in microcosm of a global principle found in a study, "Conserving Biological Diversity" by John C. Ryan, for the World Watch Institute's report *State of the World, 1992*:

> Over the past decade, many park managers have come to realize that the survival of protected areas depends ultimately on the support of local people, rather than on fences, fines, and even armed force.

Education above the trees may take several forms. In escalating order of effectiveness, consider: signs; media messages; direct in-person contact on the site; and involvement.

Educational Signs

When we started work on the Franconia Ridge, no one was telling hikers what the problem was and why they should keep on trail. So we borrowed an idea from Vermont's Green Mountain Club and the Adirondacks: educational signs, placed right at treeline. (Treeline rather than the trailhead starting point: people seem to forget the message after a couple of hours of hiking uphill.)

We had a lot to learn about signs. The first ones we asked the Appalachian Mountain Club to make for us came out (1) written in small print; (2) full of jargon; and (3) negative: "thou shalt not" leave the trail. We put those signs up, and kept putting them up over and over, because they kept getting torn down by people who apparently resented them.

Then we heard something from a real sharp New York State ranger, C. Peter Fish. According to Ranger Fish's story, the Adirondack rule once was: you can camp anywhere except where their is a NO CAMPING sign. This rule was poorly obeyed and violators rarely caught, because the signs kept disappearing. So they changed the rule to say: no camping anywhere except where there was a CAMPING ALLOWED sign, or words to that effect. *Those* signs were never taken. Moral: Keep the message positive.

So we wrote our own sign and got the national forest's approval for the wording. Hand-lettered, the message was positive:

ALPINE ZONE
THE VEGETATION HERE ABOVE TREELINE
IS BEAUTIFUL—BUT FRAGILE. PLEASE
STAY ON TRAIL OR ON THE ROCKS. HELP
PRESERVE THE ALPINE ZONE. THANK YOU.

We feel the most important words are *please* and *thank you*. These signs not only were never taken down but never had a touch of graffiti on them. The weather proved less respectful, and took its toll on our hand-lettered efforts. Eventually the forest staff replaced ours with more permanent signs, but kept the same positive message.

More recently the national forest staff has created a trailside sign for more general use wherever trails emerge from below treeline to any alpine area in the White Mountain National Forest. These signs also use the purely positive approach:

WELCOME TO THE
ALPINE ZONE
ENJOY THE FRAGILE BEAUTY.
BE A CARING STEWARD.
STAY ON THE TRAIL OR WALK ON BARE ROCKS.
CAMP ONLY BELOW TIMBERLINE.
COOK ON A STOVE.
HELP PRESERVE THE DELICATE BALANCE OF THE ALPINE ZONE.
IT'S A TOUGH PLACE TO GROW.

In our view that's a first-rate message to be sending to everyone who enters the alpine zone. Note that it doesn't say: "NO CAMPING above timberline," but "CAMP only below timberline." It doesn't say "NO FIRES," it says "COOK on a stove." Note that it invites each hiker to "HELP preserve" the alpine area. In almost every way this sign is a splendid example of good communication. (We would have added "Thank You" at the end.) These signs, be it further noted, are placed at treeline, just before the hiker steps out on the alpine area. Experience seems to show, though more could be learned on this point, that hikers will respond better to a sign seen right there on the spot, as opposed to one way down at the roadside, which neither registers meaningfully down there nor stays with their consciousness well enough through the hours of ascent.

A variation of this theme is used out West in Mount Rainier National Park. There the problem is the fragile alpine meadows, so easily damaged when visitors wander indiscriminately. So the folks at Mount Rainier have come up with a variety of educational approaches. The one that grabs our fancy is a little lapel button that reads "Don't Be a Meadow Stomper." They report that it has a salutary educational effect—and adds that important step of personal involvement when visitors themselves put on a button. Hearing about this program, some northeastern groups are copying Rainier's idea, but adapting the message appropriately (since we have, not meadows, but tundra) to read: "Don't Be a Tundra Trampler."

Media Messages

Through broader media, much has been done in recent years to educate the hiking public on environmental concerns. Backcountry managers like the White Mountain National Forest staff, clubs like the AMC, magazines like *Backpacker*, responsible outfitters like REI, EMS, and L. L. Bean, all have helped to raise public awareness of the fragility of the mountain beauty we all enjoy.

An excellent positive example is a National Geographic book on the Appalachian Trail, *Mountain Adventure*. A stunning photo of hikers on the Franconia Ridge (part of the AT) has a short but clear caption ending: "The trudging party carefully keeps on the stony path, protecting alpine tundra from an eroding stream of footsteps." Messages like that, in such widely read places, help a lot.

The converse also holds true: media messages that trumpet the *wrong* thing have a dreadful adverse effect. Recently Sierra Designs ran splashy color advertisements with a photo showing one of their fancy tents spread out right on a patch of alpine vegetation, with three climbers standing around crunching vegetation, too, with the caption:

Tested on Mt. Washington.
One of Sierra Design's testing labs is the summit of Mt. Washington, location of the highest recorded wind speeds on earth. Here, where conditions are at their worst, we found the ideal spot to test our tents for wind durability, tent pole strength, guy point placement and aerodynamics.

At a time when camping above treeline on Mount Washington has been prohibited for almost 20 years, what a message to be sending out! Incredible! The authors of that ad, the climbers who posed, and the photographer who snapped the picture ought to be strung up on a high tree well below treeline. And the highest limbs should be reserved for (1) the marketing manager who conceived the idea and (2) the land manager who approved the use of that patch of tundra for such an inexcusably destructive purpose.

Education Person-to-Person

Effective education means much more than a sign or two, or a lot of good press. In the ideal case it means direct person-to-person low-key educational encounters.

The superior effectiveness of direct interpersonal education was recognized early in Vermont. That state's Green Mountains have but two small alpine areas, a very small one on Camel's Hump and a longer exposed ridge on Vermont's highest peak, Mount Mansfield. State Officials and the Green Mountain Club were quick to perceive the growing problem of hiker impact during the 1960s. By 1969 state official Rodney Barber had designated a ranger to have full-time responsibility for patrolling the alpine zone on Mansfield. This was a radical, path-breaking move, and one pregnant for the future of alpine-area management. During the early 1970s GMC joined forces with the state to put together a small force of "ranger-naturalists"—note the polyglot terminology—to be on top of both Mansfield and Camel's Hump almost all the daylight hours during the hiking season.

The ranger-naturalists provide "low-key on-site educational encounters with the hiking public." Their job is to meet just about every hiking party as it reaches the alpine area, fall into casual, nonthreatening, friendly conversation, and make sure the message is understood: This alpine vegetation is beautiful, but fragile. Please walk on the trail or on rocks. Help preserve this unique alpine community so future generations can enjoy it too.

A key point is that they see their role as educators, not policemen. GMC leader Ken Boyd describes ranger-naturalists as "public relations people, historians, environmentalists, guides, and a friend to all hikers."

The effectiveness of Vermont's ranger-naturalist program has been unmatched among northeastern alpine areas. A University of Vermont expert summed up the results thus:

> Since the inception of this program, the condition of the alpine tundra has improved noticeably. Scars from campfires and camping have healed. Areas that were trampled and

barren of vegetation have again become covered with plants. The ranger-naturalists report that most visitors they approach are eager to cooperate and are appreciative of the effort to politely alert them about the fragileness of the area and the reasons for the regulations.

Today Mount Mansfield's magnificent summit ridge requires fewer physical obstacles than most alpine areas, because the ranger-naturalist is a far more effective inducement to good hiker behavior. The carrot works ever so much better than the stick.

During a comprehensive statewide recreational planning process in 1988, a state task group examined eight categories of "natural areas" in Vermont. Seven of the eight were found to be significantly impacted and to require at least three pages each of recommendations for protective action. Alpine areas alone required but a single page and no recommendations, because, the task group noted:

> An on-going 18-year program of tundra surveillance by summer ranger-naturalists has been effective in controlling visitor impacts and halting loss of tundra in this way.

The statement also credited "interpretive signs and literature" with a useful educational role.

In the Adirondacks, managers have paid Vermont's program the sincerest form of flattery: they've imitated it. Beginning in the summer of 1990, a "Summit Stewards" program was launched through the cooperation of the Adirondack Mountain Club (ADK), The Nature Conservancy, and the state. This program puts young people on the tops of the Adirondacks' most vulnerable summits to meet hikers and talk with them. These stewards, like their counterparts in Vermont, meet with very constructive reactions from the hiking public. "I found everyone very willing to oblige once they were made aware of the problem," reported one of the first year's Summit Stewards.

In the White Mountains, as of the summer of 1992, managers were looking seriously at the effectiveness of direct educational

programs, but in only one small corner of the range had anything
formally been initiated. In the Sandwich Range lie two lovely little
adjacent peaks, mounts Welch and Dickey. Rising to little more
than 2,500 feet, they have no true alpine area. However, both
peaks exhibit extensive open ledges, with islands of fragile vegetation between. The problem of hiker impact on these islands of
vegetation has a lot of similarity to the problems of alpine areas.

Under the leadership of the Sandwich Range Conservation
Association and its dynamic young executive director, Nat
Scrimshaw, a modest attempt to emulate the ranger-naturalist idea
was launched in 1990. The SRCA found the funds for a small trail
crew, then hired one more person than was needed for that crew.
Each day, taking turns, one member of that crew went up Welch
and Dickey to function as as ranger-naturalist, providing low-key
educational encounters with passing hikers.

You can learn something from any venture, whether completely successful or not. SRCA found that their program had
limited effectiveness. The problem seemed to be one of focus on
the part of the participating individuals. It seems universally true
that young people who work full-time on trail restoration and
maintenance develop (a) a perfectly splendid esprit de corps and
sense of accomplishment through hard work, comradeship, and
often literally blood, sweat, and tears—or at least mud, sweat, and
uproarious good fellowship. This is the positive side. It seems to be
almost a law of life, however, that (b) these positive characteristics
become associated with a certain alienation from the hiking public.
The trail crew perceives the passing hikers as generally inexperienced in mountain ways and often as ignorantly contributing to
trail erosion problems. It is next to impossible for a trail crew to
develop its own strong camaraderie and also a friendly respect for
other hikers.

Now, a ranger-naturalist simply cannot be effective unless he
or she starts from a position of genuine respect and fellow feeling
toward other hikers. If there is contempt, it will show. If there is
positive enthusiasm for shared values, that will show too—and
produce true education. In the Sandwich Range it didn't work for

someone to work fulltime for four days in the hard, sweaty, muddy, richly satisfying work of trail repair, and then take one day off to meet the public in the right spirit.

No matter: what SRCA learned is information that it and all other areas can profit by. One of the important developments of the late 1980s—and one we hope will continue throughout the 1990s—has been that managers of alpine areas are exchanging information, learning from each other, adapting programs from one range and applying them with new touches to other areas.

In the summer of 1991 SRCA hired one person specifically for full-time responsibility on the open ledges of Welch and Dickey. They hit it lucky on their choice: an offbeat, nontraditional, extremely observant and shrewd ecologist-teacher by the name of Dick Fortin. Since his arrival, Welch Mountain's little quasialpine areas have become a hotbed of interesting experimental approaches to on-site education and public involvement. Every alpine area in the Northeast will profit from what's being learned on Welch Mountain through the innovative approaches of Scrimshaw, Fortin, and the SRCA.

Elsewhere in the White Mountains, the approach for years has relied primarily on physical obstacles for keeping people on trail. None of the management groups has seen fit to allocate funds for direct educational encounters of the kind that work so well in Vermont and the Adirondacks. In part these managers hypothesize that educational programs are too vulnerable to budget cuts and hence transitory, while passive approaches like scree walls are permanent. We disagree on both counts: as we have found on the Franconia Ridge, scree walls are definitely not permanent unless well maintained by constant repair; meanwhile, educational efforts in the Green Mountains have been continuously funded for 20 years (on lower budgets than those available in the Whites)—and, once set in motion, who knows where the influence of effective education stops, as converted hikers become ongoing evangelists with other hikers, and the message spreads.

On the Franconia Ridge, faced with the lack of full-time educational support, we as trail maintainers tried to improvise what we could in the way of educational approaches. We've had only limited results. The Appalachian Mountain Club runs a "Hut Naturalist" program, under which volunteer naturalists agree to stay overnight at a hut, and in exchange for free meals and lodging they give a walk and talk for other guests after dinner. For our Franconia Ridge work, we often stay at nearby Greenleaf Hut and give such a talk. This is flying under false colors to a degree, since we are not really competent naturalists, but we can tell folks a bit about the ridge, and it gives us a chance to bring up the environmental problems in a strong way. Other hut naturalists do similar talks, most mentioning environmental concerns. The Greenleaf crews have been supportive and stress this environmental message in their numerous contacts with the hiking public, including passing day hikers. In 1990 AMC posted a handsome educational sign in the hut.

This is all on the plus side, but the hut audience is only a small fraction of the total hiking population. How to reach the bulk of the hikers on the Franconia Ridge? We try to work on the trail on weekends, and passing hikers often ask us what we're doing. *They* asked *us*—so they get a full answer. This is also a small fraction of the total, though if we talk with 30 passing hikers each summer, over 10 years that amounts to possibly 300 ridge hikers, and perhaps some of them pass on the message. They always seem receptive, interested, and quick to share the concern for that wonderful environment.

But in the long run, we think these hit-and-miss educational efforts are ineffective compared with the constant presence of Vermont's ranger-naturalists, New York's summit stewards, and the Sandwich Range's version of direct on-site education.

Involvement

Even more lasting in its influence on people's thinking is direct personal involvement. We can give you a few examples that have occurred to us over the years on the Franconia Ridge. Each turned into a work-involved encounter with people: people whose lives, however briefly, touched ours and who made an important contribution, no matter how small, to a unique alpine place; people who, because of the work they contributed, will see this place and every other alpine zone a little differently ever after. We remember:

- A Boy Scout troop (Troop 12 from Hollis, New Hampshire) that helped us build a crucial cairn near the summit of Lafayette. We gave a talk after dinner at Greenleaf Hut one night. After our talk the scout leader from Troop 12 came and asked us if his scouts could do anything to help on the morrow. *Well*, we said, there's one place we know where we have to build a brand-new cairn, a good-sized one. We're going to need a lot of big flat rocks, and they aren't too close by. Sure, they could help! This energetic boy-power enthusiastically roamed out and collected numerous big rocks from far and yon. Then it turned out that the three or four adult leaders were all engineers from those Boston research organizations. These engineers had a wonderful lot of fun erecting a huge monolith of a cairn. They became so absorbed with getting each rock perfectly stable that we finally just could sit back and watch. We told them we'd forever after refer to that as the Troop 12 cairn, and we still do. We also told them that generations of hikers, groping their way off Lafayette in dense fog, would be eternally thankful to see that Troop 12 cairn loom out of the mist.
- Often other hut guests at Greenleaf will ask us what exactly it is we do up there. The next day on the ridge, some of them work along with us for a while, then continue on their way. But as they go along, we'll see them bend over to remove a loose rock from the treadway, or clear a water bar, or restore a cairn. Then we know they got the message too.
- Every summer members of the Greenleaf crew will spend part or all of a day with us. We know several who have adopted trails of their own now. We never cease to be highly impressed with the quality of the young people who sign on to work at the AMC huts. The same goes for the GMC ranger-naturalists and shelter caretakers, and the

ADK Summit Stewards. These young people have shining
ideals and a real sense of values, from which we could all
learn. We are very grateful for their enthusiasm and their
solid support.

- Several times an AT through-hiker has thrown off his or her
heavy pack and helped us rebuild a section of scree wall or
shore up an eroded bank. They tell us they like to give something back to the trail that's given them so much. And then
they go on their way toward Katahdin or Springer. Our
experience is that no single group is so appreciative of trail
work, so willing to help, as the AT through-hikers. You can
spot them a mile off, with their shabby trail-worn look and
their staffs. Sometimes you can smell them a mile off. But they
know how much work goes into keeping up the trail.

- Sometimes we've seen a hiker or two sitting out on the
tundra where they shouldn't be. We go out and strike up
that tactful conversation which ranger-naturalists have
doubtless initiated on other mountaintops. Then when we
come back to the trail, here at the scree wall are four or five
others waiting for us with questions: Which did you say was
the really rare plant? What's the one with the big yellow
flower? What do you do to protect them? How often do you
come up here? So a little classroom situation suddenly takes
shape, and we almost want to thank that fellow who strayed
out on the tundra and got us started in the first place.
When everyone leaves, we see them bending over to
replace misplaced rocks on the scree wall or on a cairn.
They're involved.

- Most of these are one-shot assists, of course. But some come
to stay. Several of our hiking friends saw what we were
doing and how rewarding the work was, so they decided to
get a piece of the action. So they adopted adjacent trail
sections, and we all get together twice in the spring and
once in the fall to work together on whatever most needs
work. The rest of the year we work as individuals. We call
ourselves the West End Trail Tenders. We say that the
acronym stands for the kind of weather we're usually
working in.

• Those innovative folk in the Sandwich Range, who we
were telling you about a couple of pages back, have found a
neat way of involving people. They found they had a
critical shortage of rock to make scree walls for their islands
of vegetation on Mount Welch. They also observed an
abundant surplus of rocks lower down the mountain.
Putting two and two together, they began lugging rocks up,
a couple at a time. Soon finding this slow work, they
assembled little piles of rock along the trail and placed a
sign inviting hikers to join in bringing the needed rock,
with brief explanation of the intended purpose. Now
passing hikers carry lots of rock up—and you can be sure
that anyone who has added significant weight to his uphill
load is going to pay close attention to the message. That's
involvement.

Everyone a Steward

The point of all this involvement is not so much the physical work
that gets done, though surely that's a splendid contribution in its
own right. The main point is the educational value for those who
become involved. Involvement guarantees a better understanding
and deeper commitment. Furthermore, every one of those involved
individuals becomes a Typhoid Mary, spreading the virus of alpine
stewardship to all their hiking friends from then on. Who knows
how far the waves roll?

Saga 3:
Making Two Blades of Grass to Grow

Whoever could make two ears of corn or two blades of grass to grow upon a spot of ground where only one grew before, would deserve better of mankind, and do more essential service to his country, than the whole race of politicians put together.

JONATHAN SWIFT, *GULLIVER'S TRAVELS*

With education and adequate physical measures for keeping hikers on trail, impacted alpine areas begin to recover. Some tundra plants grow back vigorously given just half a chance. The spunky little mountain sandwort—the unsinkable Molly Brown of the alpine world—is ready to colonize anyplace anytime: bags packed and ready to move in as soon as you hand it the key.

However, much of the tundra vegetative community is a lot more shy, a lot slower to recover even after the threat of hiker trampling has been removed. This painfully slow recovery is a very good reason to try to prevent hiker impact *before* it happens. But it is also a reason to consider whether there is anything we can do to give the natural recovery process a boost.

Reseeding on Adirondacks' Summits

Direct action to accelerate natural recovery was undertaken more than 20 years ago by a remarkably far-sighted, creative, and aggressive Adirondacks forester, Edwin H. Ketchledge. From his position as professor at a state university, and working closely with both the responsible public agency and leading area hiking clubs, Dr. Ketchledge worked out a program for treating impacted alpine areas with lime, fertilizer, and lower-elevation grasses. The objective is for the grasses to take hold for about two or three years, after which they die, being totally unsuited to long-term survival in such a harsh environment. During those brief couple of years, however, they provide a strong cover, shelter from the wind, a trap for precipitation droplets, and more fertile soil, so that the alpine species will come back more vigorously. In the ideal situation, as the low-elevation grasses die back, a much, much stronger resurgence of summit vegetation will be observed.

Beginning with a variety of experiments on the summit of Mount Dix, Dr. Ketchledge and his professional associates worked out the formula that seemed to produce best results, a mix of Kentucky bluegrass and red fescue, together with lime and fertilizer. After the initial Dix experiment, Dr. Ketchledge moved his efforts to such trampled summits as Algonquin, Wright, and the highest of all, Marcy. Reseeding was accompanied by delineation of one track for hikers, stepping-stones through wet or mucky areas, physical obstacles designed to discourage getting off the trail, and educational signs. The energetic personpower of the Forty-Sixers, those indefatigable peakbaggers described in chapter 12, was enlisted to help carry up, over the years, hundreds of pounds of grass seed, lime, and fertilizer; to prepare the trail; and to reseed impacted areas. In the 20 years between 1971 and 1991 Dr. Ketchledge estimated that 700 people were involved at one time or another.

These labors have had significant success in accelerating restoration of the Adirondacks' alpine summits. Walk the summit ridge of Algonquin, Boundary, and Iroquois and see what it looks like now. Ketchledge has a slide show, which he will give anytime more than three people assemble at a water cooler (this man is, by instinct, equally measured, one-third scientist, one-third gardener, and one-third circus-tent evangelist), and which shows the before and after pictures for a number of tundra plots. It is a heartening thing to see the extraordinary recovery of some of those reseeded areas. In the words of Dr. Ketchledge at that Alpine Managers Gathering we described in chapter 15, such positive action sends "a message of hope" to the alpine zone.

Reseeding on the Franconia Ridge

In the spring of 1988 some officials from the White Mountain National Forest heard a lecture in which Dr. Ketchledge described his results in the Adirondacks. A no-nonsense, let's-do-it district forest ranger elected to launch a similar effort in the White Mountains. He and his staff chose the Franconia Ridge as a place to try. So for several summers now, a team of forest officials and AMC trail adopters (us) have been planting small annual crops of Kentucky bluegrass and red fescue on that high wild ridge. Sounds odd, doesn't it? But it seems to work: within two or three years, areas previously denuded seem to show much faster recovery with the artificial reseeding than without. Initially the introduced grasses spring up, bright green with youthful enthusiasm. But the weather-wracked alpine ridge is no place for valley folk like them. Within a couple of years they're gone. As the bluegrass and fescue wither and disappear, however, a vigorous growth of mountain sandwort, moss, and other native species move in to take up permanent residence. Lasting revegetation by the natives is achieved much quicker than if left to natural processes unaided.

It is important to note this is *not* an effort to interfere with the long-run pattern of vegetation in alpine areas. Alpine ecologists deem it essential not to try to change nature's patterns, or introduce exotic species. In this case, the "introduced" species does not last: it soon dies and is gone forever. All that happens is that the local alpine species then returns more quickly and effectively.

We should acknowledge that a small circle of professional botanists, mainly in New Hampshire, steadfastly resist the idea of reseeding. Their concern is lest introduced grasses take permanent hold and choke out the natives, especially threatened and endangered species. Dr. Ketchledge and others have addressed their concerns and reported no instances of these recovery programs resulting in such mischief. On some summits, notably New York's Whiteface, where human interference has taken such massive steps as road and building construction, Kentucky bluegrass has been known to become a quasipermanent resident. But in the carefully controlled reseeding of Ketchledge in the Adirondacks and of

WMNF on the Franconia Ridge, this has not happened. The concern of the botanists deserves a hearing, but unless adverse evidence is found that has not as yet surfaced, there seems no reason to refrain from active measures to promote recovery. One way to put it is this: no, we should not interfere with the normal community of alpine species; but as hikers we have already interfered, by trampling all over that vegetation. Does that not give us a moral obligation to do what we can now to restore the original community?

Toward the Regreening of the Ridge

If you give us a choice between direct reseeding, physical obstacles, and education, we'd choose...well, let's see...all three. If you do not have the physical obstacles in place and some sort of communication with hikers, reseeding would founder. Physical obstacles are certainly necessary, if only to indicate clearly to even well-informed hikers exactly where the acceptable trail lies. In that harsh environment, some form of reseeding or equivalent approach seems an advantage so as to get recovery moving faster.

But in the long run, education is the key, because an alpine area will be protected best by a hiking public that perceives its unique beauty and fragility, and truly wants to walk softly and wisely in that privileged place above the clouds.

The opportunity for education was never better. Dr. Ketchledge, in pleading for state agency involvement in alpine-areas education, pointed out the unique opportunity:

> The people causing the problem congregate at the site of the damage, which then becomes your classroom to instruct the recreating public in responsible summit stewardship, *if only you, the teacher, appear in the classroom*, there on top of Marcy and Algonquin with your students voluntarily assembled.

The goal should be to have everyone a steward of this lovely landscape. To the maximum extent possible, we want to see every hiker who walks above treeline conscious of the special kind of environment he or she has entered, and, at some level of consciousness, heedful of where to step so as to preserve the resource for future years of hikers.

We put it in terms of future hikers. Maybe some people will want to think of it in terms of the integrity of the alpine areas irrespective of human interests, the right of the mountain to exist on its own terms, a certain respect we owe to the land independent of our selfish enjoyment of it. If something of that spirit could be embraced by those who visit alpine areas, even if only for the duration of their visit to that special world, the mountain environment would be well served.

The goal is to see alpine areas such as the Franconia Ridge green again—restored to their natural splendor of alpine vegetation save for the single track needed to accommodate human enjoyment of its great beauty.

In our view, sometimes we get overly focused on the physical environment of the alpine zone—counting flowers or waxing irate about human impact, as if hikers were the enemy. We must never forget the importance of the alpine experience to the human spirit. A young friend of ours recently began a letter to us with this nicely phrased sentiment:

> I find that I can only last a week or two until I start having withdrawal symptoms to the alpine zone! I all of a sudden, somehow, someway have to get above treeline to be blown around, scramble over rocks and generally just take in the vistas (or clouds) to renew my inner self. So, Kita and I set off for a quick hike up to Glen Boulder as a storm front moved in—from sunny blue skies and trilliums to the big boulder amidst darkening skies, snow flakes, and diapensia. We even managed to see a moose and a grouse nest filled with eight eggs!

It is that kind of inspiration for the human spirit that we must protect fully as much as we protect the purely physical environment. Of course, the spiritual side cannot exist without preserving the physical. What we are saying is that it would be a hollow victory to preserve the physical at the expense of hikers' access to that spiritual experience.

Here is the essence of today's mountain problem. How can we reconcile heavy recreational use with preservation of a fragile natural environment? If hiking traffic can be encouraged to give the alpine vegetation a chance, we can eat our cake and still have it: we can continue to enjoy that magnificent Franconia Ridge and other glorious alpine areas, yet hand that precious privilege on to future generations preserved or even enhanced. We can show genuine respect for the mountain world.

But it won't happen unless the hiking community under-stands and supports the need. And it won't happen unless trail workers put in a lot of hours and creativity, both on physical measures and on improving the hiking public's understanding of the problem. It will take a lot of hard work and a lot of creative communication. We won't find a way to preserve the fragile alpine environment unless that sense of stewardship catches hold.

As Dr. Seuss's Lorax warns, the key word is: UNLESS!

17

Rock Climbers and Their Environment, 1970

*There used to be so few climbers that it didn't matter
where one drove a piton, there wasn't a worry about
demolishing the rock. Now things are different. There are
so many of us, and there will be more. A simple equation
exists between freedom and numbers: The more people,
the less freedom. If we are to retain the beauties of the
sport, the fine edge, the challenge, we must consider our
style of climbing; and if we are not to mutilate and
destroy the routes, we must eliminate the heavy-handed
use of pitons and bolts.*

ROYAL ROBBINS, *BASIC ROCKCRAFT*

YOU MAY NEVER want to go near the mad sport of rock climbing. That would be very sensible. There are easy ways up every
mountain in the East but one (the south summit of Seneca Rock in
West Virginia), so why bother with the technical difficulties,
muscle strain, and abject terror that are involved in rock climbing?

The story that follows is not intended to alter one iota your very rational decision. The reason we relate it is because we're talking here in this series of chapters about something called stewardship. And we know of no more inspiring example than what happened in the sport of rock climbing roughly 20 to 25 years before the publication of this edition of this book. There, especially at the cliffs of New York's Shawangunks, a strange and unlikely collection of outdoor recreationists (a) perceived the impact they were having on the fragile environment around them; (b) set about to change their ways so as to protect that environment; and (c) very largely succeeded through group consensus, peer pressure, and pure volunteerism, with no regulations, restrictions, or government action of any kind.

Rock Climbing

First, a word about what technical rock climbing involves, because an understanding of one or two points is essential to appreciating this story.

The rock climber, contrary to what a lot of people think, doesn't climb the rope. (Rock climbers climb rock, rope climbers climb rope.) He or she ascends the cliff by using whatever cracks, tiny ledges, nubbins, or other protrusions in the rock that may afford handholds or footholds. The fewer or less well defined these protrusions, the more difficult the climb.

So what's the rope there for? One reason: in case the climber falls. The rope and all of that jangling collection of things that climbers carry over their shoulders or otherwise attach—variously referred to as "hardware," "gear," "the rack," and so forth—are used solely to protect the climber in case of a fall, or at least most of the time these days that's their sole function.

How does this protection system work? The fundamental point is that only one climber moves at a time, and another climber holds the rope in such a way that he can catch and control a fall if it occurs.

For the second person on the rope it's all extremely simple. The leader is up there somewhere, anchored to a ledge (by means that we'll presently describe) and holding the rope. As the second climbs, the leader takes up the slack. If the second falls, he is instantly caught by the leader.

The leader is considerably more exposed. To protect himself, the leader either picks a solid tree growing on a ledge, finds a chockstone wedged in a crack, drives in a piton, or places an artificial chockstone (from the "rack") in a crack, and attaches a snaplink (or carabiner) to this "protection," through which the climber runs the rope. From then on, should he fall, the second person can control the fall through that point of protection. "Leader falls" obviously are longer, more scary, and more risky, since the leader will fall twice the distance he has climbed above his last protection—from his high point down to the protection point and then an equal distance below that—before the rope comes tight.

We trouble you, gentle reader, with all this detail only to point out one fact: the critical importance to the rock climber of this "protection." Without protection the leader would be literally risking his life on every lead, and would be strongly inclined to avoid any difficulty that he wasn't absolutely sure he could handle with complete confidence. But with good protection, new worlds open up of difficult and spectacular routes up incredibly steep and exposed cliffs. If a fall occurs it should have no serious consequences.

Now to the first point of our story: Up until 25 years ago, rock climbers almost universally employed that well-known symbol of their sport: the piton. (Pronounced like "feet-on," not "bite-on.") Pitons were variously shaped pieces of metal that were hammered into cracks in the rock. At the outside end of the piton was a hole through which a carabiner could be attached for securing the rope. Pitons were in universal use by climbers as late as 1969. Every climber carried a hammer and a rack of assorted pitons, varying in size so as to fit the various cracks that the climber might encounter on the cliff.

Where the leader runs into a blank section of rock, or one in which there are no cracks or any other way of driving in a piton or fixing natural protection, he has a new problem. In most such situations, the leader either gulps and climbs carefully until he can get to some place higher where protection is possible; or, if it looks too difficult to risk that, he simply won't climb there—he "backs off," as they say. However, another possibility is to go up to some reasonable stance on that face and then stand there and laboriously drill a bolt hole right into the rock, using a kind of star drill, place a bolt with a hanger in it, and affix the carbiner and rope. Placing bolts was a rare occurrence for most climbers, however. Many leaders climbed for years without ever placing a bolt. The piton was the standard protection used until 1969.

The Advent of Nuts

Slowly, in the late 1960s and especially the early 1970s, an environmental conscience began to hit the rock-climbing community, as an outwash from the environmentalist awakening of these years.

The climbers looked around the areas in which they were climbing. They saw that the paths they trod to get to the base of popular climbs were becoming beaten down, and erosion was starting to take place. They saw that the places they camped were too often littered and unsightly. But most of all they saw that where they were repeatedly driving pitons into the rock and removing them, the cracks were becoming scarred and disfigured. On some popular routes, places that had once taken a ½-inch-wide piton now required a ¾-inch or 1-inch piton, due to the widening of the crack as a result of repeated placements and removals.

The climbers also watched uneasily the growing popularity of their sport. They realized that all of these adverse effects were made much worse by the increasing numbers of climbers at the better cliffs. They sensed that if the sport became a popular fad, the environmental destruction could become a tragedy.

Along about this time, a few climbers came back from England with some gadgets already in use over there, called artificial chockstones or simply "nuts." Instead of banging them into horizontal cracks, you quietly slotted them into vertical cracks. The ideal nut placement is a crack of varying width (as most are)—you slide a nut in where the opening is large enough to take it in, then slide it down inside to a point where the opening is too narrow to let it out. If a fall is exerted on such a nut, it simply drives it farther into the narrow part of the crack, and it may (in the ideal case) be actually more secure than a hammered-in piton. Placing a secure nut, though, especially for those relatively new to the game, was often a bit more difficult than simply banging in a piton, and required a careful eye to the possibilities.

It should not be supposed that the first climbers to use nuts were motivated primarily by environmental concerns. Not at all. The British climbers started to use them to save money, pure and simple. The first nuts were literally machine nuts pocketed by down-at-the-heels Britishers who couldn't afford to (or didn't choose to) buy pitons. Then they began to fabricate nuts especially for climbing.

The two men whom we first encountered using nuts in the northeastern US, Willy Crowther and Chuck Loucks, did so primarily because they were intrigued with the more interesting art of placing nuts, the subtlety of the game as well as its novelty. The rest of us began to imitate them at first because Willy and Chuck were immensely popular climbers, whose style we admired and wished to emulate.

As we began to use nuts increasingly, we began to enjoy a new dimension to our climbing. Because some nut placements were tricky or tenuous, we found ourselves constantly on the lookout for possibilities. This brought us to a more continuous observation of the rock around us, a greater awareness of its qualities and configurations, a closer association with that vertical world of granite or conglomerate.

But in the climate of environmentalist concern that pervaded the years around 1970, it wasn't long before we noticed something else besides the economics and the engineering aesthetics of nuts.

When you slotted a nut and your second removed it, the rock was undefiled. No ugly scar. No hammer damage. No obtrusive banging noise. In a very short time, a number of leading climbers perceived in nuts the key to ending the environmental havoc being wrought by pitons.

By 1971 a full-scale campaign was underway among the more environmentally concerned climbers, both in the popular northeastern climbing areas and throughout the country, to preach the nut ethic. "Clean climbing" was proclaimed as the new order. Pitons were condemned as virtually immoral. Influential climbers began ostentatiously leaving their hammers at the base of the cliff, committing themselves to either finding natural protection or using nuts. Great prestige was accorded to climbers who succeeded in climbing the classic routes "all-nuts"—that is, without using a single piton, either of their own or of those left by preceding parties. If you can't find a way to protect a difficult move cleanly, said the new ethic, don't place a piton—back off and try again another day.

If pitons were frowned on, bolts became even more scorned. Drilling bolt holes was viewed as an offense several times more heinous than driving pitons.

Understand, now, that all of this was a matter of voluntary action and education. There were no enforceable rules in climbing areas, no public regulations affecting the sport (except at a few highly resented parks). Climbers are as individualistic and unregimented a group as you'll find anywhere. They will *not* be told what to do by *anyone*.

And yet, within the space of roughly three years, 1969–72, the nut revolution swept most climbing areas. In 1969 you could walk along the base of any northeastern cliff on a good weekend and hear the ring of hammers on pitons from one end to the other, on every route where there were climbers. By late 1972 the sound of hammered steel was so rare that it attracted considerable attention—and outrage. The British had a contemptuous expression: "A man who would drive a piton into British rock would shoot a fox!" Nuts reigned supreme.

The speed of this revolution, accomplished solely by moral suasion and consensus in a group that would not take orders from anyone, was and remains a miracle. It can only be explained by the intensity and sincerity of the feeling most climbers had for the environment in which they climbed.

In any reaching of consensus, there are bound to be individuals who take a more prominent role than others in articulating the impulse toward the new way of thinking. Within the eastern climbing community the leading force in getting the new ideas across was a most unusual climber named John Stannard. Well known to every climber because of his extraordinary skill at the most difficult climbs, Stannard used his prestige to advance what he most earnestly believed in: the salvation of climbing areas by the transition to "clean climbing" and by climbers accepting the responsibility to be sensitive stewards of the land on which they enjoyed their climbing. Stannard ceaselessly evangelized for the abandonment of pitons, conducted and publicized tests to prove the safety of nuts, started a newsletter to spread the good word, made an effort to climb with as many climbers as possible to show them how it could be done and earn their goodwill, and otherwise set an example of dedication to environmental consciousness that others might sometimes think weird, but that they could not fail to respect—and ultimately to follow.

In the western climbing scene, another influential and astonishing figure was Yvon Chouinard. One of the earliest of the "big wall" climbers at Yosemite Valley, Chouinard started designing pitons back in the old days and built a business that dominated the market. Everyone used Chouinard pitons (as well as Chouinard carabiners, Chouinard hammers, and so on). Then, when the Great Nut Awakening came, Chouinard voluntarily took a leading position in scuttling his own piton business to get everyone to switch over to nuts. Chouinard makes nuts too, of course, but he has never achieved the ascendancy over the nut market that he enjoyed when everyone used pitons. Like Stannard, Chouinard put his money where his heart lay: in fighting for a better climbing environment.

Others, such as Royal Robbins and Galen Rowell, were influential in advancing the new ethic, but the main point is not to single out individuals. The main point is that the overwhelming majority of the heterogeneous and zealously individualistic climbing community embraced the nut revolution and made it work. In the particular climbing area that we were closest to at the time, the Shawangunks, we would think it fair to say that the transition from pitons to nuts would have happened in a remarkably short time anyway, but that without any question the driving pressure of John Stannard's enthusiasm and example was what made it happen so very quickly.

Other Changes in Rock Climbing

There were several other ways in which the climbers' environmental concern showed up.

1. *Absence of litter.* Rock-climbing areas came to contain less litter per number of people than any other outdoor recreation area. Climbers tended to pick up not only their own trash but that of thoughtless nonclimbers. Some climbers, Stannard among them, even prowled the edge of the highway near climbing areas on Sunday mornings, picking up every shred of litter from passing motorists.

2. *Erosion control.* In the early 1970s climbers began to work out arrangements with owners and managers of the lands on which they climbed to provide for stabilizing the paths to and from the cliffs. Climbers volunteered their own labor to work on moving large rocks into eroded trail beds, digging water bars, rerouting access trails where erosion seemed unstoppable, and brushing in the abandoned routes, to give vegetation a chance to grow in. On one weekend at the East's most crowded climbing center, a bunch of climbers decided to stabilize a path to an area known as the "Beginner's Slab." The volunteer crew included four of the country's top dozen climbers, men

who could have no personal interest in a cliff as easy as the Beginner's Slab, but who gave up their own climbing for an afternoon in order to help preserve that particular area.

3. *Discouragement of publicity.* With awakening concern about damage to the rock and to access slopes, climbers began to realize that the fundamental problem was their own growing numbers. There was an expression heard often those days: We don't want to have happen to climbing what happened to downhill skiing. (Once an adventurous sport for only the most hardy, the boom in popularity brought crowded slopes, lift line queues, great expense in both equipment and weekend costs, standard-ization of techniques and style, and an army of fashion-able hangers-on, along with such abominable concepts as "après-ski" and the "ski bunny.") Rock climbers began actively to discourage publicity. Reporters and photogra-phers were treated to the unusual spectacle of people who did not thrill at the prospect of seeing their names and faces in print. The occasional climber who did a beer commercial for television was mildly ostracized by his climbing associates. Inevitably, some outsiders (and even some climbers) criticized this movement as elitist—climbers trying to keep their sport to themselves and shut off outsiders. Their criticism sadly missed the point: climbers deeply felt that the integrity of the sport and the beauty of climbing areas would be ruined for everyone if the scene were transformed into a popular fad.

4. *Rescues.* Whatever the growing cost to the public of searches and rescues for lost or disabled hikers, the rock climbers tried to take care of their own. If a climber did get hurt, as they occasionally did for very obvious reasons, it was the climbers themselves who got him off the cliff, out to a road, and to a hospital. When an accident occurred in a popular climbing area, other climbers would stop the climb they were on and take on the difficult and delicate work of littering an injured person down off the cliff face and out over the rough terrain of the approach.

Very often they didn't even call for a public ambulance at that point. In any crowd of climbers, someone usually had a van (since climbers like to be able to sleep in their cars at trailheads) and would drive the injured to the nearest hospital. In recent years, the self-help effort has been formalized in the popular climbing areas of New Hampshire with the formation of the Mountain Rescue Service, an entirely volunteer group of climbers who are available for all kinds of technical rescues, summer and winter. In many western climbing areas similar groups are on call. At other places the process may not be institutionalized, but it is still remarkably effective. Some climbing clubs schedule weekends devoted to practicing rescue techniques.

5. *Cooperation with related land objectives.* Land managers of 1970 began to find that where climbing impinged on other outdoor programs, climbers could be most cooperative. For example, researchers decided that the habitat on one popular climbing cliff was perfect to attempt the restoration of that most marvelous of endangered bird species, the peregrine falcon. Discreet signs posted at the base of climbing routes that led up by the release site were all it took for climbers to cooperate. During the crucial period for the young birds, climbers stayed off those routes.

In no other field of outdoor activity that we can think of did a group of recreationists so swiftly and so completely live up to the responsibility to safeguard the environment from the adverse effects of its own actions.

In describing these trends, we have seriously erred if we've given you a picture of climbers as stuffy do-gooders, pompously standing up for law and order, motherhood, and the American Way. Good grief, no! Climbers of that day were scruffy, bearded, sloppy, dirty, and foul-mouthed, and their devotion to most of society's laws fell somewhere between that of highway robbers and bank embezzlers.

Highly individualistic, they regarded themselves as alienated from society's strictures, sometimes even conceiving of climbing as a way of achieving a freedom that was denied them elsewhere. Some of them were tolerably well behaved, but others violated social mores at every turn. They changed clothes on the highway, swore in public places, and wound up most Saturday nights drunk or stoned. Furthermore, they smelled.

You wouldn't want them in your living room, but that 1970 generation would take good care of the most fragile of mountain environments. You couldn't trust them with your daughter, but you could trust them with the outdoors, more than any other single group.

We wish the story ended here. Alas, there is an unhappy sequel, which we'll get to later in the book. We wish we could shut our eyes to the sequel and focus only on the story we've described in this chapter.

Why have we told you this story? Because this book is about the new backwoods ethic of concern for protecting the remaining wild places of this country. It is about stewardship for the land. We think hikers and backpackers have made a good beginning toward changing their attitudes and practices in the outdoors, so as to walk more softly over the fragile land. But the hiking trails and camping sites of the backwoods still reveal that we have a long, long way to go. Too much of the time it takes official regulations to save a backwoods environment from destruction, and then we're all the losers anyway for having our freedoms curtailed and for having to confess that we couldn't exercise enough self-discipline to exist without regulations.

But look at what the climbers of 1970 accomplished and gain hope. In three years—just three years!—this band of unreconstructed individualists reached a consensus and changed their ways. Surely in a generation we hikers and backpackers can do the same. The goal is worth the try. It is nothing less than the integrity of the backwoods environment, which we all love so well.

IV

FOUR UNRESOLVED IMPACT ISSUES

Whatsoever things are true, whatsoever things are
honest, whatsoever things are just, whatsoever things
are pure, whatsoever things are lovely, whatsoever
things are of good report; if there be any virtue, and
if there be any praise, think on these things.
PHILIPPIANS 4:8

W E HAVE TOUCHED on many issues in these pages, issues where we have definite opinions. Sometimes we haven't been too tactful. Whether you agreed with what we had to say, we hope you had occasion to think about the issues raised. Whether you go along with our conclusions is not nearly as important as whether you'll think about them. The best backcountry management is based on a similar faith: not a set of absolute rules, but regulations or guidelines intended to attract our attention to an underlying moral imperative, from which we're bound to act wisely in the backcountry.

Now we want to turn to several issues where our own minds are not made up. These are case studies about which everyone involved needs to think more. If your own mind is made up, unmake it. Join us in thinking about it, exchanging views, questioning set answers, looking curiously at alternative solutions.

To have an open mind, however, does not require that it start empty. Indeed, we have no tolerance for that kind of mindless drift of dialogue where no points of reference hold any stability. We must cling to a fundamental set of values about what kind of backcountry we want to preserve. A sense of values steers any useful thought, else it is rudderless and will never know where it is going, will never get anyplace.

So when we raise questions about bushwhacking, about dogs, about rock climbing, about winter camping, we raise these questions against a backdrop of rooted belief in the value of wildness, the value of the integrity of the land, the value of a backcountry alive for people but preserving opportunities for solitude, wonder, mystery, adventure, and genuine risk.

One point we wish to make abundantly clear: we are raising questions in these final four case studies, not asserting answers. Nothing could be wider of the mark than to portray us as opposed to bushwhacking, to dogs coming into the backcountry, to rock climbers finding new routes, or to winter camping. We are in favor of all four activities. But we also think that all four can be carried on in a thoughtless, destructive, and ultimately unacceptable way. We'll go further: we think all four *are* being carried on, sometimes and in some places, in a thoughtless, destructive, and ultimately unacceptable way.

What we're trying to do here is to raise important questions about how each of these activities affects the backcountry environment and the experience of others therein, and thereby to encourage everyone involved to think them through more carefully—and, beyond thought, ultimately to act more responsibly than what we've been seeing.

Think on these things.

Case Study 1:

Low-Impact Bushwhacking

*But the stamping grounds of the lover of wild nature are
yearly growing more restricted. Some day there will be
none left. And then, a valuable species of citizen is going
to grow extinct....A plea for the Natty Bumpos,
before it is too late!*

W. T. HOWELL (WRITING CA. 1910),
THE HUDSON HIGHLANDS

IN THE EARLY 1970s Newfoundland's parkland managers initiated a program for opening hiking trails and encouraging
backcountry recreation. It proved a slow job to cut trails through
the dense northern coniferous forest, so trails opened slowly. At an
early stage, the two of us joined a good friend to do some exploration in an area as yet completely trailless. It took us three days to
fight our way along a fiordlike lakeside and up through incredibly
dense undergrowth to the top of a "mountain" that was something
like 2,400 feet high. We had no way of knowing whether anyone
had ever been there before: perhaps, but it was most improbable
country. We started to gather a few rocks to build a cairn. Then we
stopped to consider. We're immensely enjoying the feeling of being

possibly the first ones ever to set foot on this wonderful summit. Maybe that's an illusion, maybe not—but even if it is, isn't it an illusion well worth preserving? We discarded our rocks at random. Let the next party enjoy the priceless feeling of exploration too.

Ever since, whenever we go bushwhacking, we try to follow that principle: leave no trace of our passing, so that the next party can delude themselves, as we love to delude ourselves, that they're the first humans to pass through that particular piece of wild country. That feeling of exploration and adventure is one of the great joys of bushwhacking.

Bushwhacking? The very name conjures up a picture of undesirable activity: whacking bushes. Much of this book and the writings of many others emphasize the need to respect the rights of bushes and trees and delicate alpine vegetation. Please stay on trail, is the message everyone addresses to travelers above treeline. Whacking or hacking at vegetation is precisely what everyone's being asked to stop.

Yet few people go "bushwhacking" as much as we do in the White Mountains of New Hampshire. Is this a paradox? Are we monstrous hypocrites?

The New Critics

Maybe the trouble comes from the word. To hiking insiders, bushwhacking is really just jargon for off-trail travel. But to many people today the two have grown inseparable and confused. Convinced that off-trail travel involves wholesale destruction of vegetation (whacking of bushes), concerned voices are being raised in indiscriminate opposition to bushwhacking.

"Bushwhacking poses an ecological hazard," declares one AMC letter-to-the-editor writer. "Most hikers I've observed bushwhacking for fun are oblivious to their impact on the environment....It is past time for AMC to put a stop to this deliberately destructive practice."

The bushwhackers' defense is sometimes couched in terms of

safety: if people lose the trail, they need to know how to navigate without it so they can get home safely and not require rescue. That is a pretty thin argument. It seems to concede that off-trail travel is indeed environmentally destructive, but may be necessary in emergencies to save lives.

Other bushwhackers respond more positively and go overboard in stating that there is nothing at all wrong with responsible bushwhacking, and on-trail hiking can be just as damaging to the mountain environment as off-trail hiking, if carried on in a thoughtlessly destructive manner.

It is healthy that this question is being raised and discussed. We believe there are several ramifications that need to be thought through carefully. Perhaps many of us need to reexamine what we do and don't do when we go off-trail.

We find ourselves beginning to question activities we once indulged in without hesitation. Now we're hesitating. In light of the recent questions raised by critics of bushwhacking, we have to wonder whether any of us have thought through this issue clearly.

Positive Values of Off-Trail Adventure

But first: some needed perspective. There clearly are negative effects of some off-trail activity, but it is equally clear to us that other kinds of off-trail activity are not only inoffensive but provide positive values, the worth of which is so great that they should in no way be circumscribed.

Off-trail is unmistakably different from on-trail. The former is not for everyone. The footing is uncertain and treacherous, calling for attention to almost every step. Unpredictably but frequently, the bushes whack back: you can often spot a bushwhacker from the scratched arms and legs, the torn clothing. The density of some vegetation has to be experienced to be believed: many on-trail hikers are skeptical that New England krummholz *can* be penetrated—but it can, as long as you ignore reason and prudence. A veteran off-trail hiker friend of ours confided recently: "The net result of my years of off-trail travel is a much lower impact of me on vegetation than vegetation on me."

In short, bushwhacking doesn't mean people whacking bushes, it means bushes whacking people.

We understand other regions have their peculiar native miseries as well. The summertime insect population finds the denser thickets a great place to thrive, especially because their victims (us bushwhackers) are slowed to a pace that makes it easy to enjoy your meal (if you're a black fly, that is).

Positive values, did we say?

Why do some people persist in such an obviously senseless pursuit? We won't belabor the answer to that one! There is of course the obvious zest in adventure and uncertainty. Then there are the beautiful places you can find off the beaten track. But the richest value is something else. When you travel off-trail, you are perforce compelled to pay much, much closer attention to the forest you're traveling in. You become intimately aware of the changes in vegetation you're passing through. You sense the shape of the mountainside. You perceive a great many signs that speak of a vibrant natural world—dens among rocks, beech trees with the clawmarks of bears, scat of various kinds, a clutch of feathers or fur betokening some recent incident. You never know what you may see, if you keep your eyes open to what's unfolding along your route, which you *have* to do. Some perceptive few may walk trails and see as much, but most of us will see a lot more when we're off-trail.

It is not just that we see certain specific sights. The responsible off-trail traveler is likely to be far more in touch with the wildness of the natural world. That is what gives bushwhacking its ultimate value and raison d'être.

Weighing the Question

Now to return to the down side. To us, the negative test of the validity of off-trail mountain travel is whether it creates an impact

236 FOUR UNRESOLVED IMPACT ISSUES

on either the physical environment or the experience of others, with some attention to the permanent or transitory nature of that impact.

One point should be understood at the outset, and that is that bushwhacking is not a very popular pursuit. For the reasons we've touched on, few people have the slightest urge to leave trails, if it is even a little more difficult to walk. We recall that when we began hiking we considered it almost unthinkable to leave a trail. Most of the populous hiking and backpacking public have a similar reluctance to leave the official pathway. We are speaking of a small minority when we speak of bushwhackers. This is an important point. It is also one that could change, if organized clubs or schools start promoting bushwhacking in a big way, or if some activity catches on that deliberately fosters bushwhacking—like a sudden craze for orienteering all over the place, or a geometric rise in the popularity of peakbagging. If bushwhacking did become a phenomenally popular fad, much of the discussion that follows would be no longer valid.

Everyone involved in the debate should also start by acknowledging a second point: that certain kinds of off-trail travel have an inexcusably destructive effect on the natural world. One obvious example is where some rare or endangered species of flora or fauna is making its last stand. One well-known example these days is the nesting ground of peregrine falcons. Every year in our part of the world wildlife managers identify peregrine nests and post conspicuous yellow signs at specifically targeted trailheads instructing hikers not to leave the marked trails from June through August. No responsible bushwhacker would fail to cooperate under such circumstances.

Another clear-cut case is the one to which chapter 16 was addressed: wandering indiscriminately across alpine areas. A considerable effort by backcountry managers and concerned hikers has gone into propagating the message: don't tread on the fragile alpine vegetation. But in the course of discussing measures for keeping people off the tundra, most of the "policemen" have been careful to say, Please stay on the trail or on the rocks. Note the second half of the message. Some zealots have urged that there should be a categorical imperative: stay on the trail, period. We have always argued, and have been glad to find ourselves with the apparent majority of backcountry managers on this point, that we should not restrict people from wandering on open rock ledges or any terrain where they can rock-hop without treading on vegetation. The narrower view argues that it's simpler and surer to enforce the categorical message: stay on the trail, with no exceptions. We have always felt, not only that this underestimates the capacity of the hiking public to understand the subtler distinctions, but that it is far better to educate people to a broader understanding of what should govern conduct above treeline. If you say stay on the trail *or* on the rocks, you are helping people to understand that the vegetation is what we're trying to protect. We're not out to restrict freedom of movement arbitrarily, but for a very pointed objective: preserving the opportunity of the tundra to survive.

Even where rock-hopping is perfectly possible, however, the responsible hiker must exercise care as to what kind of message his or her actions transmit to casual observers. For example, in our trail work above treeline, we sometimes need to go off-trail to find rocks of the right size and shape for a cairn or a scree wall. When we do, we of course rock-hop all the way. However, we are excruciatingly conscious that other hikers coming along may see us off-trail and wonder what we're doing out there—or may even be tempted to go out where we are to see what's up. We'll often look both ways and wait for a break in the passing traffic before we go fetch our rocks. Or, alternatively, we'll make a deliberate point of initiating a conversation, so as to explain in a low-key way what we're doing and why we had to wander off the side of the trail.

How about below treeline? Is the vegetation less fragile down in the woods? Doesn't ground cover suffer terribly from a passing stream of bushwhackers?

This is a more complicated question. One point should first be understood, one that we raised earlier, in chapter 8. Nature has a remarkable capacity for restoring itself. Where there is sunlight and soil and moisture (as there is abundantly in our Northeast), there is a powerful impulse for the woods to grow, to regenerate, to remain green unless faced with overwhelmingly discouraging factors. The result is that, for the northeastern forest environment, an occasional passing pair of footprints will leave quite literally no trace under most circumstances. The problem above treeline is, first, that the alpine zone is an uncommonly harsh environment for vegetation; and second, that there is too much risk that a great many boots would tread on the same swaths of vegetation unless requested not to. With no natural barrier of trees on either side of the trail, too many people could be tempted to wander.

Impact on the Woods

Below treeline, given nature's instinct for regeneration, a modest level of off-trail travel will have virtually no adverse impact. The next question becomes, Under what circumstances will the frequency of traffic remain low enough to minimize impact? At what point and under what circumstances does off-trail traffic begin to show a destructive effect?

Here it must be acknowledged that, in any well-known hiking country, certain off-trail routes may become popular and begin to show wear. People study maps and discern off-trail lines that are obviously attractive, or the grapevine whispers about such routes: a stream valley not too far from a trail that seems to offer a probable campsite with convenient water; a ridgeline leading to an exposed summit that appears likely to have commanding views; a glacial cirque with an impressive headwall that might be fun to climb. Old logging roads abound, inviting to follow.

In the White Mountains it is not difficult to find a dozen such attractions where, over the years, the volume of off-trail hiking has been sufficient to create a slightly worn track through the forest. Naturally, as a treadway becomes established, others tend to follow it, as an easier alternative to thrashing out a fresh track. After a while, such a route becomes in effect a bootleg trail. It is neither shown on the maps nor described in the guidebooks, but experienced hikers know where these tracks can be followed.

Is this a desirable state of affairs? Are the critics of bush-whacking on sound grounds for deploring the environmental destruction that has occurred? Our first instinct is to concede that, yes, this is not good. If there is no trail in, say, Paradise Gorge, then such unplanned, unsupervised destruction is regrettable.

On reflection, however, having watched such paths evolve in some of our favorite haunts, we have to ask what the alternatives are. One alternative is to legalize and formalize bootleg trails. That is, when backcountry managers see a worn track developing from an obviously high level of off-trail traffic, they could declare it a trail, take measures to guard against trail erosion in the usual ways, and eventually put it on the maps and in the guidebooks. At some level of use and impact, such a course is probably the only sensible one. Still, we would counsel against being too hasty in declaring trails wherever a hint of a worn track appears. Such a policy could speedily open a large number of valleys and ridges that are officially trailless now. Once a trail is officially opened and maintained, the use level will jump far higher than even the most popular off-trail routes now suffer. The track will become much more obvious, the loss of natural vegetation much greater, the sense of wildness much less. Besides, maintaining the existing network of trails strains available resources, and poor maintenance could lead to more environmental damage.

Another alternative would be to try to prevent such off-trail activity completely. Should no one be allowed in Paradise Gorge? Should it be made a punishable offense to be found there? That just doesn't seem right to us. If it is a beautiful natural area, and if the only impact is a single track lightly worn by a low volume of off-trail hikers, is this necessarily bad? We'd answer by saying: well, yes, it's a *little* bad, but not bad enough to outlaw off-trail travel. A better answer, we believe, is compounded of several elements: first, do nothing to advertise Paradise Gorge so as to increase traffic therein; and second, educate the off-trail traveler to try to mini-mize his or her impact. What's involved in the latter? Obviously, don't leave litter of *any* kind. Don't break branches needlessly, and don't break *any* live branches. Try to avoid steeper, obviously vulnerable slopes, such as those covered by moss. If following a stream valley, rock-hop right in the stream to the maximum possible extent (an enjoyable, even exciting pastime anyway, and the consequences of a wet boot in warm weather are trivial—an hour later you won't be able to recall which foot fell in). When you see the very first signs of a single way becoming established, avoid taking that way. Do not assume it is too late to prevent impact. Try to do nothing that adds to that impact.

Unfortunately the present population of off-trail aficionados appears to include a small number who have not harkened to this message. We find some deplorable practices in off-trail locations: semipermanent campsites, litter such as empty food cans, and (worst of all) actual clipping of branches in areas of denser woods. There is an unforgivable arrogance to such actions: an assumption that it's OK for me to have my private campsite, or to maintain my private trail, on publicly owned land. It should be perfectly obvious that such behavior, because it would create widespread havoc if widely adopted, is therefore intolerable. We hope the offenders may read this chapter and think about the implications of their actions.

Another lamentable development is the practice by some bushwhackers of marking their routes by brightly colored plastic tape. This practice should be thoroughly deplored by anyone who values an off-trail experience. New Hampshire's bushwhacker extraordinaire Gene Daniel III has condemned plastic tape for

> confusing the inexperienced and infuriating the experienced with the implied insult from those hikers who think we couldn't find our way without their help, and drawing curses from everyone who had hoped to find a mountain relatively free of signs of human presence.

Like the unauthorized cutting of trails, littering routes with plastic tape is inexcusable.

A different aspect of the problem arises in areas that do not yet show a single discernable track. Many superb off-trail routes exist, some of them taken fairly regularly, where there is as yet no (or virtually no) trace of human traffic. For these areas, we believe there is an urgent need for all bushwhackers to behave responsibly: tread as lightly as possible, avoid taking the same way twice, stay off fragile microenvironments, and of course leave no trace of your passing. With responsible conduct by all bushwhackers, such routes may be enjoyed for years without damage to the forest.

Bushwhacking in winter is a specialized branch of the art. Here the environmental damage, at ground level at least, is far less. Extensive off-trail travel in winter has obvious safety implications, which no one should fail to consider carefully. Wintertime bush-whacking, especially under certain snow conditions, can be unbe-lievably slow—a half mile per hour or considerably slower is not at all atypical in some terrain—so itineraries need to be selected with care. Snowladen branches will relentlessly and remorselessly drench you with snow, stuffing it down between your pack and your back, where of course it melts, so that you are going to get very wet, which at 0°F has further implications that require no elaboration, especially if your long bushwhack brings you out into a strong cold wind above treeline. We repeat: bushwhacking is not for everyone.

Clouds on the Off-Trail Horizon

There are some ominous threats on the horizon, some factors that could jeopardize the validity of presently inoffensive off-trail travel.

One is the growing popularity of publicly advertised programs for teaching people the techniques of off-trail travel. The advocates of such programs doubtless feel that they provide an excellent opportunity to educate new bushwhackers in environmental consciousness and responsible, minimum-impact techniques. We hope that is a strong focus of any workshop or "how-to" session on off-trail hiking. That can be their only justification. Certainly, from the standpoint of environmental impact, any measures that encourage more people to start bushwhacking are indefensible.

More troublesome to our way of thinking is the emergence of
organized programs that systematically, year after year, send large
groups or wave after wave of small groups into trailless areas. We're
speaking of educational programs, whether of secondary schools or
hiking clubs, summer camps or Outward Bound or hosts of imita-
tors. Some of these groups make a concerted effort to minimize
impact—NOLS is a shining example. Others are far less careful.
But all are unquestionably a major presence in the wilderness. It is
inconceivable that even the most careful practitioners can go into
pristine areas year after year, wave after wave, and not have a
grievous impact.

What should the responsible outdoor educator do? At the
least, acknowledge that there's a problem here. At the least, think
about how current practices might be reshaped.

What we fear most is that sooner or later some eager publisher will commission a guidebook to "Fifty Great Bushwhacks."
The damage any such book would inflict is unthinkable. Not just
the irretrievable, inevitable physical impact on pristine valleys and
ridges, but the inexcusable destruction of wildness for everyone and
everything in those places—the ferns, the moss, the bear, the lynx,
and the occasional solitary bushwhacker as well.

Another cause for concern is a matter that Adirondack hikers
have wrestled with for years. What do you do when a specific trail,
peak, or list of trailless peaks, becomes so popular that large numbers of bushwhackers begin to beat not just one but several different "herd paths" to its top? The Adirondacks boast some 46 peaks
originally understood to be 4,000 feet high, and we've earlier
described the Adirondack Forty-Sixers who climb each of the 46.
Roughly a score of the 46 peaks have no official trail to the top.
During the 1960s and 1970s, with rapidly increasing popularity for
climbing the 46, came a proliferating rabbit warren of herd paths,
as significant numbers of bootprints took three or four or six or
seven different ways to the summits from the nearest trails. There
ensued a period of heated debate within the Forty-Sixer organization: should all herd paths be blocked off? should just one be
selected and opened as an official trail? should the organization

disband out of a sense of guilt for encouraging herd paths? should off-trail travel be banned? The issue was eventually resolved by picking one herd path and attempting to encourage its use and to maintain it as an unofficial route (but still not a designated trail), while simultaneously adopting a broadly conceived program of environmental conservation work as the principal focus of the Forty-Sixers' organization. These "trailless" peaks are still officially trailless, but everyone is encouraged to take the dominant herd path.

A similar situation now threatens a long list of New England peaks because of the popularity of peakbagging. All of New England's 4,000-footers have maintained trails. As hundreds of hikers have completed the 4,000-foot list, however, many have moved on to lists of the 100 highest in each state, or to all of the 3,000-footers. As a result, many once-little-visited peaks now are the objectives of a growing army of bushwhackers.

Toward a Bushwhacker's Code of Conduct

Before too much damage is done to all these nice little peaks, there is need for a code of conduct to be more widely adopted for off-trail travel. We've already touched on many points:

1. Do not leave litter of any kind. This stricture especially applies to the strong temptation to mark the route with bits of plastic tape. Yes, that makes it easier for the next party to reach the top or to make a return trip in winter. But isn't difficulty and challenge and mystery supposed to be part of the fun? No litter means *no* litter.
2. When selecting an itinerary, think about the kind of terrain it traverses. Some microenvironments can stand a small amount of traffic without damage, others are frightfully vulnerable. If you find yourself in a delicate spagnum bog, redirect your course if you can; and certainly reconsider any plans you may have had to bring a party of friends that way next month.

3. Keep your party small. Two or three can go up a trackless slope more or less unnoticed. It is highly doubtful whether a party of 15 or 20 could ever fail to leave a tragic swath of destruction in its wake. NOLS's low-impact instructions advocate a maximum party of four to six on bushwhacks.

4. Do not build cairns to denote turns in the route, or even on the summit. Leave the woods as fresh-looking as you found them.

5. Don't break branches needlessly, and don't break any live branches if you can possibly help it.

6. Avoid stepping on especially fragile soils, mosses, or unstable rocky surfaces—or at least minimize such measures.

7. Where a fragile area must be crossed, everyone spread out and cross carefully in different places...

8. ...unless a single worn track has already been established; in which case, everyone stick to that track.

9. Where it's an option, rock-hop along a stream bed, stepping where the high water keeps vegetation from growing anyway.

10. If returning a second time to an unmarked area, choose a slightly different route.

11. If you begin to see the first signs of a worn track, not yet clearly established, try to avoid contributing to any further wear yourself. Go a different way. Throw a dead branch or two to cover the evidence of others' thought-lessness.

12. If your objective is to get off the beaten track, then for heaven's sake don't beat your own track. It makes no sense. Every time we come across a plainly marked track off the regular trail, our principal reaction is puzzlement. Here went someone who valued getting away from the trails of others; why on earth would such a person then make his own track? So, at the very least, never, *never* commit the arrogance of making a new trail in a presently wild place.

13. Use restraint in propagating news about your route. Let others find their own way. Don't spoil their adventure, entirely apart from dispersing environmental impact.
14. Don't be overly preoccupied with this list of guidelines or any other formal itemized list. Rather, think hard about the underlying objective: to leave the wild land inviolate, or at least to minimize human impact. Understanding the problem in its general terms will be a far better guide to conduct than any itemized list of rules.
15. While you're at it, come up with a better name for all this other than *bushwhacking*. Can anyone suggest a catchy alternative with the right message?

Case Study 2:

Man's Best Friend— or Menace to Wilderness?

Love me, love my dog.
JOHN HEYWOOD (1497–1580)

THINK OF YOUR favorite wilderness camping spot: a sparkling lake set among rugged mountains or a wooded glade where you can pitch your tent on a quiet carpet of pine needles. Now introduce a dog into that idyllic picture. What's your reaction?

Some backpackers will conjure up an image of their favorite shaggy friend and recall with inestimable pleasure days of trailside companionship. But other hikers will snort with disgust at such a thought. To them dogs mean harassment, noise, pollution, and disruption of wildlife—a domestic creature jarringly out of place in the backcountry. And they will condemn the dog's owners, too, for their lack of consideration and insensitivity to a wilderness experience.

Both sides are slightly myopic in their views (the other person's opinion is always out of focus), and with increasing numbers of people in the woods, confrontations between dogs, dog lovers, and dog opponents are growing more frequent—and more provoking. Backs are up (to turn a canine phrase), and land managers, who write and administer the regulations controlling dogs in wilderness, react by instinct to the loudest voices. Some parks prohibit dogs or require leashes at all times; some limit dogs' freedom around crowded areas; others have no restrictions. An objective look at the arguments is needed to formulate rational rules of conduct and regulation for dogs—and for their owners and detractors.

Tradition honors the outdoorsman and his dog; popular culture enshrines Buck in *Call of the Wild* and King, Sergeant Preston of the Yukon's faithful dog. The ranks of those who have marched the Appalachian Trail from end to end include several dogs. One pooch has climbed Mount Robson, the difficult summit in the Canadian Rockies that has thwarted many people. Dogs often hike across Alaska's tundra. The authors' dog climbed all of the White Mountains' summits over 4,000 feet—not once but three times.

To owners of such splendid hiking companions, restrictions on dogs in the backcountry appear unnecessary and burdensome, in conflict with the freedom we all associate with backcountry experiences. We go to the woods and hills to get away from onerous restraints.

As Zane Smith of the US Forest Service put it, "One of the greater values of a national forest recreation experience is the absence of regimentation....Strict control measures are warranted only if other means fail to keep a situation within acceptable limits."

Responsible dog owners reject the notion that all dogs should be banned because a few dogs are a menace. Many argue that some children are as disagreeable as dogs—noisy, intrusive, and harassing—but we don't restrict kids in the woods.

Writing in the *Trail Walker*, the New York–New Jersey Trail Conference's official organ, A. C. Van der Kas pleads: "I am a 70-year-old hiker, and my only companion on the trails is my dog, who loves hiking. Why should I be denied my companion and my dog his joy of hiking?"

To such hikers dogs can be the finest of outdoor companions, sharing the pleasures of the walk without arguing over which trail to take or how far to go. Fresh air, especially in cooler seasons, puts a dog in a superb frame of mind. He or she bounds along, tail high and wagging. At evening the dog sticks close to camp, enjoying the companionship of his or her tired master.

Backcountry recreation can be as beneficial to the canine as to the human hiker. Veterinarians report both physical and spiritual gains. Dogs who get regular exercise have fewer heart problems and joint problems, reports a Colorado vet, Randa MacMillan, who goes on to comment on how good this is for dogs' mental condition: "Too many of our pets spend their time in a privacy fence."

If you watch a dog on the trail closely, you will notice that he observes his surroundings very differently from the way a person does. In fact, were you able to ask a dog what he experienced on a 10-mile hike, you would get an entirely different account from his master's report. We see panoramic views, birds, and trees overhead, an immensely complex visual impression; we hear birds, rushing streams, and rustling leaves; we occasionally smell some strong scent such as moist earth under a stand of hemlock.

The dog, coming back from the same hike, would report different observations, perhaps more complex and extensive. His visual impressions would have been more limited than his master's—no panoramic or overhead views. His ears heard what ours did and a bit more. But what a rich and wonderful world of smells he experienced! Furthermore, while most of us notice only the present state of things, the dog's nose records recent history: when a deer or rabbit passed by, what it did, where it came from and where it was going. Dogs' observations have a dimension of time that ours largely lack.

Despite this idyllic picture of dogs and masters in the backcountry, many backpackers object strenuously to canines in the outdoors on several counts:

    1. *Dogs harass wildlife.* Many dogs chase squirrels and rabbits and large game. At its worst, this fault extends to free-

running dogs in winter chasing down and slaughtering
deer. And some hikers complain that even well-disci-
plined dogs scare off wildlife by their mere presence.

2. *Dogs harass other hikers.* Many large, strong dogs, whose
owners are proud of their rugged image, are aggressive if
not dangerous when encountered unexpectedly. Even if
they don't bite, large, aggressive dogs can make other
hikers nervous. Families with young children can be
especially irritated when they meet a large or noisy dog
that is not carefully controlled by his owner.

3. *Dogs are noisy.* The peace and quiet of the woods can be
as rudely shattered by the yapping of a nervous pooch as
by a loud hiking party, trail bike, helicopter, or snowmo-
bile. The evening calm of a campsite can be ruined by a
dog whose owner permits barking to continue unchecked.

4. *Dogs steal food.* It's not safe to leave your lunch or dinner
unattended if there's a hungry dog around—and all
hiking dogs are hungry. Again, children can easily be
victimized by the uncontrolled dog that finds a sandwich
held at nose level.

5. *Dogs foul the trail and the campsite.* They also water the
corners of tents—and once one leaves his mark, it's
obligatory for all other males to mark the same spot.

6. *Dogs fight other dogs.* One of the rudest interruptions of
the serenity of the outdoors occurs when male dog meets
male dog on the trail. Anyone who has been in or near
the center of a dogfight knows how unnerving it is to pull
apart a pair (or more) of snarling, slashing champions of
canine virility.

7. *Dogs harass horses.* In many western backcountry areas,
horseback riders are frequent trail users. Land managers
report increasing complaints involving dogs scaring
horses.

8. *Dogs can be mistreated in the backcountry.* Some owners fail
to realize how much a dog can suffer from heat exhaus-
tion over long stretches of waterless trail. Counsels one
experienced veterinarian: "Get your dog in condition
before going too far or too hard." And park officials report

that dogs have been injured or killed in matches with bears, deer, mountain lions, snakes, scorpions, and spiders.

One annoyed state park official summed up a common view of antidog wilderness users: "It is selfish on the part of the pet owner, inconsiderate to other people, and unfair to the animal itself."

Such an indictment, perhaps too mildly expressed to suit the most ardent antidog backpacker, will strike the dog owner as grossly unfair. A well-behaved, responsibly controlled pet does none of these things, the prodog hiker insists. It's not right to condemn the entire species because of the faults of a few—or, more likely, the irresponsibility of their too-casual owners.

Some argue that dogs need not be regarded as a threat to wildlife for at least three reasons. First, a responsible owner will restrain a dog from bothering other creatures. Second, even when a dog tries to give chase, his domestic upbringing has left him incompetent to catch much more than a few ticks. And finally, the idea that a domestic dog will be the first predator to appear in the life of a wilderness creature is absurd—all nature abounds with predator-prey hierarchies, and an occasional dog adds little to the perils of everyday life for wild creatures, which are constantly eluding natural enemies.

True, most dogs are not a problem, but if all dogs run loose on the trails, how can the errant few be controlled?

Most national parks prohibit dogs on backcountry hiking trails. National Park Service regulations require that any pet in any park be leashed or physically restrained, and they give authority to individual park superintendents to prohibit pets in specific areas. For many parks this means that a leashed dog is acceptable in roadside campgrounds but may not be taken on backcountry trails. To find out whether your dog is allowed on trails in a particular park, write to the park's superintendent. You will find that most of the popular parks prohibit dogs from the backcountry.

National forests are less restrictive. At developed recreational sites leashes may be required. But on the backcountry trails of most

national forests, no general restrictive policy applies, and backpackers with dogs have more opportunities than in national parks.
Again, for any specific area, you should consult local regulations.

Regulations in state parks vary, but most allow dogs only if
leashed. In general, parks subject to intense hiking pressure have
invoked more stringent restrictions on pets. California state parks
flatly prohibit dogs on backcountry trails. Many states in the
crowded Northeast and Northwest—New Hampshire and Washington, for example—require a leash on dogs even on remote trails.
On the other hand, in Colorado dogs are generally allowed to run
loose if they are under voice control, and in Alaska there is usually
no restriction. There park officials recognize dogs as useful hiking
companions for protection against bears and for pulling sleds in
winter.

With national forests, many state parks, and countless pri-
vately owned recreational lands still open to hiking with dogs, it is
difficult to reconcile the conflicting interests of all parties involved: the rights of the harassed hiker, who feels his enjoyment of
the woods is rudely jolted whenever a dog yaps in his presence; the
privacy of wildlife, which see dogs as an ancestral predator; the
convenience of park managers, for whom dog controversies are a
headache; the rights of the dog owner who keeps pets well trained
and well disciplined; the principle of minimum regimentation of
wilderness activities; and the rights, after all, of the dog, which
loves the smells and sounds of the outdoors.

Short of prohibiting dogs from wild lands, what can be done
to improve the experience of all concerned? The answer lies very
much in the hands of dog owners, who must behave responsibly
and observe a code of ethics for dogs in the backcountry.

Here are ten points:

1. Never let your dog chase wildlife.
2. Keep your dog close to you when other hikers approach.
   If they are nervous or if your dog is aggressive, grab your
   dog by the collar or attach a leash, even if you know he
   won't bite. The other hikers don't know that.
3. Be especially watchful of your dog when small children

are around. Even the friendliest dog, if unfamiliar, can be terrifying to a child.

4. Keep your dog quiet. In the wilds most people regard barking as an unforgivable intrusion, and there's nothing more annoying than an owner who does nothing about a continually barking dog. If you can't keep your dog from barking, leave him at home.

5. Keep your dog away from all food.

6. Keep him out of all sources of potable water. When you're at a spring, make sure he drinks from the runoff and not from the spring itself.

7. Don't let him foul the trail. If he does, flick the droppings off the trail with a stick or piece of bark. Watch his toilet habits around campsites. The animal has to go some-where, but use common sense and be considerate.

8. If another dog comes along, restrain your dog and ask the other owner to do the same.

9. If horses come by, hold your dog.

10. Use common sense and courtesy.

As we have mentioned, many people want to see dogs prohibited from trails; many parks already restrict them. Responsible behavior is the best insurance that you and your dog will enjoy future hikes together.

Now, for all you dog haters: goodwill and consideration of others can go far to reduce unpleasant confrontations and increase everyone's pleasure of the great outdoors—everyone, including man's best friend.

Here is a code of ethics for dog haters:

1. Show friendliness toward the dog and its owner. Hostile behavior by dogs is often touched off by subtle displays of fear in people.

2. Exert reasonable prudence in keeping food inside packs or out of reach of hungry canines.

3. Be tolerant of a fellow creature's enjoyment of the outdoors.

4. Refrain from complaining to authorities or asking for restrictions on dogs. Remember that increased regimentation of activities in the backcountry is a burden on everyone who enjoys the freedom of the wilds.

Case Study 3:

Rock Climbers and Their Environment, 1990

*In the tumult of civil discord the laws of society lose their
force, and their place is seldom supplied by those of
humanity. The ardor of contention, the pride of victory,
the despair of success, the memory of past injuries, and
the fear of future dangers, all contribute to inflame the
mind, and to silence the voice of pity.*

EDWARD GIBBON,
THE DECLINE AND FALL OF THE ROMAN EMPIRE

IN LOW-IMPACT CAMPING, trail tending, and alpine-area
management, we read encouraging signs of a growing sense of
stewardship for wildness. We'd like to report good news on every
front, but no such luck. Let us turn to an area of outdoor recreation
where we regret to point out retrogression. In chapter 17 we
documented the story of rock climbers responding to an environmental crisis on the cliffs a quarter century ago. We painted a
picture of an eccentric, rough-edged society of cliff rats, whose

shabby exterior concealed a crusading zeal for environmental protection.

We recall that era of rock climbing now as a golden age. Not only did climbers advance the frontiers of difficulty in their arcane airborne gymnastics, but they also simultaneously elevated their ethical code. And all that time the cliffs were an upbeat, cheerful, magical place to be.

Those were sunny days to be young and a Shawangunks climber.

The New Breed

But something happened during the 1980s. The climbing population grew, changed, and grew again. New faces brought new attitudes.

Climbers began to dwell more on their own personal absorption with the difficulty of climbing and less on the lovely physical environment in which climbing took place. One of the leading climbers of the new breed confessed frankly: "I don't climb for the thrill of [being in] nature." The beauty of climbing areas, she asserted, "does nothing for me." Purely difficult moves had become everything, the surrounding environment nothing. Climbing moved subtly from a wilderness adventure to a gymnastic exercise.

The change was manifest in many ways. Climbers were increasingly fascinated with specialized equipment—belay devices, rappel devices, sit-harnesses, increasingly sophisticated protection devices. An evolving wardrobe became fashionable, featuring blaring colors and garish designs, focusing attention on the climber as a vivid individual separate from nature rather than someone seeking to become part of a wilderness environment.

The technical difficulty of the climbing became all-absorbing: each individual strove to advance the rating at which he or she could perform. To this end, physical fitness became a preoccupation: climbers trained all week, spending hours in the gym, employing specialized machines and devices to promote the development of specific muscle groups. Indoor climbing walls developed first as practice for the real thing, but gradually became the principal arena for some devotees.

At the cutting edge of the sport, the best young climbers worked with fanatical zeal to earn their 15 minutes of fame. The advance in difficulty of what was climbed was incredible. The competitive aspect of top-rank climbing loomed larger, and finally blossomed into an overt system of organized competitions, mostly staged at indoor climbing walls, with live audiences, formal rules and procedures, and intense rivalry, much of it allied to national allegiance in the manner of the Olympic games.

Meanwhile, back at the cliffs, it was a changed scene. The environmental stewardship that had spawned the nut revolution of 1969–72 had left a permanent grip on the values of some climbers. But now the enthusiasm of the new generation, and especially their zeal for mastering greater levels of difficulty, led many new faces to spurn the old ways. The ethic of not damaging the cliffs was perceived as standing in the way of climbing harder routes. Some bold new lines could not be protected by nuts, so the new generation wanted to pound bolts directly into the rock. The perfection of lightweight drilling machines reduced the time and effort needed for placing a bolt from about 30 minutes to about 30 seconds—a temptation too hard to resist. Some new lines could be opened up by chopping down a tree or two to clear the way (or to let in sunlight to dry an area otherwise usually wet). Other lines could be completed only by chipping a hold or two at one critical point.

These tactics were embraced by some of the new breed, and as hotly repulsed by those who clung to the older values, creating bitter controversies and angry emotions. But often the old guard seemed not really as concerned about the integrity of the cliffs as transparently motivated by a desire to elevate their own style and standard of climbing by condemning the new tactics. Publicized debates over climbing ethics degenerated into such shouting matches that one participant lamented:

> Climbing "ethics" are such a mess, such a fraud, that they can be used to make bad people feel good about doing almost

anything. Each such person formulates climbing "ethics" so as to justify what he wants to do and to prevent other people from doing anything different.

"Bolt wars" broke out, in which some young hotshot would bolt a blank section of cliff on one day, some enraged traditionalist would "chop" the bolts off the cliff on the next day, and the new breed would retaliate with further bolting, or perhaps a spate of tree cutting or hold chipping. The letters columns of climbing magazines became drenched in sarcastic bile, each side striving to outdo the other's invective. Fist fights occasionally erupted at the base of climbs.

While the controversies over climbing ethics and style attracted hot attention, less noticed was a decline in environmental awareness on all sides. To a climbing generation that spent much of its time in gymnasiums and on artificial climbing walls, the outdoors surroundings of a cliff were almost irrelevant. The new breed seemed not to notice their impact on trail erosion or even litter. Both the cliffs and the ground below were strewn with powdered gymnastic chalk, which dried sweaty hands, making it possible to grip tiny or poorly defined holds.

Climbers versus Land Managers

Not surprisingly, the new tactics brought climbers into conflict with land owners and managers. National Park Service officials expressed concern over indiscriminate bolting at such national parks and monuments as Joshua Tree (California), City of Rocks (Idaho), and Rocky Mountain National Park (Colorado). At several parks, officials instituted limits on bolting, amid howls of protest from climbers. The US Forest Service sought to limit human intrusions in designated wilderness areas by banning bolts at one popular Arizona rock-climbing area and limiting overcrowding on well-known mountains. The National Park Service outlawed power drills in Yosemite. The city of Boulder, Colorado, where there are literally 1,000 rock-climbing routes, undertook to

limit the use of gymnastic chalk as well as bolting. Wildlife managers placed seasonal limitations on climbing in some areas to protect
endangered species such as peregrine falcons, who like to nest on
cliffs. Other wildlands managers declared some cliffs off-limits
because of climber impact on rare plants.

The response of the climbing community has been aggressive
in pursuit of its own self-interest and often confrontational in style.
"Climbers must assure that climbing is protected through its
inclusion in management plans according to the way climbers want
climbing to take place," trumpeted Climbing magazine's "Access"
column. The column (which became a regular feature devoted to
reporting "threats" to climbing areas and marshaling political
action by climbers) as well as an "access fund" set up initially by
the American Alpine Club and later shifted to independent status,
reflected the climbers' response to any limitations on their "rights."
The focus of that response was fully and frankly defense of self-
interest.

The environmental effects of climbing seemed of little
concern to the new generation of climbers. The only thing that
mattered was their own unlimited license to continue indulging
their desire to climb whenever and wherever they wished. Bolting
was called "freedom of expression." Where climbers accepted
restraint it always seemed only a political concession, never
because climbers really wished to protect the integrity of the
natural surroundings in which they cavorted. Where they agreed to
limit bolting or other environmentally destructive acts, it seemed
always as a way of forestalling more restrictive actions by public
officials or landowners.

In an editorial entitled "Uncle Sam Raises His Eyebrows,"
Climbing magazine warned the climbing community of the position
they were drifting into:

> We're often viewed by land managers as unruly children in
> need of discipline, or worse, as pernicious vandals to be
> punished.

> The days of climbers voluntarily or even eagerly seeking to

preserve the beauty of climbing areas, for the land's sake, seemed ended. Dolefully one climber observed: "I see an insidious disregard for the wilderness ethic on the rise in our sport." Lamented another:

> We, as climbers, consider the rocks our personal domain. We talk about the rock in the extremely limited context of climbing as if climbers are the only ones who care about, or are affected by the rocks and crags we ply. We are short-sighted, isolated, egotistical and inconsiderate. It's about time we all wake up and start thinking about climbing and the rocks in terms of the big picture....

> "Consensus" among climbers is hardly consensus among open space users—that is, those who appreciate the rocks and surrounding areas for reasons other than climbing. We have no right to impact their enjoyment, regardless of whether it's derived from hiking, looking, bird watching, or whatever, just because we climb and they don't. We had better wake up to this fact and learn to coexist with our fellow outdoorsmen, lest we evoke their collective ire.

When National Park Service officials distributed a questionnaire as one means to help assess "appropriate" climbing use in the City of Rocks Natural Preserve, some climbers called the questionnaire a "threat," charged it was "calculated to elicit predetermined responses," and sarcastically termed the NPS preserve "City of Locks." Elsewhere, land managers' restrictions on bolting were referred to as moves "to criminalize bolting." Moves to protect endangered wildlife or plants were reported not under the heading of saving the climbing environment but under the heading of restricting "access"—a threat to climbers' freedoms. That was true all over the country.

Meanwhile, back at the Shawangunks, the once-close spirit of cooperation between the climbers and land managers went through a dreary period characterized by a mood of mutual distrust and defamation. The climbers circulated rumors that the land managers were anticlimbing, that their real goal was to abolish climbing from the cliffs. In turn the managers ceased to involve the climbers in work on the land and accused them, in print, of environmental apathy. The result was not pretty, either in the physical look of the Gunks or in the spirit among the climbers there. Commented one climber who remembered the old days and lamented the new: "A respect for nature and a fundamental environmental ethic is missing here."

This account has emphasized the dominant negative trend, probably more than is strictly necessary. There are exceptions to the trend, encouraging instances of climbers and land managers working together harmoniously for the good of the cliffs. One faction of Gunks climbers that had been most hostile toward the Mohonk Preserve more recently canceled a climbing weekend elsewhere in order to urge its members to come to the Shawangunks for the purpose of litter pickup and trail stabilization. The beginnings of an effective dialogue between climbers and national park officials can be noted elsewhere. We applaud such encouraging symptoms of a return to the old cliff ethic.

But so far these are exceptions. All too much of the climbing community remains single-mindedly pursuing its own narrow self-interest, bent on asserting its rights to self-indulgence at the expense of the environment. And what an environment: the beautiful, incomparable, paradoxically tough-fragile world of the mountains.

Only 20 years after the wonderful nut revolution and those halcyon days of climbers working together to preserve their beautiful cliffs, a depressing spirit of suspicious selfishness settled upon the climbing community.

It would be easy to blame the mood of the 1980s (as contrasted with the 1960s). But in the same generation, as we saw in earlier chapters, the hiking community has stepped forward to take responsibility for trail tending and alpine-area protection. Narrow self-interest is not an essential condition of this or any other generation.

What's wrong with the climbing community? What will be the stance during the late 1990s? And beyond? We have no answers, only a sad regret to see such a change in a once-vibrant, outwardly directed group who cared deeply about the incomparable surroundings in which it is privileged to enjoy its place in the sun.

The boys of summer have lost their innocence.

Case Study 4:

Winter Camping— Tracks in More Than the Snow

For that hour we would have exchanged places with no one.

PAUL VAN DYKE, EARLY ADIRONDACK WINTER CAMPER
AT NIGHT ATOP ALGONQUIN, CA. 1954

LONG AFTER SUMMERTIME camping was restricted in crowded, overimpacted areas of the backcountry, winter camping remained exempt. The assumption was that a hefty snow cover protected the fragile vegetation and soils from impact. In some national forests, for example, many regulations applied only to the period May 1 to November 1.

More recently camping on snow and ice is also being restricted. On heavily traveled mountains like Rainier, climbers on the standard route are subject to a list of restraints designed to protect against pollution of the glacier. In the Northeast, several states prohibit winter camping above treeline. In the White Mountains officials have restricted camping in the drainage of Tuckerman Ravine, that enormously popular magnet for hikers and skiers, to a few closely supervised sites.

The potential impact of winter camping above treeline makes an interesting case study of a practice that (1) can be environmentally damaging if done thoughtlessly, and (2) is liable to be prohibited if winter campers fail to correct abuses, and properly so; but, on the other hand, (3) can be environmentally harmless if done prudently, and (4) is such a priceless mountain experience that it would be a shame to see it needlessly outlawed.

Look at the White Mountains of New Hampshire, with their extensive and magnificent alpine zone and a high volume of winter climbing. Managers of the White Mountain National Forest have wrestled with the winter camping issue for years. As mentioned, they declared Tuckerman Ravine (actually the entire watershed of which Tuckerman is the most prominent feature) off-limits to camping save at a handful of carefully controlled sites. For many years thereafter, winter camping remained otherwise unrestricted. Then came an articulate "Flower Lobby"—a handful of botanists with a mission to protect rare and endangered species at whatever price it took. In the winter of 1989–90, under prodding from the Flower Lobby, the Forest Service declared winter camping above treeline unlawful. For two years that regulation was in effect—but hardly anyone knew about it, because it was not only unenforced but virtually unannounced. Signs at trailheads still proclaimed restrictions void between November and May. So the policy was essentially canceled through lack of communication or enforcement.

For the winter of 1991–92, Forest Service officials reexamined the regulation and adopted a new one: camping permitted only on two-foot snow cover. This policy was somewhat more openly communicated.

A two-foot snow cover seems to provide a remarkably useful policy guideline. In the first place, the flowers are amply protected when snows lie that deep over their heads. The notorious winter winds of the White Mountains make for extreme variation in snow depth, with much of the alpine zone blown virtually clear much of the time, while other places are draped in several feet of dense snow cover for up to an acre or even several acres in extent. An on-the-ground survey conducted on behalf of the Forest Service in the winter of 1991–92 showed that, for the most common itineraries of winter campers, a two-foot snow cover can be found convenient for camping in a wide variety of useful locations. So it would appear that the two-foot rule may be serviceable, protecting the concerns of the Flower Lobby as well as the most ardent recreationists.

Ramifications to Be Resolved

Some prickly side issues remain. For example, how does the regulation apply to snow shelters, igloos, snow caves, trenches? Same rule? The process of building an igloo often involves a great deal of tramping around, so vegetation is at risk unless ample snow cover is present. Presumably, though, snow shelter builders will normally seek extensive snow fields.

One provision of the new regulation adds a further restraint: no camping on bodies of water. There are perhaps half a dozen tiny mountain ponds in the alpine zone, some of them serving as water sources for summer hikers, all of them home to small but intensely interesting alpine ecologies. We fear that no one is looking carefully enough at the human impact on these little lakes, year-round. For example, with huts drawing water for up to 60 or 90 people per night all summer long, can it be possible that the delicate ecologies of these ponds are undisturbed? So, when it comes to winter camping, no one would question a restriction against setting up a tent right on these ponds. But how close to a body of water is too close, that is, could risk polluting the water? This is an important question because some of the best sites south of Mount Washington lie very close to the shore of one of the lakes.

A third ramification should concern the Flower Lobby: among the snow banks that may become prevalent destinations for campers under this rule, are there any locations of notably rare or endangered species? If so, questions must be asked and answered. Is the snow cover sufficient to regard the rare plants as protected? If not, how does a regulation place them off-limits without drawing uncomfortable attention to the presence of plants that thrive best on minimum public notice?

Another question: Will sites that are environmentally acceptable all winter long become environmentally threatening sites in spring as the snow hardens and slowly shrinks? Will tenting habits formed in winter months become unacceptable during late winter–early spring? A possible solution would be to add a time limit on the snowcover rule—for instance, camping permitted on two feet of snow from November 1 to April 15, or some such period. The difficulty here is that the appropriate date could vary widely according to the pattern of snowfall. Ask most winter climbers and they'd tell you that the winter of 1991–92 was a terribly low snow year; one scarcely needed snowshoes in February. Yet because of heavy late snows, the alpine area was drenched in a deep cover of protective snows during late April. You could have camped almost indiscriminately anywhere in the Presidentials on April 20 with no impact on the vegetation whatever—on *that* April 20. In other years the snows might be thin indeed by that date, and camping could be very damaging even in early April.

That question is related to the point mentioned in chapter 9: during mud season, mountain soils are especially vulnerable, above or below treeline. You really don't want people tramping around a tent site on freshly melted tundra.

Underlying any discussion of winter camping above treeline should be an understanding of and healthy respect for the safety aspects of the whole ballgame. The two-foot rule highlights this point, when you stop and think about it. Tent sites tend to form where snow accumulates rapidly during storms. Anyone tenting in these locations on a night of a storm should expect to be up several times during the night to shovel away snow from the tent, or risk serious consequences.

During Christmas week 1991 we stuck a tent above treeline in the Northern Presidentials for five nights. The snow cover was ample, in a protected site in the lee of a peak known as Adams 4.

Just to set it up was an entertaining experience. In winds that could hardly be construed as uncommon in those hills, we found we had to unroll our groundcloth very slowly, methodically holding it down with the sprawled weight of our bodies. Then we laid out snow stakes in the corners where they'd be needed. Next we slowly and carefully unrolled the tent, staking each corner as it became available. For the next stage, the din and energy of flapping tent fabric was amazing. Slowly we worked the tent poles into place and anchored each end to snowshoes cemented deep into the drift. When first erected the fabric flapped and tugged at its moorings frighteningly. Only after heavily weighting the snowflaps and sinking the side pullouts deep into compacted snow, especially on the upwind side, did we have the slightest faith in its stability. To put up the fly was unthinkable: no way would it have survived the battering of the wind. Of course, throughout the procedure, we had to be painstakingly careful not to leave any stuff sack or other light object unanchored for even a second.

Throughout the five nights and days that followed, we repeatedly found the blowing snow building up against the windward side of the tent, reducing floor space, distorting the symmetry of the living space, straining pullouts. On several occasions we dug out the fast-compacting drifts against the windward side. After those five days we felt quite proud of our dear little tent, and very grateful to it.

Understand that this was not an uncommonly windy period for the Presidentials. Peak gusts over on Mount Washington, where they measure these unpleasant details, were running over 90 miles per hour—but, we repeat, those are not uncommon speeds for winter in the Presidentials.

All of these reflections underline one final point about the new winter regulations: camping above treeline is not to be casually undertaken, two feet of snow or no. The Presidentials' strongest winds can probably dismantle any tent made. To have a tent shred in the dark during such winds is to be confronted with a life-threatening situation. Nothing should be said on the subject that does not include a recognition that above-treeline camping is a

privilege that the mountain gods grant sometimes, but always
reserving the right to revoke that privilege without warning.

Beyond the Rule

But perhaps the most useful role for the new two-foot rule and its
communication and enforcement will prove to be the educational
opportunity it can afford to managers and recreationists alike. As
we have been saying throughout this book, rules are less useful, less
effective than education. The goal of all the sound and fury over
winter camping should be not to have campers measuring whether
the snow is 23 inches or 25 inches deep; the goal should be to have
winter campers *thinking* about the problem, *aware* of their potential
impact, and *acting responsibly* not just when they set up a tent but
wherever and however they move above treeline.

We winter recreationists have enjoyed unrestrained freedom
too long, and have possibly developed some bad habits of ignoring
the fragility of the terrain we're in and the potential effects of our
actions. We all need to start thinking about where we are, what
we're doing, how we're doing it, when we're doing it.

Incidentally, in the course of attending some meetings of
winter campers on this matter, and of serving as a fill-in caretaker
at cabins in the Northern Presidentials, we've noted that the
winter campers we've talked to are receptive to thinking about
these issues, anxious to do right, willing to modify past practices,
and concerned about the magnificent alpine landscape, which
they, of all people, value highly.

The kinds of things we should all be thinking about go far
beyond where and when to set up a tent. One far more vital issue,
for example, is staying off the snow-free areas of vegetation. As
mentioned, not only do those wild winds create extensive drifts of
deep snow, but they also expose broad sections of tundra to no
snow at all, or leave only a thin crust of ice or brittle hard-packed
snow. The landscape is so altered and obscured by snow and rime
that it may be difficult or impossible to know precisely where the

trail is. Staying on trail—if discernible and feasible—becomes just as important in winter as in summer wherever there is no adequate snow depth.

Where extensive snowfields are found, the winter climber may ramble freely without impact. But herein lies a risk. With long stretches of snow and ice fields in prospect, the winter climber may feel free to wander at random along the alpine heights. This is proper, and indeed one of the rich rewards of being up there in that season on those days when visibility and other conditions make such unrestricted wandering possible. But then you come to a place where the snowfields stop and the tundra is blown clear. Now, you should be back on trail, but maybe it's way over there by now. If you don't actually backtrack to where you can step directly from snow to trail, at the least try to hop from rock to rock or step only on patches of snow and ice.

This raises a point that all winter travelers should consider, not just overnight campers. When you reach treeline, do not follow the blind rule of always putting on crampons. Stop and think about whether you need them in today's particular conditions and circumstances. Sometimes they are vital to safety and progress, but not by any means always. During the winter of 1992, for example, we found them worse than useless in December but absolutely indispensable in April.

In general, crampons appear to be far more damaging to the vegetation than boots. Furthermore, a hiker wearing boots will seek to hop from rock to rock or deep snow, and to avoid ice and frozen ground, while one wearing crampons does precisely the opposite, trying very hard to avoid bare rocks so as to step on ice and ground, where those sharp points will dig in. Some winter hikers seem to have the incorrect idea that when you go above treeline, you almost automatically don crampons. In fact, conditions often make it more advisable not to wear them. In our view, a major contribution to the protection of alpine vegetation in winter could be gained by persuading hikers that crampons are often neither needed nor desirable above treeline.

On the other hand, sometimes it will be much better for the

tundra as well as yourself to be wearing crampons. A friend told us of one recent trip to Mount Moosilauke where some members of his party had not even brought crampons. In the path above treeline glare ice had formed almost exclusively in the slight depression formed by the trail. So, to our friend's consternation, the cramponless hikers systematically stayed out of the trail and on the exposed vegetation. Obviously in such circumstances—not all that uncommon—we're all better off with crampons.

What that tricky crampons-noncrampons issue illustrates is the general principle that we winter campers must get away from memorizing regulations and start to think more about the magic world of ice and snow in the alpine zone. As Forest Service officer Buzz Durham put it during that Boston meeting we described back in chapter 15: "It's more than rules, it's ethics that are going to help preserve the alpine zone. Hikers need to be aware that this is a fragile resource and help take responsibility for protecting it."

This new obligation has the potential to expand our perceptions and enhance our overall experience. We can learn a lot about that unique community of rocks and dwarf vegetation and wind, water, snow, rime. Indeed, we must learn, so that we can fit in less awkwardly, travel less clumsily, become a supporting player, not a troublesome intruder. This should be no burden for us to bear. It is a shining opportunity for us to become a respectful and thereby a respectable visitor in that wondrous world.

Epilogue

WINTER TENTING, ROCK CLIMBING, hiking with dogs, off-trail travel—all these issues bear down on one central theme. That is the overall message toward which we believe the experience of outdoor recreationists for the past quarter century—maybe since the recreational enjoyment of backcountry began—has been tending, inexorably. It is the intended theme of this book. It is the theme of individual, personal, unshirkable responsibility on the part of all of us to see clearly what we're doing, what our proper role is in the whole backcountry, what underlying backwoods ethic must govern what we call our recreation.

In the foregoing pages we've probably emphasized specific actions (or restraints) too much, at the expense of more general philosophical concepts. That's just our limitation: we tend to be doers, not thinkers, happier tending a trail than meditating over it or scribbling about it. But we have tried to bring ourselves up and remind ourselves and you, our readers, not to memorize a set of rules but rather strive to understand the impact of our ways and to think how we can best protect the backwoods environment, which means so much to us.

Rules are not what we seek. They are inconsistent with the freedom of the hills anyway, and that spirit of freedom is an important part of the mountain experience.

What we should seek and must, if we are to pass along to the next generation the privileges and pleasures we've enjoyed, is the demands that accompany freedom inevitably: to respect the place where we are, to try to understand its processes, to think about the effect of our presence and to act responsibly to minimize that effect, and to preserve and protect the mountain world.

Those demands suggest a code of conduct that implies something beyond thinking about specific actions, something beyond even an understanding of the ecosystem that we are visiting in the backcountry. It implies a sense of values, a deeply rooted belief that we have an obligation to respect and honor this land.

Where practice moves to values, that is where etiquette moves to an ethic. In raising these environmental concerns for hikers and campers, that is our ultimate goal: backwoods ethics.

Selected Bibliography

THE OUTPOURING OF concern for the wilderness environment has produced a bewildering (odd word in this context) onslaught of printed material. Sometimes it seems like too much of a good thing. The conscientious reader could spend all leisure hours reading the literature on wilderness and never set foot in the woods. We don't wish to encourage the idea that reading about it is more important than being there.

That said, however, we believe that there is a core of "must" reading, and concentric circles of valuable—informative or inspiring—thought provokers. We list below those books that we have found useful or provocative, a half dozen of which we've marked (*) as the "must" (that is, not to be allowed to become "musty") core.

Abbey, Edward. *Desert Solitaire: A Season in the Wilderness.* Simon & Schuster, 1968.

Berry, Wendell. *The Unsettling of America: Culture and Agriculture.* Sierra Club Books, 1977.

_____. *The Long-Legged House.* Harcourt, Brace & World, 1969.

Brooks, Paul. *The Pursuit of Wilderness.* Houghton Mifflin, 1971.

_____. *Roadless Areas.* Knopf, 1964.

Brower, David. *For Earth's Sake: The Life and Times of David Brower.* Peregrine Smith Books, 1990.

Callicott, J. Baird, ed. *Companion to "A Sand County Almanac."* University of Wisconsin Press, 1987.

Cohen, Michael. *The Pathless Way: John Muir and the American Wilderness.* University of Wisconsin Press, 1984.

Cole, David N. *Low-Impact Recreational Practices for Wilderness and Backcountry.* United States Forest Service General Technical Report INT-265, August 1989.

Commoner, Barry. *Making Peace with the Planet.* Pantheon Books, 1975.

Devall, Bill, and George Sessions. *Deep Ecology.* Gibbson Smith, 1985.

Dubos, René. *The Wooing of Earth.* Scribner's, 1980.

*Geisel, Theodore Seuss [Dr. Seuss]. *The Lorax.* Random House, 1971.

Grahame, Kenneth. *The Wind in the Willows.* Scribner's, 1908.

Hampton, Bruce, and David Cole. *Soft Paths.* Stackpole Books, 1988.

*Hardin, Garret. "The Tragedy of the Commons." *Science,* December 13, 1968, pp. 1243–49.

Huth, Hans. *Nature and the American: Three Centuries of Changing Attitudes.* University of Nebraska Press, 1957.

Leopold, Aldo. *The River of the Mother of God and Other Essays.* University of Wisconsin Press, 1991.

*_____. *A Sand County Almanac and Sketches Here and There.* Oxford University Press, 1949.

Levin, Philip D. Series of articles in *Appalachia:* "Toward a Recreated Wilderness: Notes on Abolishing the Four Thousand Footer Club," June 1973, pp. 132–140; "Inward to Wilderness," part 1, December 1975, pp. 49–62; part 2, December 1976, pp. 18–35; part 3, June 1978, pp. 25–44; part 4, December 1978, pp. 57–86.

Lopez, Barry. *Desert Notes: Reflections in the Eye of a Raven.* Avon Books, 1978.

Manes, Christopher. *Green Rage: Radical Environmentalism and the Unmaking of Civilization.* Little, Brown, 1990.

Marx, Leo. *The Machine in the Garden: Technology and the Pastoral Ideal in America.* Oxford University Press, 1964.

*McKibben, Bill. *The End of Nature.* Doubleday, 1989.

McPhee, John. *The Control of Nature.* Farrar, Straus, & Giroux, 1989.

_____. *Encounters with the Archdruid.* Farrar, Straus, & Giroux, 1971.

*Nash, Roderick. *Wilderness and the American Mind.* Yale University Press, 1967; rev. ed., 1973, 1982.

_____. *The Rights of Nature: A History of Environmental Ethics.* University of Wisconsin Press, 1989.

Rollin, Bernard E. *Animal Rights and Human Morality.* Prometheus Books, 1981.

Runte, Alfred. *National Parks: The American Experience.* University of Nebraska Press, 1979.

Sax, Joseph L. *Mountains without Handrails: Reflections on the National Parks.* University of Michigan Press, 1980.

Schmitt, Peter. *Back to Nature: The American Myth in Urban America.* Oxford University Press, 1969; reissue, Johns Hopkins University Press, 1990.

Snyder, Gary. *The Practice of the Wild.* North Point Press, 1990.

Terrie, Philip G. *Forever Wild: Environmental Aesthetics and the Adirondack Forest Preserve.* Harbor Hill Books, 1985.

Thoreau, Henry David. *The Maine Woods.* Originally published in 1848 magazine articles and an 1864 book; see the Bramwell House edition, 1950.

*_____. *Walden; or, Life in the Woods.* 1854; see the Houghton Mifflin edition, 1893.

Waterman, Laura, and Guy Waterman. *Wilderness Ethics: Preserving the Spirit of Wildness.* Countryman Press, 1993.

Winner, Langdon. *The Whale and the Reactor: A Search for Limits in an Age of High Technology.* University of Chicago Press, 1989.

Index

SOUTHEASTERN COMMUNITY COLLEGE LIBRARY

3 3255 00036 6345